The Foreign Language Teacher's Suggestopedic Manual

The Foreign Language Teacher's Suggestopedic Manual

By Georgi Lozanov and Evalina Gateva

Research Institute of Suggestology
Sofia, Bulgaria

Translated from Bulgarian

Gordon and Breach Science Publishers
New York London Paris Montreux Tokyo Melbourne

© 1988 by Georgi Lozanov and Evalina Gateva. All rights reserved.

Gordon and Breach Science Publishers S.A.

Post Office Box 161,
1820 Montreux 2,
Switzerland

Gordon and Breach Science Publishers

Post Office Box 786
Copper Station
New York, NY 10276
United States of America

Post Office Box 197
London WC2E 9PX
England

58, rue Lhomond
75005 Paris
France

14-9 Okubo 3-chome
Shinjuku-ku, Tokyo 160
Japan

Private Bag 8
Camberwell, Victoria 3124
Australia

Originally published in Bulgarian in 1981 as *Sugestopedichno Praktichesko R" kovodstvo za Prepodavateli po Chuzhdi Ezitsi* © 1981 by G. Lozanov and E. Gateva c/o Jusautor, Sofia.

Library of Congress Cataloging in Publication Data
Lozanov, Georgi.
 The foreign language teacher's suggestopedic manual/Georgi
 Lozanov and Evalina Gateva.
    p. cm.
  Includes index.
  ISBN 0-677-21660-2. ISBN 0-677-21750-6 (pbk.)
  1. Languages. Modern—Study and teaching—Psychological aspects—
Handbooks, manuals, etc. 2. Mental suggestion—Handbooks, manuals,
etc. I. Gateva, Evalina. II. Title.
PB36.L63 1987   418'.007—dc19   87-24089

No part of this book may be reproduced or utilized in any form or by any means, electronic or mechanical, including photocopying and recording, or by any information storage or retrieval system, without permission in writing from the publishers.
Printed in Great Britain by Bell and Bain Ltd., Glasgow

CONTENTS

Introductory Notes	1

PART 1: SUGGESTOPEDIC FOREIGN LANGUAGE COURSES FOR ADULTS

Preliminaries	5
Enrolling in a Suggestopedic Foreign Language Course	5
Instructions	18
In Observation of the Requirements for the Suggestopedic Teaching and Learning of Foreign Languages	18
Methodological Instructions	21
For the Suggestopedic Teaching of Foreign Languages to Adults	21
I. Introduction	22
II. Active Concert Session	22
III. Pseudopassive Concert Session	23
IV. Elaborations	24
Comments on Methodological Instructions	28
Lesson One: "Getting Acquainted"	28
I. Introduction	28
II. Active Concert Session	69
III. Pseudopassive Concert Session	72
IV. Elaborations	78
Lesson Two: "Waking Up"	110
I. Introduction	110
II. Active Concert Session	111
III. Pseudopassive Concert Session	111
IV. Elaborations	113

Lesson Three: "The Eternal City"	125
Lesson Four: "The Seasons"	132
Lesson Five: "The Months"	139
Lesson Six: "At the Concert"	145
Lesson Seven: "Friendship"	145
Lesson Eight: "Goodbye, Rome"	146
Sample Course Forms	148
Further Improvement in the Foreign Language after the First Grade of Suggestopedic Courses	151

PART 2: SUGGESTOPEDIC TEACHING OF FOREIGN LANGUAGES TO SCHOOL-AGE CHILDREN

First Grade	169
Globalized Teaching of Foreign Languages in the First Year of the Suggestopedic School, with Artistic Performances and Elaborated Lessons	169
Questionnaire	169
First Global Theme	172
Friends (First Play)	172
Second Global Theme	196
Preliminary Introduction	196
Where are the Horse and the Dog? (Second Play)	198
Suggestopedic Integrative Teaching of the Russian Language to First-Graders	213
Gradual Teaching from the Second Year On	231

Methodological Instructions 231
    I. Introduction 231
    II. Active Concert Session 232
    III. Pseudopassive Concert Session 232
    IV. Elaborations 232
    V. Input and Output Levels 233

Musical Program Designed for Lessons in Foreign Languages in Suggestopedic Schools 233

Appendix 235

Index 251

INTRODUCTORY NOTES

The objectives of this edition have been to create a suggestopedic text of sufficient scope to meet the needs of foreign language teachers who are involved in suggestopedic classes for adults and children. Theoretical explanations will be rather scarce because the basic theory of suggestopedy has been already presented in *Suggestology and Outlines of Suggestopedy* (Engl. transl.: Gordon and Breach, Science Publishers Ltd., London—New York, 1978). French, German and other versions of this book will be soon available.

Additional theoretical explanations are to be found in my lectures delivered at training courses for foreign language teachers. These lectures give the clue of loading practical methods, treated in this manual, with psychological charge. This represents a *sine qua non* for the emergence (under the student's control) of a state of concentrative psychorelaxation and for the liberation of man's reserve capacities in accordance with some optimal psychophysiological laws (differing from everyday ones). The lectures conform with, and are adapted to the personality and the interests of the foreign language teachers who enlist in the training course. The lectures actually elucidate the "esoteric" core, the intrinsic factor of the suggestopedic system of teaching and learning foreign languages.

Safeguarding against theoretically unfounded and practically unvalidated claims is of particular importance for suggestopedy, since its main novelty is its domain: suggestopedy encompasses man's global reserve capacities. The term "reserve capacities" is not used here in some profane way, but in the sense of the exact objective laws and specific characteristics of the phenomenon that is strictly defined by the theory of suggestology.

Prior to working with her on this manual, it has been of great importance to me, to have attended the lectures of E. Gateva, treating problems of music, aesthetics, and linguistics from the standpoint of suggestology. It has also been important to have participated in one of her demonstrative courses and to have passed, under her guidance, through practical training in carrying on musical sessions.

All these preliminary requirements having been observed, the present manual will be of particular value for the foreign language teacher, practicing the suggestopedic system; because the more qualified the teacher is, the higher are the results.

* * *

Since its establishment as a separate scientific discipline, suggestology has been linked to the problems of paraconsciousness. It is the organization and orchestration of the more or less unrealized factors, grouped under the term "paraconsciousness"—in constant connection with the factors of consciousness—that should allow us to tap man's reserve capacities for practical purposes. In such a way suggestopedy (suggestology in pedagogy) was created and developed in both theoretical and practical aspects as one of the branches of suggestology. Presently, suggestopedy is most popular in the field of foreign language teaching and learning, although suggestopedic practice has already proved its viability and efficiency in quite a few subjects, namely in the so-called scholastic suggestopedy.

Experimental and theoretical investigation of the phenomena, factors, and objective laws of paraconsciousness have progressed hand in hand with the suggestological reevaluation of numerous linguistic, psycholinguistic, genetic, semiotic, aesthetic, musicological, psychotherapeutic, psychological, physiological, methodological, and didactic requirements. This progress has been aimed at enriching the theory of suggestopedy and at finding the optimal practical variant of a foreign language suggestopedy.

Our first mass-scale experiments (1964–1966) were carried on with the participation of two university professors in French and one in English. The basic methodological stages—introduction,* session, elaboration—were outlined, but the work was performed with standard textbooks from which words and expressions were selected and regrouped in order to facilitate their memorization. During the second half of 1967 twenty more foreign language teachers were enrolled in the Institute. They took part in

---

* Introduction—(pre-session phase; deciphering). The latest variant of the term. The change being due to completely new characteristics of the work during this stage.

the development of a series of variants; there then appeared our first textbooks. Working with part-time lecturers, however, made it difficult to qualify them in the problems of suggestology and to tap their reserve capacities in the process of teaching and learning. Most lecturers displayed a formal approach toward the methodology, lacked the necessary psychological loading, and, in many instances, completely misunderstood the problem of reserve capacities. Nevertheless, they succeeded in realizing some of the experimental formulations. Meanwhile, we had the opportunity to understand and foresee the difficulties that would be encountered in any further mass practice of suggestopedic foreign language teaching.

To overcome these difficulties we switched to a system of full-time foreign language teachers. Troubles, however, did not disappear completely. The progress in teachers' qualification maintained its slow and formal pace. Many teachers proved unable to understand the theory of reserve capacities, the global nature of the approach, or the nature of concentrated psychorelaxation. Inspiration, as a principal prerequisite in suggestopedic teaching and learning, was imperceptibly replaced by amusement. The aesthetic, ritual, cathartic, and concentrated-psychorelaxing importance of the concert session was displaced by the ideas of amusement and recreation. Sketches were introduced in a formal and sometimes psychotraumatic way—not according to the suggestological requirements of spontaneity and indirection. There was a tendency to forget our searching for reserve capacities, and not just for ordinary activation. Introducing the time honored method of activating a subject through a formalized psychological approach yielded encouraging results, but it did not tap reserve capacities. It sacrificed substance for showmanship.

Among the number of methodological variants experimented with in these circumstances, some were published while others remained to be improved upon. Several textbooks were written some of which, after pilot trials, proved fit for provisional use, while others were abandoned altogether.

Among the many experimental variants tried in our Institute and in the centers abroad which are under our methodological leadership, the variant proposed in the present manual has turned out to be in the most conformity with theory, to have the best prospects for further application, and to have the best final results. It is according to this variant that work has been carried out in all the courses in the Institute for the past seven years. Its considerable advantages have been validated through results obtained in numerous courses in Bulgaria, the Soviet Union, the United States, Hungary, Austria, Canada, and elsewhere. This great success has caused us to publish the present Foreign Language Teacher's Suggestopedic Manual—a pioneer in its kind.

E. Gateva, my collaborator on this work, was involved with the development of suggestology long before the existence of any official organization to deal with it. For fourteen years she has been working as a staff member of the Suggestology Research Institute. Her dual university qualifications—music and linguistic—has allowed her to work successfully on crucial topics of suggestopedic teaching and learning.

The present manual is intended for use in the suggestopedic teaching of all foreign languages. Examples are borrowed mainly from Italian, (Lozanov, G. and Gateva, E. *L'Italiano*. Tierp, Sweden: C. Landahl, ca. 1982) because of a number of theoretical and practical considerations. In order to make its use easier for all foreign language teachers, comparative examples have also been given with fragments of Spanish, English, French, German, and Russian texts.

G. LOZANOV, M.D., M.Sci.D.

PART 1

SUGGESTOPEDIC FOREIGN LANGUAGE COURSES FOR ADULTS

PRELIMINARIES

Enrolling in a Suggestopedic Foreign Language Course

Anyone wanting to study a foreign language after the suggestopedic method has to appear personally at the Suggestology Research Institute, where both an *application* and a *questionnaire* must be filled in. Both documents are received from and handed back to the secretary of the Institute, who keeps the blanks. This is the first encounter of the future student with the Institute and with a staff member of the Institute. During the brief conversation between them the latter makes an estimate (as cursory and superficial as it can be) of the candidate. For example, he or she estimates the candidate's willingness to enter the course, and his or her motivation, interests, culture, etc.

Here follows the text of both the *application* and *questionnaire*:

No. .... Research Institute of Suggestology
Sofia

APPLICATION

Name .... Age ....
Place of employment .... Tel. No. ....
Occupation .... Education ....
Home address .... Tel. No. ....

Dear Sir,

    I would like to enroll in an experimental suggestopedic course in the .... language.

REASONS: ....
....

Degree of command of the language (underline or fill in):
  I. I have not studied the language
  II. I studied the language
    (1) ...... years ago;
    (2) about ...... years.
  III. I know about ...... words.
  IV. I speak with mistakes; I don't speak.

I would like to have classes:
    in the morning; in the afternoon (underline!).

I have no objections to taking part as a subject in scientific investigations and in scientific documentation (photographs or films).

NOTE: ....
....

Sofia, ... 19 ...   Signature: ....

QUESTIONNAIRE

No. ....
Name .... Age ....
Place of employment .... Tel. No. ....
Occupation .... Education ....
Home address .... Tel. No. ....

1. What language do you wish to apply for? ....
2. Do you speak other foreign languages? ....
3. What foreign languages do you speak? ....
4. What is the degree of your knowledge (underline)? (speak, write; very good, satisfactory, poor). ....
5. Where did you study? ....
6. Do you like to study foreign languages? ....
7. Do you think that studying foreign languages is a hard and unpleasant task? ....
8. Have you ever discontinued studying a language because of boredom and/or dissatisfaction? ....
9. Suppose your training took part in another school (or at private lessons) at a rate of 4 school hours daily with no homework. How long would it take, do you think, to master reading and speaking the foreign language within the framework of 2,000 words and the basic grammar? ....
10. Do you presume your training in our Institute will be faster, more pleasant, and more efficient? ....
11. Does the idea of studying a foreign language in our Institute make you feel uneasy? (If yes, why?) ....
12. What kind of activity (science, art, administration, industry, etc.) is, according to you, the most suitable for yourself? ....
....
....
....

Sofia, ... 19 ...   Signature: ....

The distribution of students according to their sex and number in a group has been the subject of numerous studies in the Institute, and the results have been published. A group of 12 students has proved to be optimal. The best proportion of sexes is 1:1. After preliminary testing, the students of a given language are distributed in at least two groups: a group of relative beginners (having never studied the language) and a group of relative beginners (having some quite elementary idea of the language with little ability to communicate in it). Students above this level of knowledge are not allowed in the course, lest the necessary psychological climate of a homogenous group be upset.

As already mentioned, this distribution takes place after the *testing*. In order to make it to the testing phase, a candidate must have his or her application and questionnaire scrutinized by the governing body of the Institute. The applications and the questionnaires are ordered according to their date of filing, but preference is sometimes given to people with impending business or an important private trip in the corresponding country (who have an urgent need of the language). Particular attention is paid to the *reasons* enumerated in the application. The student's preference for morning or afternoon classes, style of filling in the forms, attitude (positive or negative) toward being subjected to scientific investigations, and documentation are also taken into consideration.

The answers to the entries of the questionnaire are studied very thoroughly and their interpretation plays an important part when making the decision to accept a candidate in a course. Still more attention is needed in composing the groups.

After their approbation, students are invited by phone to present themselves in the Institute at a fixed hour, the day before the opening of the course. The purpose of this first meeting is to carry on the testing by checking firsthand the candidates' level of knowledge of the foreign language, and to proceed afterward to the formation of groups.

Testing the candidates is the task of the respective foreign language teachers. These teachers are particularly trained in how to perform the testing in a psychologically nontraumatic manner and how to succeed in obtaining, besides purely linguistic data, certain psychological data concerning the candidates. This procedure should not be difficult for the people tested. Such psychological data are indispensable to the formation of groups. The final result of this formation is a microunit, the members of which must agree on what they expect to be taught of the foreign language for which they are applying. Therefore, the creation of a suitable psychological atmosphere begins with the student's crossing of the threshold of the Institute, and it is impossible to determine when and how it ends, since quite a few of the students continue studying (other) foreign languages, and colleagues and relatives of the students enlist in their turn in our courses, and so on.

It is clear that primary orientation concerning the future students begins as soon as applications are handed in. Primary orientation is of foremost importance for the success of the teaching and learning process. Care for each individual student exists from the very beginning and consists first in taking into account his or her psychological makeup while also considering the mutual tolerance of one another required for a group.

This preliminary work requires subtle and detailed knowledge of suggestological and suggestopedic theory, or else the results could turn out to be just the opposite of what is expected. That is why we cannot refrain from stressing: the suggestopedic theory, being an offspring of integral psychotherapy, needs a constant psychotherapeutic, psychohygienic, and psychopreventive "control."

The following pages present our original test, which has been successfully used in the Italian language courses and later in other foreign language courses. For the time being, it seems to be the most up-to-standard and best conforms to the requirements of suggestopedic testing. It consists of five stages. Before the performance of the test, a teacher or an official of the Institute cautiously informs the students that testing, intended to establish their knowledge of the foreign language, is indispensable to successfully creating the most favorable conditions for their forthcoming activities. The students must understand that each of them will derive maximum benefits from the course only if he or she is included in a homogenous group.

Testing

Stage 1—The first stage is *a translation in writing* from a short text, selected in the original literature of the foreign language, into the student's mother tongue. The student is given a sheet with the text to be translated (without a dictionary). He fills in his name and the date. If he is unable to translate a work, he writes down in his mother tongue "I cannot translate." The very same text will be offered to the student once more at the end of the course, when he or she will be asked again to translate it. During the course the test is not discussed, and nothing suggests its being given again. However, all the vocabulary and grammar used in this test is part of the textbook and of the classes throughout the course, although in a totally different form. The text to be translated includes about 150–200 lexical items (40–50 substantives, about 20 adjectives, 50–60 verbs, about 20 pronominal forms, and about 50 adverbs, prepositions, conjunctions, and other particles). The verbal forms represented in the text are regular and irregular, in the indicative mood (present, past, and future tenses), conditional mood, imperative mood, infinitive, and past participles (regular and irregular forms).

Example 1: Input–ouput level: A translation in writing from Italian.

NOME:
DATA:

I. Traducete:

FRAGOLA E PANNA

(Suona un campanello. Tosca apre. Sulla porta c'è Barbara, con una valigia. Ha una giacca di cuoio nero e calzoni blujeans.)
BARBARA: Buongiorno.
TOSCA: Non comperiamo niente.
BARBARA: Ma io non ho niente da vendere. Vorrei parlare con l'avvocato.
TOSCA: L'avvocato non c'è. E'via. E la signora è andata in paese a fare la spesa. Chi sarebbe lei?
BARBARA: Una cugina.
TOSCA: Ah una cugina? S'accomodi. La signora non tarderà. Come s'è bagnata!
BARBARA: Si. Nevica.
TOSCA: Nevica. Un tempo orribile. Ma lei è venuta dalla stazione a piedi?
BARBARA: Si.

TOSCA:	A piedi? Con la valigia? Non poteva pigliare un'autopubblica?
BARBARA:	Non sapevo che c'era tanta strada.
TOSCA:	Non lo sapeva? Allora non è mai venuta qua? E' cugina, pero non è mai venuta qua?
BARBARA:	Mai.
TOSCA:	Strano. Aspetti pure, la signora non tarderà.
BARBARA:	(tirando fuori una sigaretta) Mi darebbe un fiammifero, signora?
TOSCA:	Non sono signora. Sono una serva. E' tutta la vita che faccio la serva. Ecco i fiammiferi. Sono qui solo da otto giorni, ma non ci resto. Gliel'ho già detto alla signora che non ci resto, che me ne vado via. E'una casa troppo grande, due piani, un mucchio di stanze. Ma io non è per il lavoro che me ne vado. Me ne vado perchè siamo troppo isolati. C'è un silenzio, come essere in una tomba. A me non mi piace la campagna, mi piace la città. Il rumore. Mangiano, e non dicono è buono, è cattivo, niente. Non ti dicono mai niente. Cosi una non può mai sapere, se sono contenti o no. E poi questo silenzio! L'avvocato, io l'ho visto un momento il giorno che sono arrivata, gli ho stirato due camicie, e è partito subito. La signora, la signora non parla. Non parla con me. Tutto il giorno legge, o suona il piano. Ma non è una musica che diverte. Io sono là in cucina, con il gatto, e a sentire quei suoni mi viene il sonno. Parlo con il gatto, se voglio parlare con qualcuno. Viene qualche volta la signora Letizia, la sorella della signora. Abita poco distante.

—NATALIA GINZBURG, dalla commedia *Fragola e panna*,
atto primo

Translation:

STRAWBERRY AND CREAM

A ring at the door. Tosca opens. In the doorway is Barbara, with a suitcase. She is in blue-jeans and a black leather jacket.

BARBARA: Good morning.
TOSCA: We aren't buying.
BARBARA: But I have nothing to sell. I'd like to speak to the attorney-at-law.
TOSCA: The attorney is not at home. He went out. And Madame is out shopping in the village. Who are you?
BARBARA: A cousin.
TOSCA: A cousin? Please, step in. Madame won't be late. You are sopping wet.
BARBARA: Yes, I am. It's snowing.
TOSCA: Snowing. Awful weather. You walked from the railway station?
BARBARA: Yes.
TOSCA: On foot? With the suitcase? Couldn't you catch the bus?
BARBARA: I didn't know it was such a long way.
TOSCA: You didn't know? So you have never been here? You are a cousin and you've never been here?
BARBARA: Never.
TOSCA: Very strange. Wait a bit, Madame won't be late.
BARBARA: (producing a cigarette) Do you have a match, madame?
TOSCA: I'm not a madame. I'm a housemaid. I've worked as a housemaid all my life. Here are some matches. I have been here eight days, but I shan't stay. I told Madame already, I shan't stay, I'm going away. It's a very large house, two storeys, plenty of rooms. But it's not the work that makes me go. I'm going away because it is so isolated here. It's as quiet as a grave. I don't like the countryside. I like the city. The noise. Here, they eat, and they don't say either good or bad—nothing. It is hard to understand if they are pleased or not. And that stillness! The attorney, I saw him for a little while the day I came here, I ironed two shirts for

him and he went out right away. As for Madame, Madame doesn't speak. At least, she doesn't speak with me. All day she plays the piano. But it's not music that entertains. I'm here, in the kitchen, with the cat, and when I listen to this tune, it makes me drowsy. I talk to the cat if I feel like talking to someone. Sometimes Mrs. Letizia, Madame's sister comes. She doesn't live far from here.

—Natalia Ginzburg—from *Strawberry and Cream*,
1st Act

Example 2: Input–output level: A translation in writing from Spanish.

El déspota

Recalde era un déspota: decidido, audaz, acostumbrado a mandar como se manda en un barco.

Se casó, pasó la luna de miel; la Cashilda tuvo un niño; Recalde estuvo luego navegando tres años, y volvió a su hogar a pasar una temporada.

El primer día, al volver a su casa, quiso ser fino:

—Qué hay? Ha pasado algo?—le preguntó a su mujer.

—Nada. Estamos todos bien.

—Ha habido muertos en el pueblo?

—Sí, don Fulano, don Zutano. Y la señora de Tal ha estado enferma.

Recalde escuchó las noticias, y después preguntó:

—A qué hora se cena aquí?

—A las ocho.

—Pues hay que cenar a las siete.

La Cashilda no replicó.

Al dia siguiente Recalde fue a su casa a las siete y pidió la cena.

—No está la cena—dijo su mujer.

—Cómo que no está la cena? Ayer dije que debía estar a las siete.

—Sí; pero la chica no puede hacer la cena hasta las ocho, porque tiene que estar con el niño.

—Pues se le despide a la chica.

—No se le puede despedir a la chica.

—Por qué?

—Porque me la ha recomendado la hermana de don Renigno, el vicario.

—Bueno; pues mañana se ha de cenar a las siete.

Al día siguiente la cena estaba a las ocho. Recalde rompió dos o tres platos, dio puñetazos en la mesa, pero no salió con la suya, y cuando Cashilda le convenció de que allí se hacía únicamente su voluntad, acabó diciendo a su marido:

—Aquí se cena todos los días a las ocho, sabes, chiquito? Y si no te conviene, lo que puedes hacer es marcharte; puedes ir otra vez a navegar.

Recalde, el terrible Recalde, comprendió que allí no estaba en su barco, y se fue a navegar.

—PÍO BAROJA, *Las inquietudes de Shanti Andia*

Stage 2—The second stage is *conjugation* of a regular or irregular verb from the common usage in the present, past,* and future tenses of the indicative mood; and in the present tense of the conditional mood (e.g., "to speak," "to trust," "to start," "to understand," "can", "must", "to want," "to be," "to have," "to go," "to come," "to know," etc.).

Stage 3—One of the students who has not been able to translate anything is asked into another room, where there is a tape recorder. The student is subjected there to an *oral test* and is asked to answer questions related to the subject matter of a suggestopedic course (24 working days, 3 hours daily, within the framework of 2,000 lexical items and the basic grammar).

The student is informed that, if he or she understands the questions, and is able to answer in the foreign language, *his or her answers may be of pure invention, because the text serves merely linguistic ends.* If able to, the student answers in the foreign language. If able to, he or she translates. If unable both to answer and to translate, the student simply states this in his or her mother tongue. Everything is tape recorded and kept as documentation for the Institute and as material for research work, but also as an illustration to be used by the end of the course, to show the students their degree of progress. The same set of questions is presented to the students at the output level.

---

* Including dual past tenses as necessary, such as the Spanish imperfect and preterite.

The test is comprised of questions related to everyday life, as well as questions regarding culture, sports, etc.; narratives with themes like "My Home," "The Sights of the City of . . . ," "The Appearance and Character of Someone I Love," "The Home of My Dreams" (with the use of the future tense), and "An Exciting Moment of My Life" (with the use of the past tense).

Example 3: The oral test.

1. What is your name?
2. Where do you live?
3. Whom do you live with?
4. Are you married?
5. Have you any children? How many?
6. Have you a brother, a sister?
7. What is the name of your husband/wife?
8. How old is your mother (father, son, daughter, sister, brother)?
9. Where were you born?
10. Where have you studied?
11. Are you fond of trips? What kind of trips do you like best? Why?
12. Have you been abroad? What foreign countries have you visited? For how long?
13. Have you any friends? What is their nationality? What are their professions?
14. Would you like to describe your birthplace (or another town you love)?
15. What season do you like best? Why?
16. At what time do you get up?
17. Where do you have your breakfast? What do you have for breakfast?
18. At what time do you go to work?
19. What do you have for lunch?
20. What do you have for dinner (supper)?
21. How do you make an invitation by phone?
22. Do you like art? What type of art do you love? Why?
23. How do you feel today? Have you any indisposition?
24. Would you like to describe somebody you love, that is, his or her appearance and character?

25. Could you imagine your home in the future? What will it look like?
26. Are you a sports fan? What sports do you prefer?
27. Do you like to go shopping? Do you like buying things? What, for instance, do you like buying?
28. Would you like to tell some exciting story from your life?

Stage 4—*Reading* a text in the foreign language is the fourth stage. The reading is tape recorded. It is permissible to use the previous text and during the course this text is not repeated. It is given again only at output level.

Stage 5—The teacher reads and states aloud a couple of sentences in the foreign language. The student repeats immediately. Thus a cursory checkup of the future student's abilities for *imitation, aural perception, and articulation* is performed. These abilities will be further developed over the tide of the course. The special intonation used during the so-called concert sessions as well as the classic tunes selected to serve as musical background to these sessions, are intended to promote this very important phonetic process.

A student is asked into the room for oral testing when he or she is ready with the translation and the conjugation of verbs in writing (the test in writing takes place in another room). If more than one student is ready for the oral test, they remain with their colleagues until the oral testing of the previous student is over.

As a matter of course, well-trained teachers profit from the testing procedures by learning some psychological information about the student, which will be made use of later, during the course. Such information should be obtained by the teacher only if it is collected with the purpose of helping the student incorporate his or her personality into the microunit. The better an individual is incorporated into the group, the better the teaching and learning processes will be for the whole group.

At the risk of repeating ourselves: drawing some preliminary information from the future students at the time of their initial testing is a very subtle operation which, if not perfectly mastered by the teachers, had better remain undone. Nothing can justify a gross intrusion into a person's private life—and the results of the teaching under such conditions are totally opposite to the expectations. That is why the psychological training of suggestopedic teachers is a highly responsible task, which is to be performed only by the most competent and best qualified workers. One should never forget that suggestopedy is a medically orientated, psycho-hygienic method of teaching and learning, and therefore every move should be absolutely correct on theoretical grounds. The subtle intuitions, which many good teachers enjoy, could play false if they are not based on sound theory. On the other hand, if a skilled teacher is trained in suggestopedy with utmost care, if he or she is fully aware of dealing with an education methodology capable of revealing man's reserve capacities, he or she would trust with more assurance to the intuitive devices which are constantly made use of in suggestopedic practice. For instance: the students' specific behavior at the time of testing is, at least in some degree, a psychological signal for the teacher.

As soon as the tested candidate has left the room, the teacher takes brief notes on the future student's behavior. Afterward, these notes are compared with his or her way of presenting ideas and even (to a less degree) with his or her handwriting, since these data appear in the *questionnaire*, the *application*, and the translation of the text. All these data along with the imitation while listening to records are psychological signals and are taken into consideration for the definitive formation of the group.

The candidates are then asked to phone the Institute in order to find out if they have been enlisted in the course or if their acceptance has been postponed for some reason or other. For instance: candidates who are quite advanced in their knowledge of the foreign language or who are psychologically incompatible are tactfully informed that the present course is not the most suitable for them. Candidates who are accepted are also informed about the opening of the course.

The Opening Session

The next day, at the commencement of classes, the secretary of the Institute comes into the classroom and, after welcoming the students, reads aloud *Instruction No. 1* which outlines the requirements necessary for the suggestopedic teaching and learning of foreign languages. The printed text of this Instruction hangs on the wall of every classroom, where it is accessible to everybody at any moment. The secretary wishes the students at good time in studying, and the course begins.

INSTRUCTIONS

In Observation of the Requirements for the Suggestopedic Teaching and Learning of Foreign Languages

Given that enlisting in suggestopedic foreign language courses usually gives rise to numerous questions, we pray to have in mind the following:

1. Our courses are experimental, and students are recruited according to the needs of the experiments under preparation. The governing body of the Institute reserves the right, at any time of the course:

   (*a*) to rearrange students between groups;
   (*b*) to modify, if necessary, the program;
   (*c*) to perform physiological and psychological studies;
   (*d*) to prepare audio-visual documentation.

2. Suggestopedic education, and particularly the so-called "suggestopedic sessions," improve the students' and teachers' disposition and cause relaxation. A specific characteristic of this type of education is the spontaneous appearance of concentration on the part of the students against the background of general psychorelaxation. In order to attain this *spontaneous concentrative psychorelaxation*, the students have to observe the requirements for nonstrain, that is, for the so-called "informative" and anxiety-free attitude toward the teaching and learning process.

3. During the first "active" concert session, the students keep an eye on the textbook, watching both the foreign language text, read aloud by the teacher, and the corresponding translation in their mother tongue. The foreign language text is read by the teacher slowly, with a pure and distinct diction and a particular intonation. The students have the opportunity to take brief notes.

During the second ("passive") concert session, the students listen to the concert and to the foreign language information, delivered by the teacher with a natural colloquial intonation, without the textbook.

During both sessions the teacher reads with the accompaniment of suitable musical pieces, which are professionally selected and experimentally ascertained.

Whether the student's attention is directed to the music or to the text makes no difference.

4. The students take part in the next stages of the educational process

of their own free will, in a playlike form, without being afraid of the mistakes they might make in the beginning of their education. The mistakes are corrected by the teacher with skill and tact, an ability in which the teacher is particularly trained.

5. The suggestopedic method (in its present-day phase) results in an acceleration of learning, a laying of the foundation of the foreign language, and a creation of possibilities to make active use of the material which consists of about 2,000 lexical items and the whole basic grammar. A positive psychotherapeutic and psychohygienic effect is observed at the same time.

From midcourse on, directions are constantly given concerning further studying and perfecting the foreign language on the student's own, after the course is over.

6. The correct implementation of both the teaching and the experiment requires strict observances of the following:

(*a*) Classes begin and end at the fixed time sharp.

(*b*) Students are allowed to be absent with valid reason *once*. A second absence results in the removal of the student from the course, without depriving him or her of the possibility of enlisting in a similar course at some future time. The attendance of every student is duly recorded.

(*c*) Students are requested, if unable to attend or if compelled to be late, to inform well in advance the administration of the course by phone.

(*d*) Smoking is permissible only in the courtyard.

(*e*) *Bringing tape recorders into the Institute and taping in the classrooms are forbidden.*

(*f*) In order to derive maximum benefit from the method, students should avoid overstraining themselves with other tasks during the course. They should possibly stay away from psychotraumatic situations; abuse of alcohol is highly undesirable, as is going to bed late in the evening. Generally speaking, students must observe a natural, normal hygienic regime.

(*g*) Any opinions, assessments, and proposals arising during the course are to be addressed to the governing body of the Institute. By the end of the course, the students will have the possibility to express their opinion in written form.

(*h*) A foreign language course for beginners takes 24 working days, 3 school hours daily, with no homework.

(*i*) We recommend: *before going to bed in the evening* or *after getting up in the morning*, spare 15–20 minutes for the reading of the new text from the foreign to the native tongue, and vice versa. Such a reading should be merely informative (as one skims through a newspaper) with no attempt to learn parrot-fashion. All kinds of records in the foreign language may be listened to, as a background activity, without paying special attention to them and without trying to memorize them.

Have a good time in fruitful studies!

THE INSTITUTE

As a rule, students are seated in a semicircle in easy chairs with small tables. The easy chair for the teacher is slightly set apart and placed in such a way to allow the teacher a good view of every student in addition to allowing every student to see and hear the teacher as well as possible. Students may change their seating arrangement at any time during the course.

Fresh-cut flowers are always present in the classrooms. The latter are always aired very well. In the cold seasons they are well heated. The colors in the classrooms are of soft and pleasant shades. The walls are hung with grammatical posters of the most important paradigms, which are rearranged or replaced according to the concrete needs of the class. The posters exhibit an artistic presentation, with pictures that suit the didactic material as a background or as illustrations. A map of the country of the language being studied, photographs, and/or souvenirs are also hung.

The students are in a sort of suspense. The teacher's very first contact with the students creates the kind of dynamism, warmth, and easiness which are so necessary for suggestopedic education. From the first moment the teacher speaks only in the foreign language.

As has been already pointed out, the qualification of the teachers is of crucial importance for the effectiveness of the suggestopedic courses and the suggestopedic learning in general—henceforth for the continuing self-instruction of the students.

The following pages contain the brief *Methodological Instructions for the Suggestopedic Teaching of Foreign Languages to Adults*, which represents a plan–synopsis for the work of qualified suggestopedic teachers. Afterward, we shall examine the sections of this document in more detail.

METHODOLOGICAL INSTRUCTIONS

For the Suggestopedic Teaching of Foreign Languages to Adults

I. Introduction

1. The introduction is designed to be the teacher's first encounter with the students. Furthermore, it should be the first contact of the students with the subject matter to be dealt with during the following days.

By means of short *artistic and didactic songs*, where the most important lexical and grammatical forms can be found, the teacher offers to the student an imaginary autobiography. The teacher presents him- or herself with a nationality and a stage name borrowed from the foreign language, with a bogus occupation, birthplace, etc.

At the teacher's very first contact with the students, he or she introduces a spirit of *dynamism, easiness,* and at the same time, of *delicacy* into his or her attitude toward the group as a whole and toward every student as an individual.

Every student is included in this act of introduction very naturally, according to a plan in which each student chooses a *nationality and name* in the language under study, in addition to a bogus occupation, etc. Imitating the teacher, the students introduce themselves to one another and take up their new roles.

The introduction in the ensuing lessons takes place under a similar artistic presentation, always bearing in mind that it should embrace the most important lexical and grammatical highlights.

Note: The introduction in the first lesson might take about 20–30 minutes, and in the next lessons, no more than 15 minutes. Use may be made of tiny props, musical records, slides, films, as well as other suitable materials. It is recommended that this not be overdone to keep on the safe side of the grotesque.

2. The artistically drawn grammatical posters, designed for the needs of the lesson, should be properly placed. They should preferably be perceived by the students *peripherally*—and this is particularly important in the beginning. Later on, when the material requires them, they can be

quickly glanced at. The need for such posters must gradually fade as the course progresses.

II. Active Concert Session

1. The musical compositions for the active session are very emotional, with a wealth of melody and harmony in them.
2. The teacher's *behavior* is solemn, as it should be when a concert is about to begin. The teacher waits quietly till the end of the introductory movement of the music. After a clearly perceivable *caesura* (a breath, a short pause), *the reading* of the text begins, the teacher's intonation varying solemnly *according to the character of the musical piece.*
3. The teacher should, in his or her mind, keep a little ahead of the accompaniment, so that as he or she comes to read each subsequent sentence, it is tuned in to the music: movement in *major* scale (jubilant mood), in *minor* scale (intimate and lyrical mood), the different tempi (slow, fast, moderate), and the volume (low, full or medium).
4. It is suggested that the teacher consult the program before each session. Information is given in it about some of the characteristic features of the respective musical compositions—for instance, the scale (major or minor); the tempi of the movements: andante (at a walking pace), allegro (rather fast), moderato (at an easy pace); and so on. In the ideal case, the teacher should listen to the musical composition in its entirety before playing it for the class.
5. In reading, the teacher's voice should be harmonized with the nuances of the musical phrase. The diction should be pure and distinct, every word clear-cut and phonetically well-molded. The voice should be well taken up in the resonance box. The reading should be slow and rhythmical, the breathing regular. The active session normally should not last more than 45–50 minutes (with the only exception of the first concert session).

(*a*) In order to obtain self-control over the rhythm of reading, the teacher should first read the sentence to him- or herself and afterward—slowly—aloud.

(*b*) The musical phrase should always be kept in mind: the reading should begin when there is a strong (accentuated) note, and finish, if possible, when the musical phrase comes to an end. The teacher should naturally follow the brightest melodic line, regardless of the part where it appears.

(*c*) When the musical line ranges to a higher register, the voice which follows it should not become high-pitched, but softer and deeper.

Metaphorically speaking, the reading voice should join in the orchestra as a *suo modo* new instrument, which emphasizes the musical phrase and makes its psychological charge easier to apprehend.

6. Those new words in the text which bear lexical or grammatical information of particular importance, should be brought out with a kind of intonation different from that used in the rest of the sentence.

Note 1: In reading, the teacher should often lift his or her eyes from the book, and show attentiveness to the students through a glance at them or through a gesture.

Note 2: The more the reading is kept in harmony with the character of the chosen piece of music, the more varied, original, intriguing, and eagerly expected will the students find it. Also, the more easily memorized and the more readily reproduced will be this reading matter later on.

The most important part of the work should be finished when this "particular" kind of reading is done.

III. Pseudopassive Concert Session

1. Here the *musical compositions* are characterized by austerity of form, content, and intellectual depth.

2. The teacher sits down comfortably, correctly, and is very calm and relaxed. He or she waits for the students to imitate him or her spontaneously.

3. The reading is normal, like everyday speech, and as artistic as the dialogue requires it should be (i.e., the timbre of the voice varies slightly according to the lines of the characters and the emotion in them). The rate of reading should be that of the colloquial speech of the respective foreign language. In this session, the music is used mainly as a background for relaxation, but is as loud as at a normal concert.

The two suggestopedic concert sessions are the acme of the ritual cycle. They should not be underestimated.

IV. Elaborations

1. First Day After the Concert Session

First elaboration: The text is divided into several parts. The reading of the first dialogue is performed mostly in chorus. Cursory phonetic explanations are given on the spot. The students read the parts in the foreign language, taking a look at the translation of the text. During the next days the students assume different roles, each one reading the lines of the character he or she is impersonating. The students pass the roles on to one another, so that each student gets the chance of reading each role in one of the parts of the text—in other words, one student reads the lines of a certain character in one part of the text, while another reads the same character's lines in another part of it. (Another possibility is to give different variants of one and the same role.) The reading mistakes should be corrected tactfully, the teacher only repeating the word in the correct way, as if by chance. When the given part is read, the translation is taken away (or folded up) and the whole of the same part is translated by the students.

In a more advanced phase the teacher decides which passages should be translated and which not. In the last lessons of the course, only a few words and phrases have to be explained by means of synonyms.

While the translation is being done (without the text in the native tongue), some details of the part, which are important from the point of view of their lexical and grammatical features, are acted out through games and songs (and even through easy dances). All students should participate. The location in the text and the duration of the games are previously specified. Quite a lot of subject matter can be presented through these games.

Then comes the next part.

Note: There should be a group reading with the teacher from the very first session if reading difficulties in certain languages have to be overcome. Some passages should be tried out with students who can read, though not quite correctly. Generally speaking, all possible suggestopedic means of mastering the reading should be used. (Most often this should be the technique of "learning how to ride a bicycle.")

If the whole dialogue cannot be dealt with in one day's period, of course, it can be worked out to the end of next day. This primary elaboration of the text should come as a confirmation of the student's conviction that they have mastered the material at the translation level. Now, the teacher must make certain that there is an *easy, quiet transition to active speaking.*

2. Second Day After the Session

Second elaboration: The group goes on with the work begun the previous day until they get through the grammatical units in the lessons. The students are activated in two ways: (a) directly, through reading and translation, interspersed with easy games and play-acting; and (b) by playing suitable games apart from the text. The choice of which to use is left to the teacher's intuition.

Note: During reading and translating, all opportunities for analogy should be made use of. For instance, when reading a sentence, the verb therein could be quickly conjugated on the spot, in chorus, and its link to the verbs in the posters could be shown furtively. In a similar fashion, sentences or phrases could be remade.

The teacher reads aloud slowly the description of an event, and the students translate *the new reading matter*, either in chorus or individually (in the latter case, at their own wish). The text should form a summary of the most important lexical and grammatical units used in the dialogue, in a new way, using direct and indirect speech. (If any student wishes to, he or she can try and narrate in a few words some similar event.) The text should provide a basis for some of the students to tell a story of their own the next day. They should think about what they will be able to narrate within the framework of such a theme (summarizing, in fact, the most important points in the lesson). The rest of the group should turn its interests to another part of the lesson. The stories should be in direct and indirect speech. At the beginning they should be rather short, but with progress made in the respective language, they should grow longer and more detailed. They can be connected with the students' new identities and with the roles they play in class. From the middle of the course on, the students can tell suitable anecdotes and speak about small happenings in their own lives. The contents of these narrations should be interesting. The teacher should be careful in choosing the theme to be thought over at home. Of course, nothing should be written down.

Suitable games and/or songs should also be included in the secondary elaboration. They should always be loaded with lexical and grammatical information and be of artistic value, with a view to the general educative sides of the instruction—familiarizing the students with the culture of the respective country.

3. Third Day After the Session

In the initial stages of the course, the teacher might write suitable questions on the blackboard, so that when the students give answers to these, the answers begin to form a story with a plot.

By skillfully steering the conversation around the theme (or themes) of the different stories given the day before, the teacher can, in an encouraging way, invite the students to retell them. Only the most inadmissible mistakes should be corrected.

As soon as the first spontaneous attempts of a student to cut into another student's story appear, the teacher must immediately take the situation in hand, and stimulate and maintain this process of spontaneous communication as much as possible and see that it becomes a regular procedure in the course. (Not "early," but "spontaneous" activation!)

Generally speaking, one should from the very beginning take the utmost care in the double-plane, tactful, delicate, and suggestive directing of the students toward spontaneous conversation. This conversation should be natural, with no pressing requirements, nor creation of special role-playing situations (except in cases when the students either seek or create them themselves).

The teacher should think of various ways of inspiring different forms of general conversation among the students about their everyday life (stressing positive things, of course), either with the group conversing in chorus or individually.

From the very beginning of the course, those students who have some previous knowledge of the language should be handled very cautiously. Skill and tact must be used in keeping the part they play in the lesson well in hand, so that they do not monopolize it, and to save time and keep up the spirits of the real beginners who cannot understand all that the students with a smattering of the language are saying. After a certain amount of general progress has been made in the whole group, these students with some prior knowledge can be allowed to display their knowledge to the full.

In general, *activation should come in a more vigorous way after the third or fourth dialogue*. The students then can be given roles to play more often if they express a spontaneous wish to do so.

Note 1: Conversation between two or three students, either with or without textbook, should not be allowed outside the teacher's control. Such conversations are not in line with suggestopedy and psychotherapy. (The beginner poses the wrong questions, thus surprising and perplexing the other beginner.)

Note 2: Every new working day should begin either with reading aloud a text in the foreign language, or with the teacher narrating some intriguing everyday story in the foreign language—taking into consideration the students' easy understanding of it.

Part of the output level (according to the established suggestopedic tests) should be given cautiously a few days prior to the end of the course, for instance, in the form of challenging written tests, conversations, etc.

During the course, the students should be given *easy tests to stimulate them*, mainly translations into their mother tongue, including meaningful parts of dialogues and extra texts (after the latter have been translated during the elaborations). These fragments can be given either in written form or can be read slowly by the teacher and translated *extempore* by the students.

The closing day should be thought out carefully. If a so called "final performance" is given, it should be only if the students really wish to give it. The course can also have a more solemn ending.

SPEAKING ONE'S MOTHER TONGUE DURING THE COURSE IS UNDESIRABLE. THIS HOLDS TRUE BOTH FOR THE TEACHER (EVERY TIME HE OR SHE COMES INTO CONTACT WITH THE STUDENTS) AND FOR THE STUDENTS (WITH THEIR GRADUAL PROGRESS).

Note: Suggestopedy is neither a direct, nor a directive, teaching technique, but a way of encouraging the spontaneous creativity of the learner with tact and double-planeness.

The teacher should not display his or her abilities—instead he or she should suggest to the students that they display theirs. That is why, in the beginning of the course, the teacher is very active and social, diplomatically stimulating the students. Then, gradually, the teacher should retract upon him- or herself, assuming merely controlling and consultative functions.

COMMENTS ON METHODOLOGICAL INSTRUCTIONS

Lesson One: "Getting Acquainted"

I. Introduction

1. Each presentation of new subject matter (i.e., every new lesson) begins with introducing it. But the introduction is so short emotionally and so condensed logically, coded and algorithmed in such a way that the essence of lexis and grammar stipulated to underlie a suggestopedic lesson, is presented in the most synthetic form. We call the lesson "suggestopedic," because it is totally organized on the basis of suggestology and according to the principles and means of suggestopedy (see G. Lozanov, *Suggestology and Outlines of Suggestopedy*, Gordon and Breach, New York, 1978).

The first encounter is of decisive importance. This is an established truth in general psychology, and we have obtained abundant experimental validation thereof. The expectation; the surprise; the novelty; the extraordinary, emotional, and at the same time convincing and logically satisfying (for the student) organization of the first encounter—all these premises constitute the basis of any further work. From the very first moment of introduction the teacher should solidly embrace the whole group and the individual student with skill, delicacy, and competence, in order to successfully implement from the beginning to the end of the course a highly efficient suggestopedic work, that is, tapping to the maximum the reserve capacities of the individuals he or she is going to teach and for whom he or she will lead the way toward self-education. Everything in this work is designed to engender from the very first moment, from the very first communicative "spark" between teacher and student, the dynamism that is so necessary in the suggestopedic process. The intensity of this dynamism is dictated by the teacher according to the predominating stereotypes of the group. The aim is to achieve maximum acceleration of the students' psychological processes without bringing about a state of strain. That is where the teacher's mastery lies: to be able to conduct with precision the transition between the three tempi of work: fast, slow, moderate; to introduce light and shade in the dynamism: high, low, medium; to fix the duration of these states according to the rules of the golden section which, for the time being, is still the soundest psychological criterion for a good balance.

Here we propose a model scenario for the initial encounter and introduction in the first suggestopedic lesson in a foreign language (namely, Italian). This model scenario has lately won recognition as a very successful variant and is being applied widely by teachers in other foreign languages as well.

The teacher comes into the classroom and shakes hands with each student. He or she speaks mostly in the foreign tongue, translating into the native tongue with "mistakes" and an accent.

Buon giorno, buon giorno!	Hello, hello!
Non mi conoscete.	You don't know me.
Io vi conosco.	I know you.
Mi chiamo Lucia.	My name is Lucia.
Sono italiana.	I am Italian.
"La storia mia è breve..."	My story is brief.

(The last line is spoken by Mimi in Pucini's *La Bohème*, and the teacher sings it.)

Ecco la.	Here it is.

The teacher distributes among the students the song *Stories*. The teacher, Lucia, then sings this song, which is both artistic and didactic, designed to present the modal verb "to be." The teacher's singing places particular emphasis on the different forms of the verb. The students gradually engage in singing. The text of the song is given with a translation in order to make it possible for the students to follow. The teacher imparts a slight irony to the meaning of the text.

Note: Similar artistic–didactic songs are worked out for all the lexical and grammatical topics that are important for the learning of a foreign language. When didactic material is presented in songs, recitatives, recitals, and even in the simplest rhythmic form, it is assimilated much easier, in much larger amounts, and with much greater retention. (For more details see E. Gateva, *Development of Language and Melody*, 1979. Selected elements in their experimental aspects are treated in G. Lozanov's work, *Suggestology and Outlines of Suggestopedy*, Gordon and Breach, New York, 1978.)

Storie	**Stories**
1. *Sono* sola, sola, sola (solo)...	I *am* alone, alone, alone...
2. Dove *sei*, amico (-a) mio (-a)?	Where *are* you, my friend?
3. *E'* un giorno tanto bello!	It *is* such a nice day!
1. Ma *siamo* separati.	But we *are* apart from each other.
E perchè?	And why?
Sapete voi?	Do you know?
2. Forse non *siete* soli?	Perhaps you *are* not alone?
3. *Sono* storie banali!	These *are* banal stories!
Basta, basta!	Enough, enough!
Ho morti amici.	I have many friends.
Ecco Rocco.	This is Rocco.

(Lucia carries a large traveling bag. From it she produces a gaily colored, funny-looking figure: a Rocco doll.)

Rocco è molto intelligente.	Rocco is very intelligent.
E' straordinario.	He is extraordinary.
Solo io lo capisco.	Only I understand him.
Sentite la storia di Rocco.	Listen to the story of Rocco.

(Lucia distributes another didactic song, *Beautiful Flower*, for the verb "to have." She sings the song, which has a dance tune. Lucia makes the class get up and dance for a while, instructing them to jump when a form of "to have" is pronounced. Everything should be done in a very captivating and tactful manner.)

Un Bel Fiore	**Beautiful flower**
1. *Ho* un amico.	I *have* a friend.
Gli dico un giorno:	I tell him one day:
"Non ho denaro.	"I have no money.
2. *Hai* mille lire?	*Have* you a thousand lire?
Voglio comprare	I want to buy
quel bel fiore."	that beautiful flower."
Lui mi guarda.	He looks at me.
3. *Ha* mille lire.	He *has* a thousand lire.
Cerca piano.	He searches slowly.
Ma io ho fretta:	But I'm in a hurry:

Storie

Allegro
Parole e musica: E. Gateva

1. Sono sola, sola, sola. (solo)

2. Dove sei, amico mio (amica mia)

3. E' un giorno tanto bello!

1. Ma siamo separati.

E perche? Sapete voi?

2. Forse non siete soli?

3. Sono storie banali! Basta, basta!

1. "*Non abbiamo*   "We *have* no
   più tempo, Rocco."   more time, Rocco."
   Due ragazzi   Two boys
   hanno comprato   have bought
   quel bel fiore.   that beautiful flower.
   "Dite, ragazzi,   "Say, boys,
2. *avete* bisogno   do you need
   d'un bel fiore?"   a beautiful flower?"
   "Certo, signori.   "Of course, gentlemen.
3. Tutti *hanno*   All *have*
   un bel fiore!"   a beautiful flower!"
   Ecco il fiore di Rocco.   Here is Rocco's flower.

(Lucia produces a somewhat peculiar looking artificial flower out of her bag and hangs it on the wall. Then she produces other dolls, and shelves them in particular places.)

Note: During the introduction, the teacher translates in accordance with the students' reactions.

Un bel fiore

Allegro
Parole e musica: E. Gateva

1. Ho un amico. Gli dico un giorno:

2. Non ho denaro. Hai mille lire?

Voglio comprare quel bel fiore.

meno mosso

3. Lui mi guarda. Ha mille lire.

più mosso

Cerca piano. Ma i' ho fretta:

1. —Non abbiamo più tempo, Rocco.

Due ragazzi hanno comprato

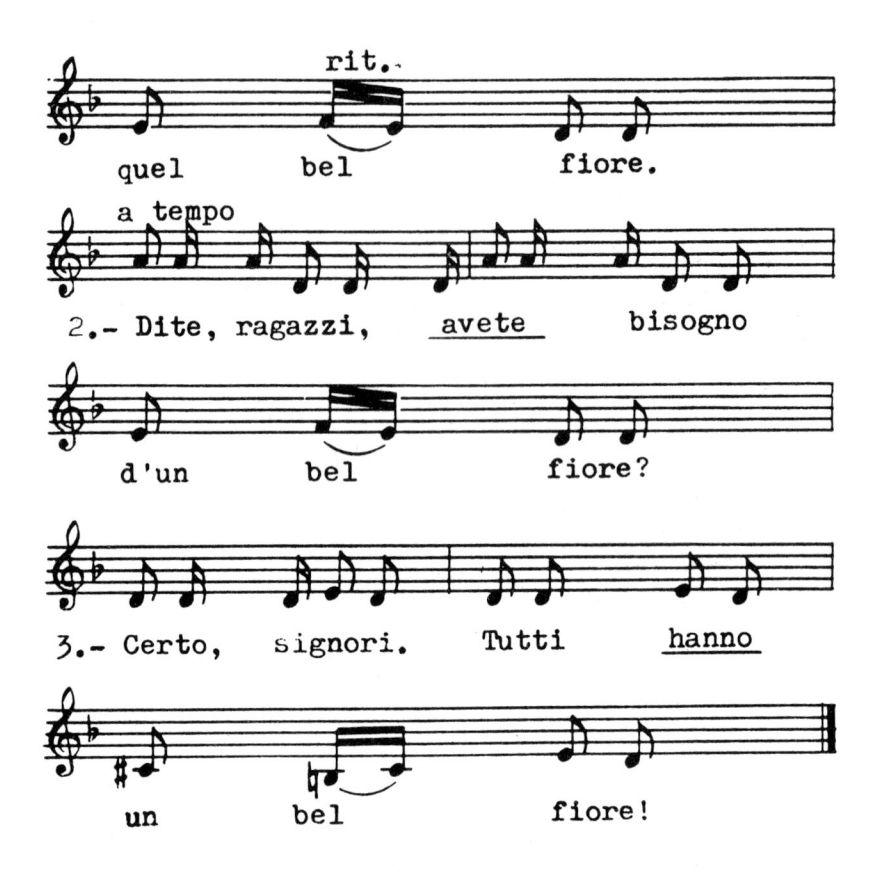

quel bel fiore.

2.- Dite, ragazzi, avete bisogno d'un bel fiore?

3.- Certo, signori. Tutti hanno un bel fiore!

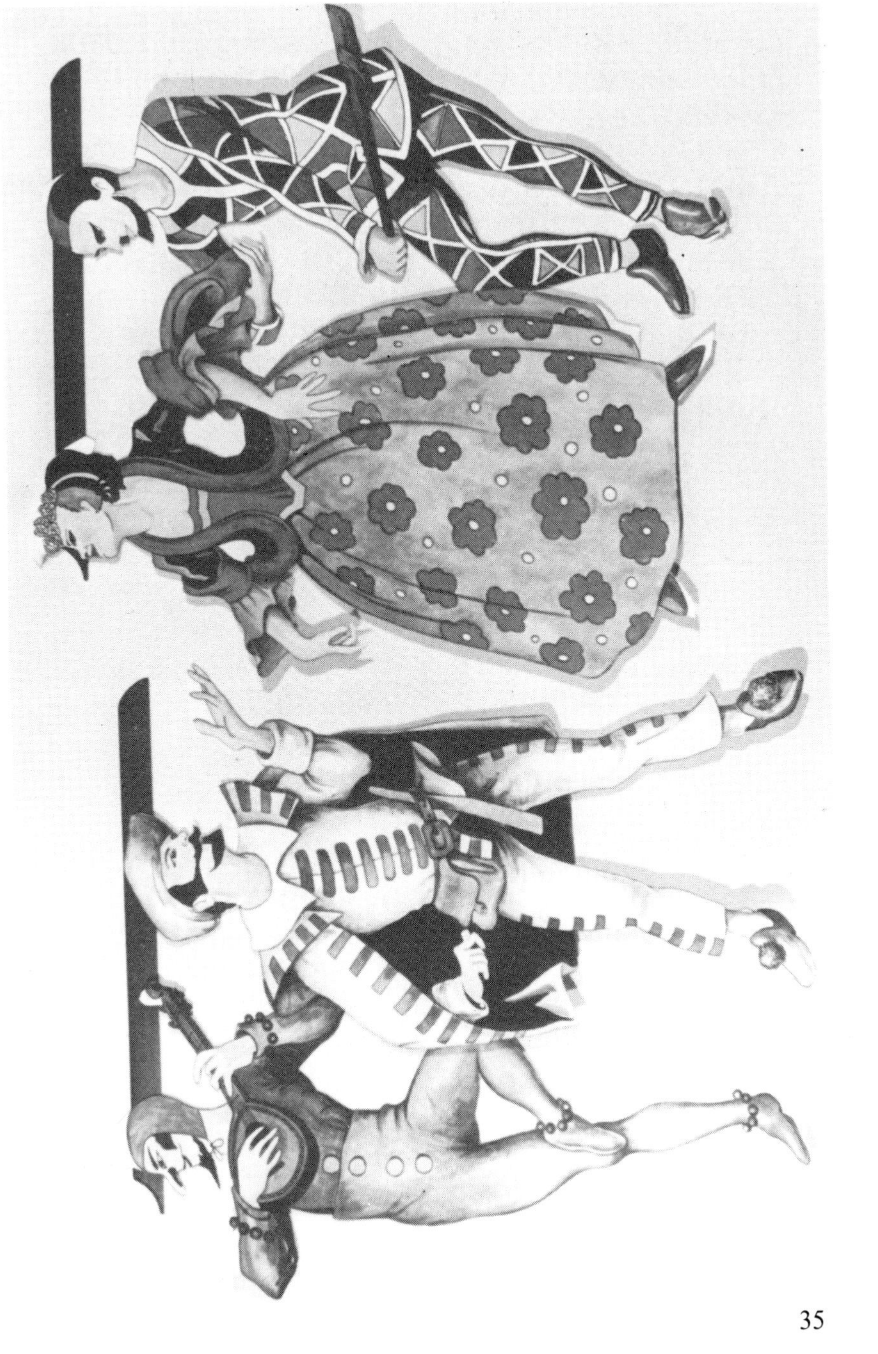

impiegato, -a	Vincenzo	Beatrice
contadino, -a	Francesco	Cecilia
marinaio	Cesare	Lucia
attore – attrice	Cicerone	Lucrezia
pittore – pittrice	Marcello	Chiara
scrittore – scrittrice	Luciano	Angela
direttore – direttrice	Carlo	Gilda
avvocato – avvocatessa	Domenico	Gina
giudice	Claudio	Giulietta
medico – dottoressa	Gioachino	Gisella
studente – studentessa	Scipione	Margherita

ragioniere — architetto
ingegnere — farmacista
autista — dentista
regista — generale
giornalista — ufficiale
musicista — ministro
poeta — avventuriero
commerciante

Fig. 1 - Italian language—names and occupations.

Nome	
Singolare	Plurale
Maschile	
il quadr*o*	*i* quadr*i*
lo {*specchio*, *zucchero*}	*gli* specchi
l' italiano	gli italiani
il padr*e*	*i* padri
Femminile	
la copert*a*	*le* copert*e*
l' italiana	le italiane
la città	le città
la madr*e*	le madr*i*

	avere	
Presente:	*Ho*	un bel fiore
	Hai	" "
	Ha	" "
	Abbiamo	" "
	Avete	" "
	Hanno	" "
Passato p.:	*Ho avuto* un bel fiore.	
Futuro:		Imperfetto:
avrò		avevo

Fig. 2a - Definite and indefinite article, nouns in masculine and feminine, singular and plural. b - Auxiliary verb "avere" ("to have"). Present, past perfect, past imperfect, and future tenses (indicative mood).

essere	Presente	
1 Io	*sono*	Lucia.
2 Tu	*sei*	un bambino.
3 Egli Lui Ella Lei Lei	*è*	il padre. la madre. molto gentile.
1 Noi	*siamo*	amici.
2 Voi	*siete*	studenti.
3 Essi Esse Loro	*sono*	ospiti.

Passato prossimo

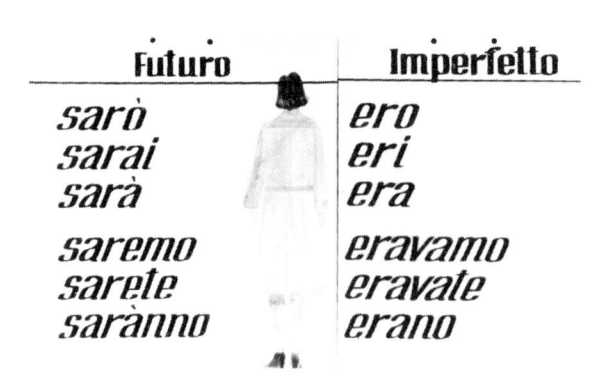

sono stato,-a

Futuro	Imperfetto
sarò	*ero*
sarai	*eri*
sarà	*era*
saremo	*eravamo*
sarete	*eravate*
saranno	*erano*

Fig. 3 - Auxiliary verb "essere" ("to be"). Present, past perfect, past imperfect, and future tense.

Presente

	cantare	vedere	partire
1	cant-o	ved-o	part-o
2	cant-i	ved-i	part-i
3	cant-a	ved-e	part-e
1	cant-iamo	ved-iamo	part-iamo
2	cant-ate	ved-ete	part-ite
3	cant-ano	ved-ono	part-ono

Passato prossimo

ho cant-ato	ho ved-uto (visto)	sono part-ito (ita)

Futuro

cantar-ò	veder-ò (metter-ò)	partir-ò
-ai		
-à		
-emo		
-ete		
-anno		

Imperfetto

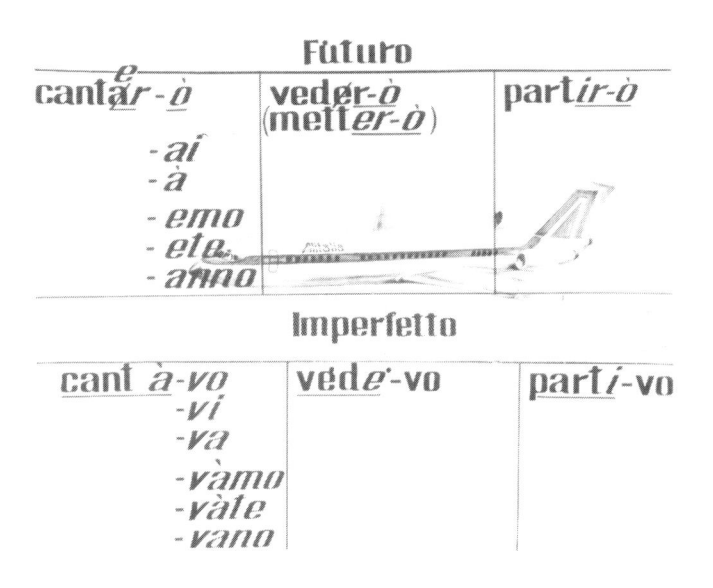

cant à-vo	vede-vo	parti-vo
-vi		
-va		
-vamo		
-vate		
-vano		

Fig. 4 - First, second, and third conjugation of the Italian verbs in present, past perfect, past imperfect, and future tenses.

dovere	potere	volere
Presente		
devo	posso	voglio
devi	puoi	vuoi
deve	può	vuole
dobbiamo	possiamo	vogliamo
dovete	potete	volete
devono	possono	vogliono
Passato prossimo		
ho dovuto	ho potuto	ho voluto
Futuro		
dovrò	potrò	vorrò
Imperfetto		
dovevo	potevo	volevo

andare
Presente: vado
vai
va
andiamo
andate
vanno
Passato p.: sono andato,-a
Futuro: andrò
Imperfetto: andavo

fare (facere)	sapere
faccio	so
fai	sai
fa	sa
facciamo	sappiamo
fate	sapete
fanno	sanno
ho fatto	ho saputo
farò	saprò
facevo	sapevo

Fig. 5a - The modal verbs: "volere" ("to want"), "potere" ("can"), "dovere" ("must"). b - The irregular verbs: "andare" ("to go"), "fare" ("to make"), "sapere" ("to know").

	dire (dicere)	uscire
Presente:	dico dici dice diciamo dite dicono	*esco* *esci* *esce* usciamo uscite *escono*
Passato p.:	ho *detto*	sono uscito,-a
Futuro:	dirò	uscirò
Imperfetto:	dicevo	uscivo

	venire
Presente:	ven*g*o v*ie*ni v*ie*ne veniamo venite ven*g*ono
Passato p.:	sono venuto,-a
Futuro:	verrò
Imperfetto:	venivo

leggere — *letto*
scrivere — *scritto*
bere (bevere) — *bevuto*
mettere — *messo*
muovere — *mosso*
scendere — *sceso,-a*
succedere — *successo*
prendere — *preso*
chiudere — *chiuso*
decidere — *deciso*
correre — *corso*
risolvere — *risolto*
scegliere — *scelto*
togliere — *tolto*
vincere — *vinto*
chiedere — *chiesto*
rimanere — *rimasto,-a*
rispondere — *risposto*
aprire — *aperto*

Fig. 6a - The irregular verbs: "dire" ("to say"), "uscire" ("to go out"), "venire" ("to come"). b - Irregular forms of the past participle: "to read," "to write," "to put," "to move," "to descend," "to become," "to take," "to close," "to decide," "to run," "to resolve," "to choose," "to remove," "to win," "to respond," "to open."

Gino mi (мe) guarda.
" ti (me) "
" lo (ѕo) "
" la (я.Bu) "
" si (ce) "

" ci (ни) "
" vi (Bu) "
" li "
" le (ѕu) "

Gino gli (мy) dice un aneddoto.
" le (ú.Bu) "
G. dice loro (uм) un aneddoto.

Fig. 7a - Personal pronouns as direct and indirect complement (short form). b - A collective painting on the subject "Seasons" (course in Italian, Sofia, 1980).

ser
Modo indicativo – Presente

1 Yo	soy	español.
2 Tú	eres	mi amigo.
3 Él	es	de Madrid.
Ella	”	muy hermosa.
Usted	”	mi profesor.
1 Nosotros	somos	españoles.
2 Vosotros	sois)	
3 Ellos	son	mis amigos.
Ellas	”	mis amigas.
Ustedes	”	mis profesores.

Pretérito imperfecto	Futuro	Pretérito indefinido
era	seré	fui
eras	serás	fuiste
era	será	fué
éramos	seremos	fuimos
erais	seréis	fuisteis
eran	serán	fueron

Fig. 8 - The Spanish auxiliary verb "ser" ("to be").

estar		tener	
Modo indicativo		Modo indicativo	
Presente		**Presente**	
Estoy	contento y alegre	tengo	tenemos
¿Estás	aquí?	t*ie*nes	tenéis
Está	muy bien	t*ie*ne	t*ie*nen
Estamos	en el hotel	**P. indefinido**	**Futuro**
Estáis		tuve	tendré
Están	listos	tuviste	tendrás
P. indefinido		tuvo	tendrá
estuve	estuvimos	tuvimos	tendremos
estuviste	estuvisteis	tuvisteis	tendréis
estuvo	estuvieron	tuvieron	tendrán
Futuro: estaré		**P. imperfecto**	tenía
P. imperfecto: estaba			

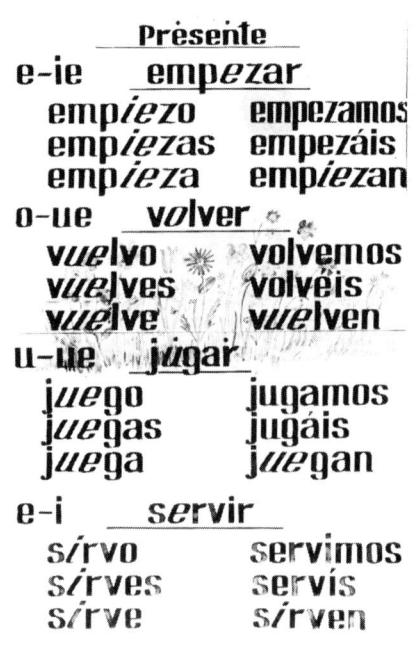

	Presente	
e-ie	emp*e*zar	
	emp*ie*zo	empezamos
	emp*ie*zas	empezáis
	emp*ie*za	emp*ie*zan
o-ue	v*o*lver	
	v*ue*lvo	volvemos
	v*ue*lves	volvéis
	v*ue*lve	v*ue*lven
u-ue	j*u*gar	
	j*ue*go	jugamos
	j*ue*gas	jugáis
	j*ue*ga	j*ue*gan
e-i	s*e*rvir	
	s*i*rvo	servimos
	s*i*rves	servís
	s*i*rve	s*i*rven

Fig. 9 - Spanish verbs "estar" ("to be") and "tener" ("to have"). Partially irregular verbs.

44

lachen	Präsens
ich *lache*	wir *lachen*
du *lachst*	ihr *lacht*
er sie *lacht* es	sie *lachen* Sie *lachen*

lachen	Imperfekt
ich *lachte*	wir *lachten*
du *lachtest*	ihr *lachtet*
er *lachte*	sie Sie *lachten*

lachen	Futur
▸ich *werde* lachen	

lachen	Perfekt mit "haben"
▸ich *habe* gelacht	

fahren	Perfekt mit "sein"
▸ich *bin* gefahren	

werden	Präsens
ich *werde* Tee trinken	wir *werden* Tee trinken
du *wirst* " "	ihr *werdet* " "
er sie *wird* " " es	sie *werden* " " Sie *werden* " "

Fig. 10 - German language. The verbs "lachen" ("to laugh") and "werden" ("to become").

Verbes du premier groupe
Chanter
Futur
chanter-*ai* chanter-*ons*
    " -*as*   "   -*ez*
    " -*a*   "   -*ont*

Imparfait
chant-*ais* chant-*ions*
    " -*ais*   " -*iez*
    " -*ait*   " -*aient*

Passé composé
J'ai chanté
Je n'ai pas chanté
Est-ce que tu as chanté?
As-tu chanté?

Béatrice	Gérard
Mireille	Gaston
Solange	Charles
Germaine	Georges
Claudine	Jean-Marc
Sylvie	André
Blanche	Henri
Françoise	Louis
Hélène	Bernard
Jacqueline	René
Marie-Rose	Julien
Monique	Léon
Agnès	
Antoinette	

Adjectifs possessifs

mon   ma   mes
ton   ta   tes
son   sa   ses

notre   nos
votre   vos
leur   leurs

Fig. 11a - French language. Names. b - Possessive pronouns. c - The verb "chanter" ("to sing").

can, may, must

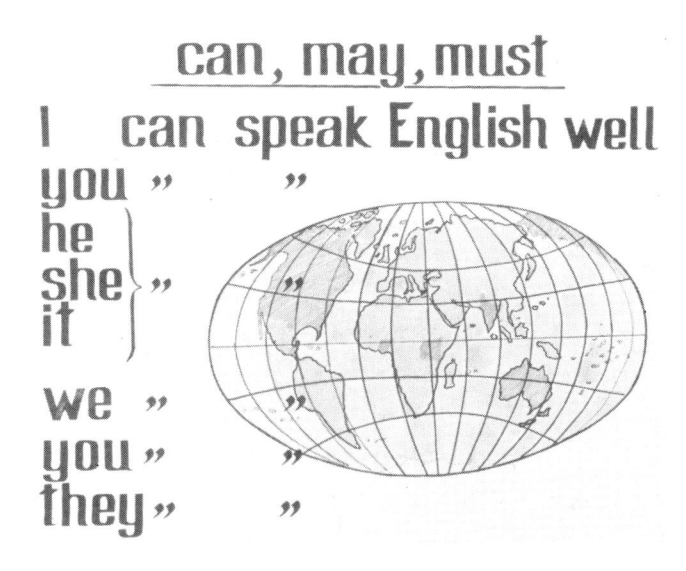

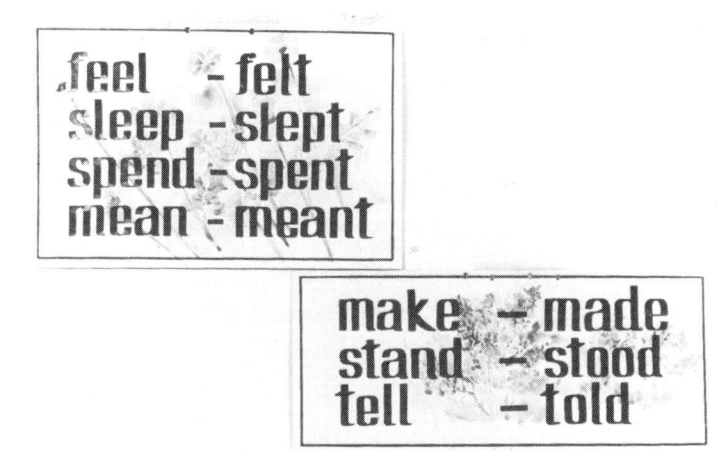

I can speak English well
you " "
he
she } "   "
it
we " "
you " "
they " "

feel — felt
sleep — slept
spend — spent
mean — meant

make — made
stand — stood
tell — told

Fig. 12a - English language. The modal verb "can." b - Some verbs in past simple.

Fig. 13a - Some of the props used in the Italian course. b - The items from the bag.

Figs. 14–16 - Art reproductions used during the elaborations of some themes (course in Italian).

Fig. 15

Fig. 16

Los marineros

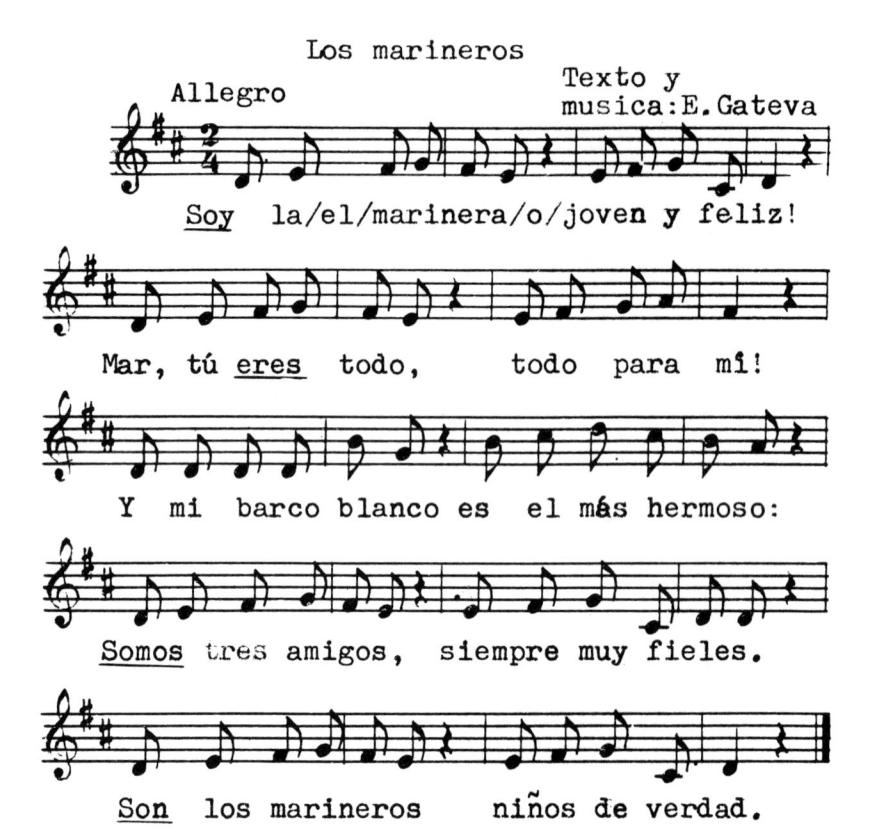

Allegro
Texto y musica: E. Gateva

Soy la/el/marinera/o/joven y feliz!

Mar, tú eres todo, todo para mí!

Y mi barco blanco es el más hermoso:

Somos tres amigos, siempre muy fieles.

Son los marineros niños de verdad.

Estoy muy contento

Allegro moderato
Texto y musica: E. Gateva

Es<u>toy</u> muy content<u>o</u> /-<u>a</u>/, contento de la vida. Es<u>tás</u>, mi vida, cerca, te siento, te adoro. Está mi vida llena de sol, de alegría. Estamos juntos siempre, tú y yo. Conmigo los amigos <u>están</u> alegres.

I Am a Happy Man

Words by L. Kozhuharova
Music by E. Gateva

Allegretto

I am, I am a happy man. You are, you are my good old friend. He is my friend, she is my friend, we are good friends, all

1. happy friends. // 2. hap- py friends.

La famille heureuse

Par. Z. Ivanova
E. Jordanova
Mus. E. Gateva

Allegro

Je suis joyeux. Je suis heureux.

Je suis content. Tu es charmante.

Tu es très bonne. Tu es si belle.

Il est mignon, le bébé.

Elle est mignonne, la fillette.

Ils sont charmants nos enfants.

Vous êtes joyeux tous les trois.

Vous êtes contents, mes chéris.

Nous sommes nombreux mais heureux.

Bon anniversaire

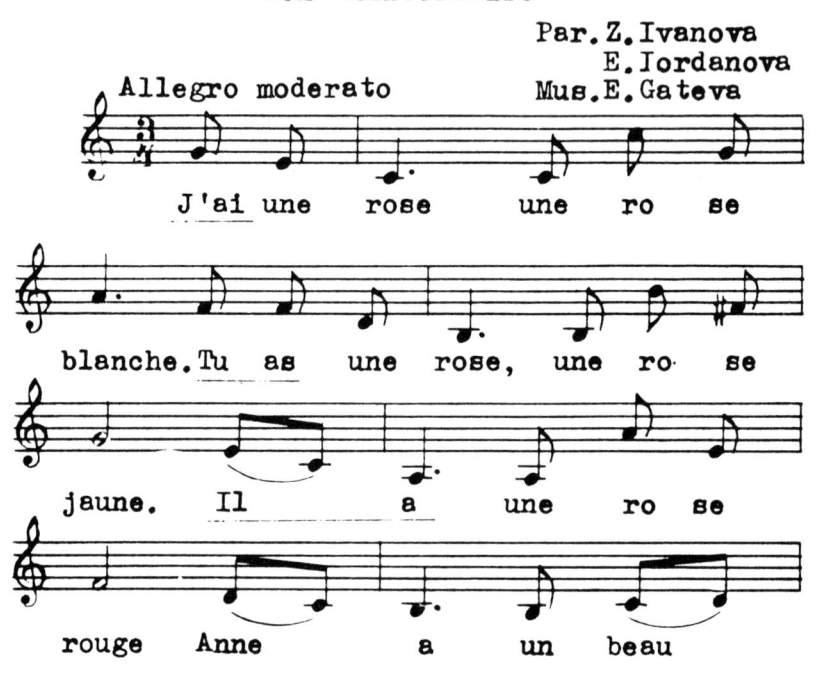

Par. Z. Ivanova
E. Iordanova
Mus. E. Gateva

Allegro moderato

J'ai une rose une rose blanche. Tu as une rose, une rose jaune. Il a une rose rouge Anne a un beau vase. Elle y met nos fleurs. Toutes les roses ont des é- pines, mais leur parfumes exquis. Nous avons un grand plaisir. A votre fête Anne vous avez de bons amis. Trois vrais et bons amis. Bon an ni vairsaire chérie!

Die Blume

Worte: M. Tschukova
Musik: E. Gateva

Allegro

Ich habe eine Blume in meinem klei- nen Garten. Ich möchte sie dir geben. Sie hat ein kurzes Leben.

Du hast die schöne Blume
Bei dir in deinem Hause.
Wir haben sie zusammen.
Ihr habt nicht solche Blume.

Der Tag

Allegro moderato
Worte: M. Tschukova
Musik: E. Gateva

Der Tag ist voll Licht. Er ist voll Blüten. Ich bin sein Gesicht. Du bist die Stimme. Auf unserem Weg sind wir der Morgen. Und seid ihr mit uns, sind wir ohn' Sorgen.

Eccoci la Biancaneve con i due nani: *il Saggio* e *l'Astuto.*	Here is Snow white with the two dwarfs: *the Wise* and *the Wily.*
Ecco la Lepre Coraggiosa, i buoni amici: il Gallo e la Volpe.	Here is the Courageous Rabbit, the good friends: Cockey and Foxey.
Io sono *regista.*	I am a *director.*
Collaboro con Fellini.	I collaborate with Fellini.
Adesso *si gira il film* "Bella ed antica," forse per l'Italia, forse per la Bulgaria . . .	Now *we are shooting the picture* "Beautiful and Ancient," may be about Italy, may be about Bulgaria . . .
Io cerco i personaggi piú interessanti.	*I am searching* the most interesting characters.
Ho sentito dire di voi.	*I was told about you.*
Ed eccomi qua.	And here I am.
Vorreste partecipare al film?	*Do you want to participate* in the picture?
Pago bene.	I'm paying well.
Ho bisogno dei personnaggi: Brighella, Arlecchino, Pantalone, Colombina, Coviello . . .	*I need* the (following) characters: Brighella, Arlecchino, Pantalone, Colombina, Coviello . . .

(Out of her bag, Lucia produces a rolled up sheet of cardboard and unrolls it on the floor. On it are the Italian words for different occupations and some Italian names. The phonetic characteristics of the tongue, as well as some particulars of the substantives (endings for masculine and feminine gender) are stressed by means of different colors. This way of presenting things is used for other foreign languages as well.)

While the students, more or less perplexed with the proposal to "take part in a shooting," are fussing about and choosing a role and a name, the teacher drops hints in the foreign tongue making use mostly of international vocabulary, that is, words that are not hard to understand with a minimum effort of imagination. "Entering" the foreign language takes place right then, imperceptibly. Here is a possible variant:

Ho bisogno di una Beatri*ce,* la *donna eterna* di Dante,	I need a Beatrice, the eternal lady of Dante,

l'eterno *ideale*.	the eternal ideal.
Ho bisogno anche di una *Ceci*lia	I need also a Cecilia,
la *Santa* romana	the Roman Saint
o la matrona romana.	or the Roman gentlewoman.
Cerco una Lucrezia,	I'm looking for a Lucrezia,
una vera Lucrezia Borgia.	a real Lucrezia Borgia.
Bella, intelligente.	Pretty, intelligent.
E *Gi*lda?	And Gilda?
Chi sarà Gilda del *Rigoletto*?	Who is going to be Gilda from *Rigoletto*?
Chi sarà *il maestro* Vincenzo?	Who is going to be maestro Vincenzo?
Il maestro V. Bellini, *naturalmente*!	Maestro V. Bellini, of course!
Ho bisogno di un *Cesare*,	I need a Caesar,
di un vero Cesare romano	an authentic Roman Caesar,
un imperatore o	an emperor or
un eroe semplice dei *Racconti Romani*	simply a character from *Racconti Romani*
di A. Moravia.	by A. Moravia.
E chi sarà il famoso Marcello,	And who's going to be the famous Marcello,
M. Mastroiani, *l'attore* della *La Dolce Vita*?	M. Mastroiani, *the actor* from *La Dolce Vita*?
E Rosina?	And Rosina?
Rosina del *Barbiere di Siviglia*?	Rosina from *The Barber of Seville*?
Avrò bisogno anche di Michelangelo,	I'll need also Michelango,
il grande scultore.	*the great sculptor.*
Chi sarà?	Who's going to be?
E *l'avventuriero* Luciano?	The *adventurer* Luciano?

(And so on, according to the time available.) In the general excitement the students make their choice of names and occupations.

E adesso facciamo la nostra conoscenza.	And now let us get acquainted.
Mi chiamo Lucia.	My name is Lucia.
Sono regista.	I am a producer.

Per favore, come si chiama Lei?	Please, what's your name?
Quale è la Sua professione?	What's your profession?

With these questions the teacher addresses each student in turn, and the latter introduces him- or herself. Then all the students get up and meet each other, shaking hands.

Sono italiana. Sono di Roma.	I am Italian. I am from Rome.
E Lei, signora (signore)?	And you, madam (sir)?
Parlo l'inglese, il russo,	I speak English, Russian,
il tedesco, lo spagnolo.	German, Spanish.
Capisco il francese, il bulgaro,	I understand French, Bulgarian,
il greco,	Greek,
capisco un poco il cinese	I understand a little Chinese
e il giapponese.	and Japanese.
Ma andiamo a Roma,	But let's go to Rome,
a Civitavecchia,	to the old city,
la città dei film.	the film city.
Ecco l'aeroplano.	The plane is here.
Prendiamo i posti!	Let us take seats!
Mentre viaggiamo,	The time we're traveling
studiamo la sceneggiatura del	let us study the screenplay for
film *Bella ed Antica*.	the picture *Beautiful and Ancient*.
Ecco il libro.	Here is the book.

The teacher distributes the textbooks (one per student). Everybody opens it to pages 5–6. The students get acquainted with the characters of the textbook. Very brief explanations are given (if necessary, at translation level) concerning the *dramatis personae*. At that moment the P.A. system of the Institute gives the musical signal for a break. The students are allowed to go outside. Smoking in the building of the Institute is forbidden. In thirty minutes the work is resumed.

The most time-consuming introduction is the first one, and this is easily understandable, since the first encounter requires a flexible approach both toward the group and toward the individual. The teacher must include everyone in the game from the very first day. Suggestopedic teaching requirements are particularly insistent on not pursuing such long introductions further on in the instruction. When such long, explanation-burdened introduction procedures are kept running beyond the first lesson, they generally serve to keep the teaching on a conscious level, and this effect is opposite to the desired one. Authentic suggestopedic teaching quickly "immerses" the student into the core of the purposefully globalized subject matter, without being afraid of presenting an ever larger mass of it (naturally, things are so ordered that the student understands the main point and feels that the material is compiled in a way to render prompt and efficient practical results). For instance, the first lesson in a foreign language for adults contains 600 to 800 lexical units (the exact number fluctuates according to the language) and the basic grammar. Suggestology relies to a considerable extent on man's paraconscious psychological capacities of perceiving and learning. To rely only on the conscious level for acquiring such a large amount of information within the time schedule of the course is not possible, given the existence of universally accepted social learning norms. On the other hand, the human brain is capable of accommodating via the perceptions and mechanisms of paraconsciousness a complexity of information and is able to cope with it without any loss of energy. This is the original, natural state of the human mind. And we are addressing ourselves here to the possibilities of organizing this phenomenon.

Thus, we do not need a long introduction in the next lesson, lest the students be overburdened with too much information, which is destined to be assimilated on only a purely logical level. Experiments have confirmed that even the most organized presentation of more or less extensive information at the conscious level does not result in its assimilation. In fact, under such circumstances boredom and "switching off" of the brain are evident. It has been amply proven nowadays, that such practice of conscious teaching and learning gives rise to didactogeny, fear of learning. Against it, neither the interpolation of the "relieving arts," nor the specially organized shifting of themes have turned out to be of any help.

During the so called "concert session," our students are given the possibility to take part in the process of education both consciously and paraconsciously. The presentation of the material is performed in such a way as to allow everyone, within the boundaries of his or her individual capacities, to make the best use of the conscious and paraconscious mechanisms of acquiring and processing information.

Before going on to the next item (comments on section II of the instructions: "Active Concert Session"), we would like to first give certain explanations concerning the foreign language suggestopedic textbook.

The Foreign Language Suggestopedic Textbook

When compiling a suggestopedic textbook one must bear in mind several important prerequisites. We will refrain from giving here the whole of our views because the theoretical aspects are rather wide reaching, while the present work aims, first of all, at partially satisfying the ever increasing interest in the practical aspects of suggestopedy. Nevertheless, some of the more important theoretical aspects cannot be skipped.

In the last year, aesthetics has been raising questions concerning the intellectual satisfaction of the two simultaneously existing models within man's psychophysiological nature: the systemic-structural model and the diffuse-voluminal one. These questions are of immediate concern to suggestopedy with its trend toward carefully considering and making the best use of man's capabilities of perception—both consciously and paraconsciously. These questions are also connected with the formal problem of compiling a suggestopedic textbook. It is equally important for us to be familiar with the controversial questions of linguistics as they are posed by different schools, beginning with W. von Humboldt; passing through A. Schleicher's naturalism; H. Steinthal's, Potebnya's, and W. Wundt's psychologism; the neogrammarians (Junggrammatiker) from the German school and the "Gestalltpsychologie," Croce's aesthetic idealism; the French sociological schools from F. de Saussure to R. Barthes; the functional (structural) linguistics with its multitude of tendencies from the remote past to the present day; and also with the Marxist linguistical standpoint on the cardinal problems of language and thinking. This list is naturally extended to include the problems of semiotics and symbology, of semantic logic, of programming, and of cybernetics, which are each of particular interest for suggestology.

Profound knowledge of the culture, the belles lettres, and of the style of the most prominent representatives of the different literary tendencies, are also a prerequisite for compiling a foreign language suggestopedic textbook. The pursuit of a delicate balance between the colloquial speech for everyday practice and the literary style needed for a more comprehensive penetration into the culture of the nation, whose language is studied—thus raising to a higher level the communicative possibilities and even the creative capacities of the individual—underlies the foundation of a suggestopedic textbook.

The textbook in Italian (Gateva, Lozanov; 1974/1978) is also a manual which can be used as an example in compiling other suggestopedic textbooks. It is consistent with the latest requirements of the suggestopedic system. The material is drawn from life on a communicative level. Following the plot of the light didactic story, the students become familiar with various aspects of the characters' psychology, with the characteristic features of Italy, with its ancient and modern culture. They penetrate into the beauty of the foreign tongue. In this way the difficulties of mastering a language recede into the background and are overcome imperceptibly.

The textbook is consistent with the basis of suggestology as well as with the principles and techniques of suggestopedy. Its correct use makes it possible for the teacher to help students to realize their reserve capabilities, that is, to learn the material with considerable ease at a creative level and without unpleasant fatigue, without harmful effects on the nervous system, with favorable educational effects, and with ever-growing motivation.

Besides giving the whole plot of the didactic play, this textbook also has the following advantageous points from the standpoint of suggestopedy:

1. Most of the subject matter (800 new words and a considerable part of the essential grammar) is given already in the first lesson. So use is made of the particular suggestive features at the "first meeting," when learning is the easiest. At the same time, the students have a wide choice of words, phrases, models, and grammatical forms. In all the lessons for the elaboration of the new material, they do not feel "conditioned" and restricted within the framework of a few words and models when expressing their thoughts in the foreign language. In the following lessons, the number of new words and grammar units decreases, so that learning them is easier.

2. The different parts of the sentences, as well as the word groups, have been put on separate lines so that they can be changed easily. In this way, hundreds of parts of models of the spoken language that can be changed are learned more easily. Structuralism per se is avoided, but its rationale is used imperceptibly, naturally, usefully, and with vigor.

3. The visual aids in the textbook are connected with the subject matter and are globalized, and do not illustrate merely isolated elements. In this way, audio-visualization is carried out on both a semantic and a double-plane level, with great liberty for creative initiative, and avoiding conditioning by the narrow framework of a small number of visualized

elements pertaining to the objective world. A useless return to the elementary mechanisms of perception, characteristic of early childhood, is also avoided.

4. The music and the words of the songs are consistent with suggestive requirements for the emotional and artistic "introduction" of important semantic, phonetic, and grammatical units.

5. Students are given translations of every lesson in the textbook to grasp the initial vocabulary better and to satisfy the needs of the adults' cognitive process in the initial two phases of the suggestopedic process of learning: deciphering, and active concert session. On the second day, the translations are taken away from the students. This is in line with the requirements for learning the foreign language and for a more rapid transition to thinking in the foreign language.

6. Underlining the words from Lesson One to Lesson Five aids the student in directing his or her efforts toward mastering the vocabulary of high frequency (which, of course, is in an unbreakable link with grammar). Some words of high frequency, appearing for the first time in the lesson, are not underlined—either because of a new selection of frequency within the framework of the lesson, or because of their being regular derivatives of already familiar ones.

7. Every lesson is followed by an outline of lexical and grammatical units, which are then elaborated upon. The elaborations of some subjects are more fundamental, while those of others are more cursory, depending on their importance, as well as on their natural reiteration in the course of learning. This outline is of particular importance to the teacher, giving him or her the possibility of self-control in the course of the elaborations and of a natural progression to the work, according to the preliminary planning. This outline serves also to satisfy the need for order for most of the students.

8. The summary reading materials following Lessons One, Two, and Three are of artistic and didactic value. Their role in the elaborations is that of an illustrative example for the students. The latter are provided with useful suggestions in how to make up a short, interesting, and not merely didactic story, containing direct and indirect speech, by themselves. To the lessons are added complementary texts: easy anecdotes, within the understanding capacity of beginners, which play a similar role—model to imitate. Through such imitation, the students look for suitable anecdotes and transform them with the help of the vocabulary

they have already acquired, thus creating a lively and healthy educational atmosphere, which helps them further master wittier forms of expressing themselves.

9. A good balance between dialogues and monologues has been sought because this is the natural state of communicative speech. Incorporation of songs and original authors' texts into the dialogues has been done for the same reason.

10. The characters' parts are not exempt from half-expressed ideas or of allusions since these also occur in living speech. Here and there some logical incoherence seems to appear, but this is only a superficial impression due to the "dismemberment" of the idea. Nowadays, this is the normal state of our protean minds. Stronger tendencies in this direction are dangerous, however, the text being part of a suggestopedic textbook and not a piece of belles lettres.

11. All the quotations, taken from the work of the great names of Italian culture, as well as the captions of the pictures, never fail to be linked to the text of the lesson. Sometimes this link is allegorical, sometimes it is symbolical; in very rare instances, it is direct.

12. The quotations in the beginning of the textbook and in every lesson, the original poetry, and the art reproductions have been included to stimulate an interest in mastering the language, not only with the purpose of satisfying purely utilitarian communicative needs, but also to make it easier to understand the original culture of the respective nation.

The original quotations, marking the beginning of every lesson, are translated by the students with the teacher's assistance when the work with the active grammar is over. Very brief, but interesting explanations about those quotations are given.

13. Beyond Lesson Five there are no more underlined words. Up to Lesson Six both vocabulary and grammar are basic (of very high frequency). They are elaborated more thoroughly. After Lesson Five the material becomes easier; new words are less frequent; words of less important frequency make their appearance in a natural way; the more difficult part of the grammar is presented in less imposing form; and elaborations are more passive and directed mainly toward translation. During the concert session, the students are given the possibility of underlining by themselves whatever they judge as suitable and important. In that way, after having fully mastered the technique of reading (attained in the

suggestopedic courses by virtually 100 percent of the students), students are oriented toward unaided education.

Another thing that comes after accomplishing the elaborations of Lesson Five is the "stop day" (a day for revision), to be discussed later on. In general, that happens about the fifteenth day of the course, or after 60 hours of study (school hours, 45 minutes each).

14. The material, following Lesson Eight (i.e., the last one) is naturally placed outside the lessons, being outside the dramaturgic time. It consists of two letters of the principal characters and the Epilogue of the suggestopedic play (pages 94 and 95 of the Italian textbook).

15. The grammar, carried in the last pages of the textbook, is presented in the most synthesized form possible, the way it should be dealt with during the course. Examples are exclusively derived from the text of the lessons. In suggestopedic practice, one deals with grammar after the concert presentation of the new material, when the greatest part of the analytical and synthetic tasks of the brain are performed spontaneously at the conscious and—in to a much larger extent—at the paraconscious level. The grammatical examples are already automatized in an important degree. During the elaborations they have only to be specified and extended.

The layout of the textbook gives a good idea of this principle of presenting grammatical structures: their location in the lines, and the placement of those paradigms that the student might need to refer to at any given moment on the right half of the page, the translation half, are relevant. Peripheral perceptions do the remaining work for the student's mastering of the material with no loss of energy or motivation. The body of grammatical information at the end of the textbook is of particular importance for the teacher, in order to keep a tight rein, that is, to prevent the student from professionally plunging into details of the lexical and grammatical pattern of the foreign tongue.

16. If willing to characterize the dramaturgy of the suggestopedic textbook, we have to look up the newer literary trends. The characters are rather hinted at than typified. The characters' countenance is subjected to perpetual modifications, it is at one moment sketchy, at another clear-cut, amorphous, orthodox, and controversial. The plot and its development are also subordinated to the requirements of the textbook. A beginner would feel bewildered and upset in the maze of a complicated dramaturgy. The natural easiness, a hint of fantasy and playfulness, the dominating optimism and buoyancy, determine both the typology of the

characters and the course of events in the suggestopedic textbook. All basic psychological temperaments find their place in the characters. The latter are more or less in a state of evolution: past, present, and future. Acute dramatic situations elapsed, in view of the didactic purposes of the book. The purposefully obviated conflicts are replaced with original fragments of the respective nation's literature. The characters' unburdened thoughts and easy speaking are well within reach of beginners.

On the other hand, the organization of suggestopedic teaching offers to the students a great many possibilities to make frequent changes of their "roles" as the course progresses. Such changes occur in different ways: accepting freely and spontaneously a role from the suggestopedic play, from the supplementary texts and the original fragments, from the games played during elaborations, and, last but not least, accepting roles derived from the student's own preferences. In this way the individual is afforded the possibility of a repeated spontaneous personification (affecting himself or the whole group) in an atmosphere of ease and friendship.

The organization of the suggestopedic teaching and learning processes has always been consistent with various psychotherapeutic techniques (artopsychotherapy, psychotherapy through hypnosis and through suggestion, Moreno's psychodrama, psychoanalysis, etc.), but under the common denominator of the theory of suggestology. The latter has found its substantiation in integral psychotherapy (G. Lozanov). One should never lose sight of one of the chief goals of art: catharsis. One should also keep in mind the different dramaturgical, artistic, and psychological theories (Ibsen, Wagner, Stanislavsky, Vigotsky, Brecht, Berg, Ionesco, etc.), again from the standpoint of suggestology. It is impossible to attempt to convert the students to patients or artists. However, reckoning with the abovementioned theories in the course of the suggestopedic education, results in a complementary (and absolutely spontaneous) psychohygienic effect.

So, the students hold in their hands the playlike textbook they are going to work with. We proceed to the second stage of presenting the subject matter—the presenting of the first lesson by means of the so called *active concert session*, according to the Methodological Instructions.

II. Active Concert Session

The students are seated quietly in their easy chairs. The air in the room is fresh, the lights are adequate. In front of each student there is a little table, with the textbook on it, open at Lesson One. On the right of the pages is fixed the translation. It is printed on separate free sheets of paper and corresponds line for line to the foreign language text. The teacher will read aloud with a special intonation the whole text (only in the foreign language) against the background of an integral musical piece. More than one piece is prepared for Lesson One, which is the longest. As specified in the Musical Program, the music compositions to be heard during the active session are predominantly by the Viennese classics: Haydn, Mozart, and Beethoven, as well as by the classic romantics. Numerous and extensive experiments in the Suggestology Research Institute have proved in an incontestable way that the most suitable conditions to put into practice the purpose of suggestopedy—revealing the reserve complex of the personality under the conditions of concentrative psychorelaxation—are brought about by classic art. It is widely known that classical art has always been a powerful stimulus to the inspiration of the great artists. Nevertheless, not all compositions by the old masters are suitable a priori for the needs of suggestopedy. The structural principles of a classical composition exert their influence through a humane philosophy, expressed in a pefect form. They create within human beings the necessary conditions for a natural transition from chaos and disharmony towards order, harmony, consistency, logic, inspiration, and delight. These principles create also the conditions needed for a regulation of the naturally arising psychorelaxation, the state of mind where reserve capacities are revealed and tapped.

A detailed analysis of the questions on the role of art in the suggestopedic teaching and learning process, as well as on the role and effect of suggestopedic art, will be the subject of another work. Some cardinal topics concerning these problems are to be found in the report and the part taken by G. Lozanov at the UNESCO Symposium on the suggestopedy held in Sofia in 1978, as well as in the part taken by E. Gateva at the the same symposium and at the First Congress on Symbology held in Rome in the same year.

The items and the notes (from 1 to 6) in Section II, from the Instruction "Active Concert Session," do not need any comments. It is evident that teachers should be trained in the elementary theory of music, the history of music, musical analysis, and articulation (of speech and singing). Musicality is one of the virtues of suggestopedic teaching. The timbre of the teacher's voice, the clearness of his or her diction, the quality of his or her artistic performance, and his or her mental and physical plasticity and mobility are of incontestable importance for suggestopedy. We cannot spare any space here for the musical analysis of the compositions for the concert sessions because as already mentioned, this will be the subject of a separate work and of separate lectures designed to be delivered to suggestopedic teachers.

During this recitallike reading, the character of the compositions, suitable to an active presentation of the new material, is cause for the teacher to stand upright, solemn. He or she may change place during the pauses between the parts of the composition. The students have the possibility of making notes in the textbook itself (marking off phonetical peculiarities, accents, and so on).

The course of the musical thought often is quite different from the text of the lesson, but this mild paradox (mild, because of the effect of classical music) is a source of surprise, novelty, and uncommonness—all contradictory feelings that fix more firmly the information presented. On the other hand, by means of his intonation the teacher does his level best to bring the speech, in its quality of mere acoustic flow, closer to the relief of the muscial composition. This organized intermingling of several planes in the presentation and the acquiring of information is characteristic of suggestopedy; it discards the necessity of exerting effort to focus one's attention on acquiring information in a purely conscious way: something that closely approaches coercion.

Reading the text of the first session aloud needs more time, that is why the teacher should have made solid preparations. The estimate of time necessary should be the soundest possible, lest the session be either begun or terminated at the wrong moment. By the end of Concerto No. 5 for violin and orchestra by Mozart, the teacher announces a pause (the word "rest" is never uttered) lasting 5 to 6 minutes, and then leaves the room, which is reaired. Then he or she comes back and resumes the activities. Another pause is allowed, if needed, following Mozart's Symphony No. 29. When the reading of the whole material is over, the teacher closes the book and, without sitting down, awaits the end of the musical composition or switches off the tapedeck. (In the Institute, the musical program is fed from a central panel, in a separate room.) The end of the composition is awaited for as long as one minute. Then comes a 7-minute pause. The room is reaired. During the pauses the teacher leaves the classroom in order to allow the students to go outside, if they feel like it, but the teacher never forgets to let them know beforehand the exact time they are accorded and never fails to heed that time to the minute (no oversight is admissible from the first to the last day of the course).

The teacher's reading in the active session is interrupted by short pauses which allow the students to have a look at the paradigms in the right-hand half of the page. The need for order is particularly important in the case of adult learners.

III. Pseudopassive Concert Session

At this stage, presenting the information for the second time, the teacher should present the material with a normal intonation consistent with a true-to-life artistic coloration depending on the requirements of the text. The teacher should also suggest through his or her behavior that the moment has come for complete relaxation, identical to the relaxation occurring at concerts. *The textbook is closed.* The teacher is comfortably seated in his or her own easy chair, waits for the music to grip the audience (about 1 minute), and then begins to read. The music is baroque and is intended to bring about the necessary atmosphere for meditativeness and self-concentration, for breaking away from everyday problems and conflicts and taking an anxiety-free attitude toward them. The mind is now in a state of alertness, and the state of the student's spirit is critical. Abundant experimental and theoretical evidence has been collected showing this. Presented against the background of this concert the information becomes directly correlated with the motivation of the student toward the subject matter he or she desires to learn, which has already been subjected to critical evaluation during the active session. It is worth mentioning the capacity of classical and baroque music for creating conditions conducive to a creative inspiration of the highest order.

Concert sessions are intended to create spontaneous states, and not to urge the students to forcefully imitate the teacher's behavior. The teacher's conduct is soft, in line with a true understanding of suggestologic and suggestopedic theory and practice. The wrong conduct results in the artificial creation of training states, which will progressively cause conventionality, incorrect associations, negativism, and all that is associated with these things.

During the pseudopassive session, reading becomes more like colloquial speech (without going to extremes; diction should be of maximum didactic clarity), its speed is faster, and the need of pauses drops off. In the beginning of this stage, the students' degree of understanding of the text is lower; however, their delight in the "music" of the foreign language is high, because of their natural motivation. With each subsequent lesson understanding becomes more and more complete, and the delight taken in this session becomes more and more intense, thus increasing interest in the language and, quite naturally, the degree of motivation for its learning. In this way the processes necessary for the mastering of any given subject matter are in a permanent state of mutual stimulation.

It is quite natural for the students in the initial stage of their education to pose the question whether they should turn their attention to the text or to the music. Experimental data along these lines are in favor of the personality's inward spontaneous choice. From the psychophysiological standpoint this is the most natural course of events.

In this session, as in the previous one, the end of the reading is followed by a calm awaiting of the music to fade away; then the teacher unobtrusively rises and takes leave. The teacher should leave immediately so as not to break the atmosphere of serenity. The students leave the Institute under the influence of that last stage of the working day. According to Instruction No. 1, the students should ideally "skim through the material as one skims through a newspaper" once in the evening, once before going to bed, and again eventually in the morning. It is not so serious if the students completely neglect to read the material at home, because the Institute anticipates such a development. In any event, the material will be re-read in class the following day.

What follows is the Musical Program of the active session with the duration of the parts marked in parentheses.

Musical Program for the First Grade of Foreign Language Suggestopedic Courses

Session One

1. *W. A. Mozart*
   Concerto for Violin and Orchestra in A Major No. 5
      Allegro aperto (9:35)*
      Adagio (11:05)
      Rondo. Tempo di Menuetto (9:50)

---

*Numbers in parentheses are the playing time in minutes and seconds for that music selection.

Symphony in A Major KV 201 (No. 29)
  Allegro moderato (8:40)
  Andante (7:25)
  Menuetto (3:50)
  Allegro con spirito (5:40)
Symphony in G Minor KV 550 (No. 40)
  Molto allegro (8:10)
  Andante (7:35)
  Menuetto allegretto (4:47)
  Allegro assai (4:50)

2. *J. S. Bach*
Fantasia for Organ in G Major BWV 572
Fantasia in C Minor BWV 562

Session Two

1. *J. Haydn*
Concerto No. 1 in C Major for Violin and Orchestra
  Allegro moderato (9:30)
  Adagio (4:40)
  Finale (4:10)
Concerto No. 2 in G Major for Violin and Orchestra
  Allegro moderato (8:35)
  Adagio (7:05)
  Allegro (3:45)

2. *J. S. Bach*
Prelude and Fugue in G Major BWV 541
Dogmatic Chorales

Session Three

1. *W. A. Mozart*
Symphony in D Major "Haffner" KV 385
  Allegro con spirito (4:55)
  Andante (4:30)
  Menuetto (3:30)
  Finale presto (3:55)
Symphony in D Major "Prague" KV 504
  Adagio–allegro (11:55)

Andante (8:50)
Finale presto (6:00)

2. *G. F. Handel*
Concerto for Organ and Orchestra in B-flat Major, Op. 7, No. 6

Session Four

1. *J. Haydn*
Symphony in C Major No. 101 "L'Horloge"
Presto (8:00)
Andante (8:00)
Allegro (4:00)
Vivace (4:00)
Symphony in G Major No. 94
Adagio cantabile. Vivace assai (12:00)
Andante (7:00)
Menuetto. Allegro molto (4:00)
Finale. Allegro molto (4:00)

2. *A. Corelli*
Concerti Grossi, Op. 6, Nos. 4, 10, 11, 12

Session Five

1. *L. van Beethoven*
Concerto for Piano and Orchestra No. 5 in B-flat Major, Op. 73
Allegro (19:30)
Adagio un poco mosso (8:00)
Rondo. Allegro (10:40)

2. *A. Vivaldi*
Five concertos for flute and chamber orchestra

Session Six

1. *L. van Beethoven*
Concerto for Violin and Orchestra in D Major, Op. 61
Allegro ma non troppo (24:30)

Larghetto (11:20)
   Rondo. Allegro (9:30)

2. *A. Corelli*
   Concerti Grossi, Op. 6, Nos. 2, 8, 5, 9

Session Seven

1. *P. I. Tchaïkovsky*
   Concerto No. 1 in B-flat Minor for Piano and Orchestra
   Allegro non troppo e molto maestoso
   Allegro con spirito (21:50)
   Andantino semplice
   Allegro con fuoco (15:15)

2. *G. F. Handel*
   "Wassermusik"

Session Eight

1. *J. Brahms*
   Concerto for Violin and Orchestra in D Major, Op. 77
   Allegro non troppo (22:05)
   Adagio (9:25)
   Allegro giocoso, ma non troppo vivace (8:05)

2. *F. Couperin*
   Sonatas for Harpsichord:
   "Le Parnasse" ("Apotheosis of Corelli")
   "L'Astrée"

3. *J. F. Rameau*
   Concert Pieces for Harpsicord "Pièces de clavecin" No. 1 and No. 5

Session Nine

1. *P. I. Tchaïkovsky*
   Concerto for Violin and Orchestra in D Major Op. 35
   Allegro moderato (22:00)
   Canzonetta (7:00)
   Finale. Allegro vivacissimo (10:00)

2. *J. S. Bach*
   Dogmatic Chorales for Organ BWV 680–689
   Fugue in E-flat Major BWV 552

Session Ten

1. *W. A. Mozart*
   Concerto for Piano and Orchestra No. 18 in B-flat Major KV 456
      Allegro vivace (11:55)
      Andante un poco sostenuto (10:10)
      Allegro vivace (7:35)
   Concerto for Piano and Orchestra in A Major No. 23 KV 488
      Allegro (11:00)
      Adagio (7:05)
      Allegro assai (8:05)

2. *A. Vivaldi*
   The Four Seasons, Op. 8
   Spring
   Summer
   Autumn
   Winter

    We propose this Musical Program for suggestopedic sessions after having tested it with thousands of subjects. Bearing in mind the endless and most often useless theoretical disputes on "European" versus "Non-European" music, disputes of both professionally-subjective and pancultural character, where the genre and national context is the rule rather than the exception, and where use becomes restricted within the narrow limits of extreme concepts—we have accepted the experimental proof for our Musical Program as a sufficiently strong argument. Moreover, suggestopedic sessions do not consist of listening to concertos in the common, musically-educative sense. They are intended to create conditions for concentrative-psychorelaxational states of mind, under which students' reserve capacities of learning are revealed and tapped to their utmost extent.
    Another fact that has been established is that by weaving the teacher's voice (when reading in the well-trained manner already spoken of) into the texture of the concertos, the most important components of the musical expression (melody, harmony, rhythm and metrics, timbre, tempo and

dynamism, themes, musical forms, caesura, conception) are emphasized. The students feel and understand better the psychology and architectonics of the compositions. It often also happens that by the end of their studies at the Institute, students become more enthusiastic toward attending concerts. Their contacts with singing, dancing, and painting, established during the course, have much to do with this.

IV. Elaborations

Didactic Games in Suggestopedic Practice

The usual way of elaborating the grammar consists in organizing games of the types listed below. We have already emphasized that games in suggestopedic practice are not intended to provide amusement and relief, because such a design would succeed in nothing but reaffirming the social suggestive norm concerning the painstaking nature of education. The games are of psychological importance for establishing an anxiety-free and cheerful atmosphere, which is conducive to the students' shaking off any psychotraumas or strains, and to the creation of confidence, a lack of constraint, and a feeling of security, because the game gives rise to the spontaneous unlocking of many psychological capacities. When the students are engaged in games, their mistakes should not be corrected pedantically; everything seems like fun; everything is at first glance simple and unambitious. (We will refrain here from going into details about this topic which, as already mentioned, has solid theoretical grounds in suggestopedy.)

The games should be so selected and applied that the students' conviction of having learned sufficient amounts of material is reinforced on a double-plane level. Any game that does not use to the best advantage a considerable amount of information is a game for entertainment, and this type of game results in further reinforcing the idea of agony in studying.

The games of choice should be easy, with no sophisticated and showy riddles, because the object of didactic games in suggestopedic practice is different. Their strategic logical objective is mastering the foundations of a foreign language. The games, considered as a general approach in suggestopedic practice, and not considered singly, should affirm the delight of having mastered the material in amounts that exceed the norm. That is why they should be organized with dynamism, without wasting time on mere entertainment.

What follows is a model list of games, applied with success in the Italian courses and which are gaining an increasing popularity in the suggestopedic courses in the other foreign languages. Most of them are exposed in more detail in the section dealing with them directly.

Didactic Games for Use in the Suggestopedic Foreign Language Courses

1. At the time of deciphering and elaborating, the songs are performed making slight dancing steps, at least part of the gestures having some didactic purpose (see below).
2. Guess a nationality from a name or a characteristic gesture. Points go to the first one to guess.
3. Where have I been? What is that place? Photographs of famous places and cities are displayed. Points go to the first one to make the right guess.
4. The most popular states, cities, and towns. The first letter is written on the blackboard and the blanks are filled up by the students. Ten points for a letter; 50 points for the first to guess the whole name of the place.
5. An auction or an exchange of belongings. Dice may be used.
6. Invitation to breakfast, lunch, or dinner. Played with cards, the cards are dealt out, one for each student. Those having cards of the same suit or the same value (or of another common feature, depending on the kind of cards) form a group, where the individuals are ranked according to the succession of the cards they have. The one with the highest card is the host. He or she addresses invitations to dinner. The one with the second highest card addresses invitations to lunch, and so on. The invitations should specify the meals: first, second, and third course; the day of the week; the hour. On the appointed day a comical situation mimicking an official dinner (luncheon, breakfast) is created in class. The invitations should also include information about entertainment, transportation, etc.
7. The teacher selects a text suitable for illustration. He or she reads aloud slowly, while the students draw. Then the drawings are exhibited on the walls. A preliminary announcement states that abstraction is allowed. Abstract drawings, when exhibited, should be explained by their authors.
8. The theme "The Four Seasons" is illustrated by a collective "canvas." Each student has to tell something about a particular season and draw an illustration as best as he or she can.

9. For the purpose of the individual narrations preceding the new lesson, the students are offered a bagful of small things. Each student picks one. Everyone then selects the theme of his or her story for the next day chosen from among the themes proposed by the teacher in accord with the list following the lesson. The story should be related both to the student's new identity and to the thing he or she has chosen.

10. A text is read without the teacher vocalizing and the students try to lip read. Points are awarded for the students with the best guesses.

11. Solving riddles, which conceal a plot of a surprise. Points are awarded for every solution.

12. At the time of the individual narrations, a student turns his or her back to the group and tries to identify a speaker from the group by his or her voice. Points are awarded for the right guess.

13. A text is supplied which must be memorized in a couple of minutes. Then it is reproduced by the "players." According to the exactitude and the peculiarities of the retelling, the teams are given names: the lions, the panthers, the nightingales, etc.

14. Group reading with "stop." The teacher establishes the rhythm of the reading. At a given moment the class goes on reading to itself, trying to keep pace. The teacher cries "Stop!," and each student in turn then resumes the reading aloud, thus showing whether he or she has kept pace with the rhythm. This game is used to accelerate the reading. Points go to the most rhythmical, the most precise.

15. A text is read with intentional mistakes (first by the teacher, then by the students). The mistakes are corrected by the joint efforts of the class. Unfamiliar parts of speech may be added.

16. A familiar text (from the readings or the songs) is taken apart. The words and phrases are written on small cards, which are shuffled and dealt out. The students then rearrange them to obtain the original text.

17. The group is thought of as a "computer." Each student represents a "key," loaded with information, for example, some grammatical category. When "pressed," the key displays the exact information. In such a way, by "pressing" the different "keys" in turn (all the students should take part), the teacher gradually arrives at a meaningful text. This game is particularly suitable to review lessons.

18. Phrases are number-coded. A number corresponds to a letter, a word, or a sentence. Each student receives a coded message that he or she must decode. A suitable situation should be set up previously. The contest is by teams. Points go to the team with the best plot.

19. Guessing phrases (possibly out of the textbook). A student picks a phrase, writes the first word, and marks the number of remaining words with dashes. The rest of the group tries to fill in the dashes. Points are awarded to the winners.

20. A story is made up based on a given word. (This game is particularly useful for grammatical elaborations.)

21. Phrases with or without a sense of motion are recited. When the phrase bears a sense of motion, the players must stand up. Those who stand up late drop out. The leader of the game stands up at every phrase to confuse matters.

22. A student makes a drawing and as soon as it is ready, hides it (or erases it, if it is on the blackboard). The player who succeeds in redrawing the picture from memory has the right to make the next drawing. The subjects of the drawings are assigned by the teacher and should be related to the lessons (old and new).

23. Telephone. The class form a circle. A very short story is then told by one student in the next student's ear. The last student in the circle retells the story out loud. If the result is nonsense, the path of the story is followed back. The student who has made the wrong transmission must become the source of a new short story.

24. The students write on a sheet of paper pairs of antonyms for: *time* (early–late, day–night, morning–evening); *place* (left–right, near–far, up–down); *attributes* (heavy–light, white–black, cold–hot, etc.). The student who has written the greatest number of antonyms in the time fixed by the teacher and who is able to include his or her antonyms in phrases on the spot is the winner. The contest may also take place between teams.

25. Funny disguising. The participants are divided into two teams. Each team picks two players: the "models." The latter are thoroughly examined by the group for one or two minutes. Afterward they "disguise" themselves, that is, they add something or remove something from their apparel (a necktie, a shawl, spectacles, a wristwatch, a handkerchief, a ring). The "models" go outside the classroom and make the changes undisturbed. The groups re-examine them and try to recognize the changes. Points go for every right guess. The game is pursued with another pair of "models." The tempo is very fast.

26. Decoding a text, written without capital letters or punctuation marks. The individual or team that decodes the text the quickest gets points.

27. Relay race. The participants are divided into two teams. Each participant receives a number. The blackboard is divided in half, one half to each team. There are several questions written on the blackboard, numbered according to the number of participants. The answers to these questions form an elementary story. The teacher holds the cards with all the numbers. The contest begins. The teacher lifts two cards with numbers on them. The respective participants must immediately go to the blackboard, find their respective question, and answer it in writing. Points are accorded for speed and for correctness of the answer. Spelling mistakes are not taken into account. The teacher remarks on the answers in-between "plays." Only the correct meaning of the answers is considered in the initial stages.

Now let us go back to the first elaboration of the first part of Lesson One. The first paradigm in the textbook in Italian is of the auxiliary verb "to be." We recall the song *Stories* from the first working day. The class sings this from memory, each student being ready to emphasize the forms of "to be" by a gesture, a facial expression, or a movement that corresponds to the phrase where the verb "to be" is included. One of the students is the jury, passing judgment on the performance of the song. From that moment on, each individual or collective victory is given 10 points. Each student keeps his or her own scorecard to keep track of the number of premium points earned during the course.

We now note a peculiar aspect of the Italian language: the frequent neglecting of personal pronouns. It follows from this that the verb system is of utmost importance. Using the sentence "*Lei è il signor Civinini?*" we explain that the polite form of the verb is the third person singular. (The same explanation is given when dealing with German, Spanish, etc.) By the way, reading the sentence we explain that the polite form is the third person singular: "Usted, señorita, habla muy bien español!," or the third person plural "Sind Sie allein?."

To help the students at this stage we allow them to use the second person plural, corresponding to the polite form in Bulgarian. Nevertheless, we emphasize that the accepted polite form in Italian is the third singular. As they progress through the grammatical section, the students find the "rule" concerning substantives from the masculine gender. By use of phrases where this grammatical aspect is included, even though continued, we clarify as necessary.

It should be emphasized the grammar in suggestopedic courses is always dealt with in some context and is always included in practical work. Easy phrases are used: "Ecco il mio biglietto da visita" ("Here is my visiting card"). The students are given cards of the proper size and they make for themselves visiting cards with their new names, occupations, and addresses. Then they exchange the cards between one another. The teacher explains that the word "biglietto" means "a note" in the broadest sense, as well as "a ticket." It is masculine. In general, substantives from the masculine gender in Italian end in "o" in the singular and in "i" in the plural. If they begin with a vowel, the definite article is "il" for the singular and "i" for the plural (as in the example under study). The indefinite article for the singular is "un."

We go on translating and stop at the sentence, "You speak Italian very well." The teacher says by way of a joke that he or she speaks almost all languages and asks one of the students which languages he or she speaks. The teacher always makes use of the polite form: third person singular. The student, who should understand now how to construct a sentence in the first person, gives an answer.

As has already been mentioned, during the active session the teacher reads with short pauses to allow the students to have a look at the paradigms in the right-hand side of the page. In the vicinity of the verb "to speak" there are the names of other languages, coinciding with the name of the respective nationality. Thus the students are in a position to answer the question about the languages they speak, either truthfully or making it up. If necessary, the interrogative form is explained. An example will make it quite clear to everyone that this is achieved by inversion or by a change in intonation. "*Do you* speak English?" (Russian, German, Spanish, etc.). The affirmative response is more than evident: "Parlo." The negative reply is also quite easy. The negation "non" is put in front of the verb: "Non parlo." In the textbooks in English and in French the first lesson should be saturated with simple interrogative and negative sentences in order to avoid burdening the students with superfluous and inhibiting explanations concerning the "special" forms (e.g., "Do you like . . .?"; "Je n'ai pas de frère").

At this point, the time has come for a little game of guessing nationalities. Each student must think up a name or act out a short scene, characteristic of a particular nationality. The participants are divided into

Ça me suffit

Par. Z. Ivanova
E. Iordanova
Mus. E. Gateva

Allegretto

Je n'ai pas beaucoup d'argent

J'ai beaucoup d'enfants

Je n'ai pas d'objets en or rit.

Ma femme est un trésor
a tempo

Je n'ai pas d'appartements

J'ai beaucoup d'amis

A Paris ça me suffit.

A Paris ça me suffit.

Spring Time

Words by A. Karaslavova
Music by E. Gateva

Allegro

Did you stop? Did you stop?
Did you stop to hear that tune?
Did you pick? Did you pick?
Did you pick blooms in the plane?
Did you try? Did you try?
Did you try to reach the Moon?
Did you like? Did you like?
Did you like the Spring-time rain?

two teams. A right guess wins 10 points. Then the points are summed up to determine which team has won.

The class reads aloud the paradigm of the verb "parl*are*" ("to speak"). The teacher reads the endings in a well-shaped intonation, *fixing them with an appropriate circlelike or jerky movement of his or her hand*: "o" for the first person singular, "i", for the second person singular, "iamo" for the first person plural. The teacher states these endings (first person singular, second person singular, first person plural) are valid for all verbs in the present tense, regardless of the conjugation. In the remaining persons, the characteristic "a" from the infinitive persists. The teacher points at the poster.

We continue with the translation of the first part of Lesson One. Here the sentence is "The performance of 'Aïda' is wonderful." On the right-hand side is written the rule: some substantives that are masculine and begin with some consonants accept the definite article "lo" in the singular and "gli" in the plural. The teacher reminds the class of the phonetics of the construction "gli," pronouncing "famiglia" (i.e., "g" is not pronounced when followed by "l", but softens the "l"). The indefinite article, instead of "un," is "uno." The teacher jokes that Italians are very musical and do not like piling up consonants. That is why, instead of "il" and "un" before the grouped consonants in the words "*spe*ttacolo," "*sc*ultore," "*scr*ittore" (all of them masculine), they place the clearer-ringing "lo" and "uno."

We proceed with the translation and find the sentence "Hanno sei bambini" ("They have six children"). On the right-hand side there is another paradigm, the verb "to have." Here the teacher reminds the class of the song "Un bel fiore"—the story of Rocco. The students learn the song by heart. Then they dance while singing it, making a jump forward any time a form of "to have" appears in the text. The students dance hand in hand. "Rocco" also takes part in the dance and, held still by the teacher, makes his jumps in place.

The teacher says he or she has one child. The teacher then asks the students how many children they have. The group is told that invented answers are preferable. In such a way, using diverting questions, the theme of "acquainting" is developed through the accumulation of facts, mostly invented by the students. After translation of the sentences, including verbs of the first conjugation ("viagg*iare*" and "ritorn*are*"), the students in chorus quickly conjugate these verbs according to the analogy of "parlare." With appropriate movements of his or her hand, the teacher consolidates the endings.

In connection with the transposition of the *accent* in the third person plural, the teacher gives some explanations of the placement of the accent in Italian. In most cases it falls at the last-but-one syllable and is not marked in the texts. As a rule, the accent is written only if at the last syllable. In all the remaining cases, when the accent is neither at the last-but-one syllable, nor at the last one, it is marked in the textbook as an aid to the students.

The teacher pauses at the questions "Perchè?" ("Why?"). He or she writes it on the blackboard preceded by a No. 1, and remarks that "Why?" is one of the basic questions for the progress of mankind. The students put down in the notebooks "No. 1" in front of the word "Perchè?." The next question is No. 2, "Chi?" ("Who?"); No. 3, "Le piace ... ?" ("Do you like ... ?") follows. Here the game "Do you like this city?" is introduced. Two teams are formed. The teacher displays some picture postcards with famous sights of cities from around the world. A correct guess earns 10 points. Then the points of the participants are summed up to determine the victorious team.

The next interlude is a game based on the question "May I introduce you to my daughter?" (my son, my husband, my wife, my father, my mother). Each student chooses another to be his or her relative and introduces him or her to their "neighbors," inventing a name, an occupation, a birthplace, some preferences (for languages, cities, places where the "relative" has been, etc.).

This is the end of the translation stage and the elaborations in respect of the first part of Lesson One (page 9 of the textbook). The musical signal from the central panel of the Institute marks the beginning of a 30-minute pause. The teacher immediately brings the lesson to an end. After the pause the activities are resumed.

1. The First Day After the Session

First Elaborations

It is advisable that those people interested in suggestopedic practice have at their disposal the textbook in Italian (translated and adapted to be of use to students speaking Russian and English). In recent years, relying on numerous experiments held in Bulgaria and elsewhere carried out mostly in the courses in Italian and Spanish, substantial corrections of the existing suggestopedic practices have been put into effect and many new elements have arisen (in line with the theories of suggestology and suggestopedy).

The Italian tongue, as heir to Latin and Greek, is particularly characterized by features of an Indo-European tongue in its phonetical and morphosyntactic development. That is why Italian turned out to be ideal as a tongue for methodological experiments and conclusions.

On the day following the initial session the teacher checks and substitutes (if necessary) the posters and other things in the room, and prepares the aids and props he or she will need for the elaborations. First of all, however, the teacher makes up a schematic plan of his or her activities for the day, evaluating and distributing the time-schedule he or she has been accorded. Experience and flair are both of great help at this stage. Improvisations are allowed only to the extent that such original ideas which sometimes arise in the course of exactly programmed events are natural and psychologically justified. The bulk of the teacher's activities are subjected to the most strict programming: any looseness, guesswork, self-asserting inventiveness, jumping from one subject to another, incoherence, etc., corrupts the suggestopedic work, and the results do not meet expectations.

It is rather common that when otherwise artistic and inventive teachers are faced with poor results in their work, they have probably failed to work out a meticulous plan and have not concentrated their efforts in preparing models of their activities. Such models must, of course, be embroidered with the unavoidable improvisations of a good professional. The individual work of every teacher is of great importance. From the first moment of class he or she is in control of establishing the exceptionally important prerequisites of order and harmony in both actions and relations and, like a first-class orchestra conductor during rehearsals, he or she then develops the masterly virtuoso performance of the composition by all. Each gesture, each facial expression, each word of the teacher-conductor should belie his or her expertness at drawing out the philosophical intentions of the author. The teacher insists scrupulously and without counterfeit pathos on obtaining such results from the performers in order to present them in the purest possible form to the audience. From the very first the suggestopedic teacher must show a sincere faith and a profound scientific conviction in the sweeping capacities of every individual student and of the group as a whole. And that takes place at the time of the first multi-planed encounter, of the first spark between teacher and students. It should be mentioned here that the concept of "infantilization" dealt with in suggestopedy is not to be taken literally. The concern, sense of responsibility, and outward and inward psychological organization of the teacher are factors that determine a true confidence between the expert in a given domain and his or her pupils. Any hint of "falling into a second childhood" is out of the question. The games, props, toys, and other aids used in suggestopedic teaching to adults (and, to some extent, to children) serve another purpose. They are meant, through reminiscences, fantasies, and associations, to turn the attention of the student away from the "pain and torture" of studying. This is the crucial point of games in the suggestopedic theory.

So, the day following the first session begins with the teacher coming in promptly, cheerful, smiling, and optimistic. He or she greets each student in turn and asks (using a very simple phrase in the foreign language) about any news in the student's bogus occupation. Both the questions and the answers become more complicated as the course progresses. In the beginning the teacher answers him- or herself the questions that have been posed, in order to facilitate the student's getting into the swing of the work. Then he or she reminds the students of the necessity to study the scenario, opens the book, and then everybody begins *to read Act One*. The latter is subdivided into several parts. For instance, the first lesson in Italian is subdivided, according to lexical themes as follows: Introduction, Occupation, Family, Foreign Languages, Days of the Week, Drinks, Landscape, At the Airport, At the Hotel. Usually the reading begins in chorus. It is also possible to separate the men from the women, the former reading the lines of the male roles and the latter the lines of the female ones (later on, the roles can be reversed). In both groups it is the teacher's voice that dominates, the students reading softer, to ascertain once more the pronunciation. Most phonetical problems should have been resolved during the active concert session, when the teacher's reading should have been slow, in a clear-cut voice, that would have allowed the distinct hearing of every word and phoneme. The students should have also taken notes.

Elaboration of the First Part of Lesson One

Pages 1 and 2 of the text L'Italiano are read aloud slowly, with maximum clearness of diction. The teacher keeps a close watch on reading mistakes. As already mentioned, most of the phonetical peculiarities should have already been mastered, consciously or paraconsciously, during the active and passive concert sessions. The elaborations are intended only to consolidate them. Taking advantage of some mistake, the teacher interrupts the reading and, without correcting the mistake, gives a cursory explanation of the phonetic rule. For instance, suppose the word "successo," (page 9 in Italian text) is pronounced in the wrong way by some of the students. Making use of the list of names and/or professions hanging on the wall, the teacher reminds the class of the pronunciation of the names "Cesare," the profession "attrice," and so on. He or she then explains that the consonant *c* is soft, palatal, only if placed before *e* and *i*. He or she then reminds the class of the prononuciation of "*Ci*vinini," "*Ce*cilia," "musi*ci*sta," etc. In all other cases it sounds hard, velar: "ami*co*," "*Ca*rlo," "*scu*ltore," "*Chi*ara." By a similar approach the teacher explains the rest of the basic phonetical rules, the exceptions and the particular cases being skipped and left for explanation at a more advanced stage of the course.

Following is a list of some phonetical particulars, explanations of which are given en passant during the first elaboration of Lesson One. The lists refer to the Italian and Spanish languages, but similar procedures are being introduced in the courses in English, German, and other languages as well.

ITALIAN LANGUAGE

PARTICOLARITÀ DELLA PRONUNCIA DI ALCUNE CONSONANTI

c	ce	certamente, felice, successo
	ci	Civinini, Lucía
	ca, co, cu	cantante, Scala, Pellico, scuola
	chi, che	chidere, marchesa
g	ge	dipinge, intelligente
	gi	giro, regista
	ga, go, gu	ragazzo, Rigoletto, guardo
	ghe, ghi	colleghe, colleghi
	gli	figlio, biglietto
	gn	signore, ingegno, montagna

s	(a) sempre, studentessa
	(b) francese, casa
sce	conoscenza
sci	scientifico
z	(a) zucchero, zero
	(b) servizio, ragazzo

L'ACCENTO

1. Parole piane:

      2 1   2 1   2 1 2 1

   signore, cantante, mare, rosso

2. Parole tronche:

   città, università

3. Parole sdrucciole:

     3 2 1 3 2 1 3   2 1 3 2 1

   telefono, libero, zucchero, parlano

SPANISH LANGUAGE

c	(a) cena, precio
	(b) comer, nunca
ch	muchacho
g	(a) ingeniero, imagínate!
	(b) llegada, luego
j	mujer, caja, viaje
ll	llegada, llave, apellido
ñ	niño, mañana
q	quiero, pequeño
z	vez (cena)

EL ACENTO

1. mesa, hermano, nosotros, hablan
   lámpara, médico
   aquí, interés, balcón

2. dirección, profesión (profesiones)

3. director, libertad, actriz, capital, subir
   (a) fácil, difícil, útil, carácter

4. él habla, el muchacho
   más
   cuánto (cuándo, dónde, qué)?

5. imagínate, tomándolo

ENGLISH LANGUAGE

1. Vowels

a = /ei/ (in open syllables)   Kate, plane, day
all, alk = /o:/   ball, talk
e = /i/ (in most cases)   Peter, be, teacher, see, people
e = /e/ (in close syllables)   men, red, let, tell
i = /ai/ (in open syllables)   Mike, driver
oo = /u/ (in most cases)   book, good
er, ir, ur = /ə:/   farmer, girl, burn

2. Some consonants:

c   can, cent
ch   child
sh   shop
w   wife, woman
th   this, with
ph   photo

GERMAN LANGUAGE

1. The long accented vowel:

    (a) Seen, Boot
    (b) wohnen, fahren, sehen
    (c) viel, wieder
    (d) fragen, Ferien

2. The short accented and unaccented vowels:

    Fenster, alle, Wand

3. Dipthongs:

    ei   Stein
    eu (aü)   Freund, Fraülein

4. Some consonants:

    sch   schreiben, Schubert
    tsch   deutsch
    ch   lachen

Gradually, with progress in the vocabulary the remaining specific phonetical cases can be elucidated. The tendency is to select examples from the vocabulary that has been mastered, both auditorily and visually, during the sessions. In that manner, with the necessary short breaks, when the phonetical specificity demands it, we read aloud the first part of the text. During the reading the students are able to refer to the translation in their mother tongue attached to the side of the page. Afterward the translation is taken away (or folded back). We begin again from the beginning and translate. This time the phrase in the foreign tongue is read quickly, unlike the first time, when the reading is slow, reminiscent of the first concert session. We begin by translating in chorus. Anybody needing to look up a word or phrase in the translation is allowed to do so. In fact, this serves as a self-check for the student letting him or her know how far the material has been mastered at the passive level.

The teacher should not forget that the psychological momentum during translation is of no less importance than during reading. Everything in the teacher's conduct suggests that the material has been mastered. A great many students, dominated by the social suggestive norm, lack confidence in having mastered everything at the passive level. Others are impatient and want to obtain full and prompt evidence of their achievements at both the active and passive levels. They forget that a time-consuming period of individual audio-articulative adaptation does exist, a period when one slowly penetrates the specificity of thinking of the nation whose language is being studied. Certain individual differences are more than natural between nations, and these differences effect the structure of the language as well.

The basic linguistic paradigms, marked off at the right-hand side of the page (only in the initial lessons), impose temporary diversions in the course of translation.

Elaboration of the Second Part of Lesson One

Now we can reverse the roles: the men read the women's parts and vice versa (and act them at the same time). The reading will sometimes seem comical but it will also bear a psychological charge. We read the whole of Lesson One. During the reading, time is spared again to bring the phonetical explanations to an end (those figuring in the grammar to Lesson One). Once again, the phonetical explanations are connected with names and occupations, as well as with examples from the first part. In translating, the students' attention is fixed on the phrases, containing verbs of the first conjugation (suonare, abitare, mancare, assomigliare, studiare, incontrare, invitare, visitare, insegnare, cantare, portare—respectively, to play, to live, to miss, to resemble, to study, to meet, to invite, to visit, to teach, to sing, to carry). The verbs are listed in the order of their appearance in the text. They all belong to the most common frequency. Conjugation is performed by the class as a whole. Some students may refer to the poster on the wall. Instead of reading the sentence in the textbook again, each student asks his or her neighbor (using the respective verb): "Do you play the violin?" (the piano, the guitar, etc.?); "Where do you live?," "Who do you live with?;" "Who do you resemble?;" "Do you like studying foreign languages?;" "Where do you work?" (here the teacher helps by thinking up and translating different working places); "Do you sing?;" "Where were you born?;" "How old are you?;" "Have you ever been to . . .?" (the question relates to different states). In the last case, names of the states should have been previously written on the blackboard. The questions are relatively easy, because they are posed immediately following a sentence of the same sense. The theme of "acquainting" is broadened more and more via the individual answers of the students. This mild activation serves mostly audio-articulative purposes.

The time has come to play a game: guessing "by telepathy" the name of some state, chosen by the teacher (and not one written on the blackboard). The teacher writes the name on a sheet of paper and keeps it at his or her desk (for verification). On the blackboard he or she then draws as many dashes as the number of letters in the name of the state. If a student identifies the state at once, the student earns ten times as many points as the number of the letters in the name. If nobody succeeds, guessing is begun letter by letter. Each successful guess earns 10 points. The points are then summed up for each team.

(This game is particularly useful when studying English by non-English speaking students, because of the characteristic peculiarities on the pronunciation, mostly of the vowels.)

We turn our attention to the sentences in direct relation to the grammar on the right-hand half of the page: the definite article for the masculine gender before a vowel "l" and "gli," the substantives of feminie gender, ending usually in "a" in the singular and "e" in the plural. The definite article agrees: "la" for singular, "le" for plural. The indefinite article in the singular is "una."

In the second part we find the important questions No. 4 and No. 5, and write them down in the manner of the first three: No. 4, "How much?" ("How many?") and No. 5, "When?" To answer question No. 6, "Where were you born?," the teacher distributes amongst the students maps of Italy with the different regions and the main cities outlined. While the students think of an answer, choosing a birthplace, the teacher summarizes in two or three sentences a few of the more important facts from the history of the respective region or city. For instance, the teacher says that Piemonte was the center of the Italian Rissorgimento—the Italian unification movement. The vocabulary is easy, the words sound familiar—the roots are mostly Latin, that is, international. The teacher might also say something about Venice, such as that the city was founded on islands because of the raids of barbarians on the mainland, etc. Picture cards from the cities of Italy are displayed.

When elaborating on the theme "The days of the week," the teacher explains without undue seriousness the origin of the names of the days, explaining that they are for the most part the names of planets, which in turn are related to Greek and Roman mythology.

Each student asks his or her neighbor: "Which day of the week do you like?."

Then the teacher offers to the students the "forgotten" diary of Mr. Civinini—the opera singer and principal character. The diary is an original Italian one. The pages of the respective dates and days of the week are filled with Mr. Civinini's notes about his participation in performances of La Scala and his concerts. The students choose a performance they are going to attend.

The elaboration of the second part of Lesson One is over. This is also the end of the first day of the concert session. After the musical signal announcing the end of class, the teacher wishes everyone a good time for the rest of the day (or evening) and leaves the classroom at once, to avoid redundant questions. The questions of the students should progress in nature as the course progresses. Moreover, staying for a while to chatter destroys the discrete distance between teacher and students, which is so important for the process of education. This is why the teacher's leaving the classroom immediately after class is the essential both at the end of the working day and during pauses. The well-trained suggestopedic teacher does not show off this distance; his or her conduct should be thoughtful and natural, so that the distance appears and is maintained by itself. Such relations are profitable to the students, and have much to do with the efficiency of the course. Even the best interpersonal relations—in the broadest sense of this word—are easy to spoil in the absence of diplomacy, discretion, and nobleness.

2. Second Day After the Session

Second Elaboration

The third part, from the appearance of the air-hostess on is read. Women read the female parts, men the male ones. Women read the underlined words very softly, men more loudly.

When it is time for translation, the class act out the ordering of something to drink. The students choose some drink for each of them (from the textbook). One student plays the role of the air-hostess. The teacher has brought the necessary props: children's tableware, empty bottles, battered glasses, a lovely apron, and a uniform cap for the air-hostess. Comical situations are looked for (the text permits it!), in order to create the free-hearted atmosphere suitable for spontaneous activation within the limits of familiar knowledge.

The polite conditional forms with "should" and "would" are one of the topics of the day. We write down question No. 7: "*What* would you like?."

On page 13 of the Italian textbook we elaborate on the sentence "Emilio, are we not grownups?" in all the persons, thus mentioning the personal pronouns. The latter are always at the students' disposal, because they are included in the posters with "to be" and "to have," hung on the wall. Once more we mention that in Italian (in Spanish also, as in Bulgarian) the personal pronouns are often neglected.

In other languages, explanation of the personal pronouns is given in didactic songs, written mostly for the verbs "to be" and "to have," as well as via other songs that are also suitable.

We use the artistic–didactic songs "Mother, I Love You So Much" and "My Beloved Land" (Italian textbook, page 14).

Mamma,	Mother,
ti voglio tanto bene!	*I love you so much*!
Mamma,	Mother,
tu mi *aspetti* sempre.	*You* keep *waiting* for me.
Guardo il tuo viso	*I look* for your face
un po'invecchiato,	A little aged,
capisco molto bene	*I understand* very well
i tuoi sacrifici,	Your sacrifices,
la gioia, il dolore,	Your *joy*, your *pain*,
l'amor per tutti noi,	Your love for all of us,
nascosto nel tuo *cuore*.	Deep in your *heart*.
E *cerco*, cerco sempre	And I keep *look*ing for
la strada bella e vara,	The beautiful, the true *way*,
e *vengo* innocente	And *I come*, innocent,
a *riposàr* da te ...	To *have a rest* close to you ...

Ti voglio tanto bene

Moderato
Parole e musica: E. Gateva

Mamma, ti voglio tanto bene!

Mamma, tu mi aspetti sempre...

Guardo il tuo viso un 'po' invecchiato, capisco molto bene i tuoi sacrifici, la gioia, il dolor. l'amor per tutti noi, nascosto nel tuo cuor. E cerco, cerco sempre la strada bella e vera e vengo innocente a riposar da te.

Terra mia cara

Parole e musica: E. Gateva

Moderato

Terra mia cara, bella ed antica! Guardo le montagne, il cielo più sereno, i laghi, i fiumi, le valli, il mare più azzurro; l'animo agi-tato trema di gioia pura. Terra mia cara, abbraccia con amore, con fede e speranza un figlio che torna!

Terra mia *cara*,	My *beloved* land,
bella ed antica!	Beautiful and ancient!
Guardo *le montagne*,	I am looking at *the mountains*,
il cielo piú sereno,	The clearest *sky*,
i laghi, i *fiumi*,	The lakes, the *rivers*,
le valli,	The *valleys*,
il mare piú *azzurro*—	The *blue*st sea—
l'animo agitato	My agitated soul
trema di gioia pura.	*Trembles* with a pure joy.
Terra mia cara,	My beloved land,
abbraccia con amore,	*Embrace* with love,
con *fede* e speranza	With *faith* and hope
un figlio *che* torna!	A son *who* is coming back!

These songs (and all the songs of the textbook) are related to the Italian way of thinking, to the musical setup of a nation where Christian and pagan conceptions intermingle in a very particular manner. And that is not fortuitous. These songs are related to the Italian Renaissance, at which time the Mona Lisa was painted: (the Italian textbook, page 15).

The artistic–didactic songs in other languages, some of which are included as examples in the present Manual, reveal certain psychological characteristics of the respective nations in a similar way.

We elaborate and consolidate the verbs of the first conjugation by conjugating them completely. These verbs are: aspettare, guardare, cercare, riposare, tremare, abbracciare, tornare (respectively, to wait, to look, to look for, to rest, to tremble, to embrace, to come back). Such a conjugation might seem "mechanical" at first sight, but it satisfies the inner needs of the students to automate the verbal system of the language. Within the framework of a vast, but *carefully selected for practical purposes*, system of material, such mechanical work, when its link to semantic units is necessary is not only devoid of dullness and repulsiveness but, on the contrary, is expected with eagerness because of the evident benefit it causes. This mechanical approach might seem at first glance contradictory to suggestologic principles. It is not so. In suggestopedy it makes up part of a body of information that substantially differs from the situation observed in conventional teaching. The latter presents the material to be learned in small doses and insists on its complete mastering at the conscious level. Then comes the automation of these small doses by means of reiterating tedious structures. Only then is a new small dose presented to the students. Meanwhile, this kind of logical analysis has destroyed any motivation for studying, interest has waned, and the objective of education—a creative synthesis that should always be foreseen in perspective—has been forgotten.

In suggestopedic teaching the trend is toward bringing about, through a purposefully elaborated program and making use of psychotherapeutic methods and artistic devices, the natural conditions necessary for the spontaneous analytical–synthetical activity of the brain in its receiving and processing information.

The songs are prerecorded, performed by a professional opera singer. The text reads that right now on the radio sounds Mr. Civinini's voice. We listen to the "performance" of Mr. Civinini, the opera singer from La Scala and principal character of the textbook.

Next follows the day's pause.

After the pause *we read the text to the end.* In the case of the other lessons the reading is done the day after the session. It is possible to try having students read roles out loud, particularly those students the teacher has already built up confidence in to be able to read with relatively few mistakes. When these students read, the mistakes should not be corrected overtly. The teacher should merely repeat the word, gently, in the correct way, as if speaking to him- or herself. The fourth part of the lesson (after the songs and up till the arrival at the hotel) is read in this manner. (If the reading makes good progress, we continue.)

For the fifth part of Lesson One small objects are given to the students, which are related to the "roles" they have chosen to read. The use of these props is not insisted upon. The students have to express a spontaneous wish to choose one of them. The purpose is clear: during the reading of roles one should create a figurativeness and an emotiveness which will be of help to the reproduction later on. Dr. Walter gets elegant spectacles (only the rims) and a traveling bag. Mrs. Walter gets a lovely hat, much like the one in the picture. The Italian driver gets dark glasses, Italian make. Francesco is a modern youth; he could also get dark glasses. The hotel-keeper gets a bunch of keys to be suspended on his belt and a couple of hotel keys with number plates. The chambermaid Mirandolina, whose name and behavior evoke associations with C. Goldoni's "La locandiera," gets a stylish wig and a little lace apron. Elsa, another modern young person, gets a handbag and a thick book. It is in this book that

Francesco looks up in vain the joke he wants to tell (the joke from the end of Lesson One). The book turns out to be on philosophy. Francesco gives it back to Elsa with a gesture of contempt. Maestro Rossini (from the joke) gets a bowtie, and the lady long white gloves.

The time has come to attempt individual translation of the dialogue in the fourth part (after the songs), beginning with those students for whom the prospect of success is the most likely. Step by step, all the students will become involved.

The teacher stresses the verb "vedere" ("to see") of the second conjugation, placed on the right-hand side of the page. The teacher relates his or her explanations to the paradigms of verbs of second and third conjugation, emphasizing first the identical forms and then the small differences in the endings for the third person singular.

The particular characteristics of different conjugations are also on the right-hand side of the textbook, so that the student learns some of these points by means of the already discussed mechanism of peripheral perception.

We come to question No. 8: "*What* is this?" and write it down under the other questions. We open Dr. Walter's traveling bag, and one of the students takes on the role of a customs officer, asking questions (from the textbook) about the chosen contents of the bag, which the teacher has chosen beforehand.

We come across the modal verbs "dovere" ("must"), "volere" ("to want"), and "potere" ("can"), each of which are irregular. Here the teacher also gives comparative explanations (e.g., which forms are similar, which are regular, which are distorted), thus promoting memorization. Furthermore, these verbs are going to be used quite widely. With the help of modal verbs we are able to make a great many combinations, and, on the whole, they will be of great use in the work to come. First of all, from a purely practical standpoint, the needs of intensive learning (which, in its essence, is suggestopedy) will be met perfectly by the possibility of partly replacing the imperative and subjunctive moods (still out of the student's reach) with structures including the modal verbs. The same holds true for the future simple tense: Asking questions and formulating answers is greatly facilitated.

We now address question No. 9: "*What* is your address?". Each student asks his or her neighbor. The model for answering is once again found in the textbook. In general, during the elaboration of Lesson One the students' activation is directed exclusively toward simple questions and answers, solely in connection with a concrete sentence or situation from the textbook. The sentence (situation) is slightly modified—person and number of the verb, gender and number of the noun—to fit the student's chosen role.

Here we can broaden the scope of some questions, for example, "Which floor do you live on?," or "Which floor would you like to live on?"

We give a brief explanation of the verbs of the type, "prefer*ire*," "capire," "finire" ("to prefer," "to understand," "to finish"), which are of the third conjugation and have their characteristics explained on the right-hand half of the page.

If time permits, we go on with the translation and the elaboration of the grammatical topics.

3. Third Day After the First Session

The detailed elaboration of Lesson One that we propose requires more days than is usually devoted to the following lessons, so we proceed to the translation of the last (sixth) part.

Quite often we interrupt the translation in order to conjugate on the spot some verb from the sentence just translated.

After having translated the description of the hotel room, we transform the text into questions and the students answer them. For instance: (1) Is your house (flat, room) quiet and cosy? (2) What does it face? (the garden, the street, the mountains, the lake, the river, etc., choosing from the familiar vocabulary); (3) Is the carpet new? (the curtains, the armchairs); (4) Where is your bed? (near the window, far from the window, near the door, by the wall); (5) Do you use one or two pillows? (6) Have you any pictures on the walls? What kind of pictures? (modern, classical); (7) Is there a wardrobe in your room? (a mirror, a little table, a bookcase, a telephone, a radio, a TV set); (8) Does the radio (TV set) function? (9) Have you a balcony? (10) How does your bathroom look? (11) Do you have running hot water? And so on.

We stress again to the class that the students are encouraged to invent the answers and even to answer for a third person: a friend, a relative, an acquaintance.

In order to consolidate the concordance of the noun with the definite and indefinite article both in the singular and the plural, as well as with the adjective, use is made of the game "Auction."

The student sitting at the teacher's left (or right) is the first to assume the role of "broker." He or she casts a die. The number of the die indicates how many of his or her belongings are to be sold. (The items are those figuring in the description of the hotel room in the textbook.) The "broker" can refer to the textbook (if at a loss for an item) and announces the item to be sold (the verb "vendere"—"to sell"—is of the second conjugation, like "vedere"—"to see"—from the poster). Let's say the number having appeared on the die was "2." The "broker" announces: "Vendo *i* tappet*i*. Sono due tappet*i* nuov*i*" ("I am selling the carpets. They are two new carpets"). The next student casts the die. In order to win his or her neighbor's belongings, this student must make a prompt calculation of which of his or her own belongings, sold in the quantity indicated by the die, are worth the items already announced. For example, the die the student has thrown indicates "5." The student makes a rapid calculation as to which items he or she should "sell" to make a profit and win the two new carpets. The student offers five pieces of antique furniture. If the offer does not cover the value of the previous one, the other students intervene, make valuations, and the unsuccessful "broker" drops out of the game. Then comes the turn of the next student, and so on. The student who rolls a "6" wins everything. As already mentioned, the purpose of the game is to consolidate the particular characteristics of the declension of nouns and adjectives in gender and number, as well as of some forms of the verb "to be." Cardinal numbers from one to ten are declined, too.

By the end of the game the wealthiest player makes a handsome gesture and donates the belongings he or she has won to the course. We mark the donation at the blackboard and congratulate the donor.

In our further explanations of lexical and grammatical characteristics we consolidate the greetings: "Good morning" ("Good afternoon"), "Good evening," "Good night," as well as the phrases: "to be in a hurry," "to be hungry," "to be thirsty," "to feel sleepy" (with auxiliary verbs). The teacher calls the students' attention to the way of constructing the past perfect tense (passato prossimo), which is quite common in coloquial speech, by means of the anecdote about Rossini and suitable examples from the text. ("*Ho mangiato* un magnifico pollo alla panna." *Siamo arrivati.*) (In the German language—"das Perfect": "*Ich habe* den Brief *bekommen.*" "*Sie ist abgefahren.*" In the French language—"Passé composé: "*J'ai choisi.*" "*Il est venu.*")

Once more stress is placed on the importance of the auxiliary verbs "to be" and "to have." That these should be learned by heart should be sufficiently motivated that a definite consolidation of their forms should be evident during the first few days of the course.

After the pause, the teacher reads aloud the complementary summarizing story "Patrizia." He or she shows a photograph of Patrizia to the class. Then each student reads a sentence and translates it.

The teacher assigns the next day's subject: "On the analogy of the story about Patrizia, make up a similar one, referring to some of your friends. Make it short in order to be able to tell it easily. We shall be glad to see a picture of your hero. Please do not write anything. Just think it up in your native language, and first try to find a suitable picture."

These explanations once again put emphasis on the importance played by the stimulation of artistic thinking in suggestopedy. Anyhow, teaching of foreign languages to adults cannot do without translation. On the contrary: the skillful and natural use of translation as a visual (but not auditory) mainstay of the class is another way of more quickly delineating objective and abstract notions. Intensifying the adult student's artistic thinking lays the foundation for global perception. That is why audio-visualization in foreign language suggestopedy for adults does not stimulate primitive pictorial thinking (a result that is fundamental in the case of children), but activates imagination, fantasy, artistic thinking. Thus stimulated and emotionally refreshed by such artistic thinking, the student has activated in him- or herself the processes of memorization and of motor activity.

4. Fourth Day After the First Session

As usual, we open the daily work with some familiar songs, accompanied by an easy dance.

The fourth day after the first session is the day when the cycle is closed and the next lesson (in this case Lesson Two) is to be taught. We take a cursory look at the grammar presented at the end of the textbook, relating to Lesson One. Suggestopedy tends to avoid the absolute consolidation of all the material presented: in this way we provide the paraconscious mechanism with the possibility of performing a complimentary automatic processing. Another reason for this tendency is the natural repetitiveness and variability as the material is presented. As already mentioned, it is the high frequency material that is taken into consideration, both for the vocabulary as well as the grammar. In this way, the subject matter is mastered completely in a given period very naturally.

As for the Italian grammar provided for Lesson One in the textbook, the problem of simple and compound prepositions, being a problem of some particularity, is left at a purely translational level. A very cursory explanation about the conjunction of simple prepositions with the definite article is given on the spot. The particularity in question is readily mastered at the audio-articulational level because of its frequent use. Some linguistic characteristics of other foreign tongues are treated in a similar manner. For example: learning the declensional systems in Russian and German; the interrogative and negative forms in English and French; the use of the two forms of auxiliaries "ser" and "estar" and the partial irregularity of conjugations in Spanish; the continuous tenses in English, Spanish, and Italian and the declensional forms of personal pronouns; the frequent use of some forms of the subjunctive mood in most languages; the sequence of tenses; etc.

The grammatical explanations pertaining to Lesson One of the Italian textbook contain almost all the verbs figuring in the lesson itself. They are about 90, of high common frequency. We proceed to a short game. Once more, the teacher selects the verbs according to their frequency and proposes that a student make a simple sentence using one of them (for instance, with the verb "to study"). The next student should continue with the next verb, suggested by the teacher to link the meaning of the second student's sentence with the first. The overall purpose of this exercise is to obtain a meaningful story, every student taking part in it with a verb proposed by the teacher. The intention is to bring into being intriguing motifs that create an interesting plot. Practice has shown that such development occurs without strain, the students showing great imagination and fantasy. In this way the different sides of the verbs having the greatest practical value are revealed, and the vocabulary having just been taught is clarified.

Next follows an imperceptible entrance into the swing of the language. Taking advantage of the game, we give the floor over to the students. They should tell their individual stories on the subject "Patrizia." The students join quite readily, if the invitation is made in a mild and tactful way. More often than not they have brought photographs, portraits, or simple press clippings, and they look at them and narrate in a calm and confident tone the unpretentious things they have prepared for this first monologue of theirs. Then the photograph (the picture) makes the round of the audience while another student takes the floor, and so on.

These first narrations are not interrupted if the student makes grammatical (and even lexical) mistakes. The goal is to make the students "loosen their tongues." As already mentioned, the main problem for the majority of learners is the audio-articulational one, as well as the difficulty of thinking in the corresponding language. In this connection, the tactfulness and patience of the teacher come to the fore as decisive prerequisites to any further success of monologic speech which, according to the Methodological Instructions, if skillfully directed by the teacher, will develop into *spontaneous* dialogic speech. At that stage the students will have overcome to some extent their articulation problems and will be able to pose questions to one another in a relatively correct manner. A question that is posed incorrectly and unclearly both in phonetical and grammaticolexical respect often perplexes the student, bringing about confusion and anxiety. The reasons are more than evident. The teacher's tactfulness and patience should be noticeable to the students. A similar conduct amongst students themselves is cultivated in such a way. Socialization within the group is further increased, as well as the concern to obtain the maximum educational profit for everyone.

Further on, during the next lessons, the teacher corrects the monologic speech only if the mistake is such that it might interfere with communication. As already emphasized, mistakes are not corrected bluntly; the teacher merely repeats the word or phrase in the right way, as if by chance.

The teacher should try to stimulate and encourage intervention on the part of the students in the form of questions or comments (the sole condition being that they must be in the foreign language) that interrupt the speaker's monologue. The model is given by the teacher, who interrupts the speaker at an opportune moment, in a tactful and intriguing way, asking an easy question in relation to the story. The teacher is "master of the situation": he or she once proves his or her tactfulness if some of the students' narratives turn out to be too long or too intricate. The teacher intervenes very cautiously and assists the student to shorten and simplify the story. The same holds true for those students whose progress in the language is more rapid. Later on the whole group learns to apply this mechanism to "curtail" the most talkative individuals without hurting anyone's feelings.

After the break a short introduction to Lesson Two is given, followed by the sessions. This is a completed cycle. The work is conducted in a similar way when dealing with other lessons. The teaching and learning of all foreign languages takes place according to these same principles.

We have already spoken about the phonetical explanations in English, Spanish, French, and German. The rule of thumb is: the grammatical highlights, printed on the right-hand side of the page, should be elaborated on by means of games and songs at the time of the translation. The first lesson in the abovementioned languages includes a vocabulary and a grammar that are analogous to those included in the Italian textbook. The verbal system of the language is worked out on the grounds of the verbs of the first frequency. The priority given to the rapid mastering of the verbal system results in an easier attainment of successful reproduction by the students. The psycho-physiology of the phenomenon has been investigated, but we will refrain from discussing it.

Even in English we pay special attention to the verbal system, despite the apparent simplicity of the conjugation itself. As a matter of fact, this is the underpinning for the automation of the examples "to be" and "to have," the modal, the regular, and the most frequent irregular verbs that result in the regrettable mistakes of neglecting the ending "s" in the third person singular, and the mixing up of the auxiliaries "to be" and "to have." The situation is similar in German, where the change of radical vowels in the conjugations, the problem of divisible and indivisible prefixes of some verbs, and the structure of the sentences are of particular importance to a student's rapid entrance into the swing of the language. The declensional system is left, as already mentioned, to be learned at the translation level. Learning the rules is of no help; only the accumulation of sufficient lexical material at the communcation level promotes natural reproduction by the students with comparatively few mistakes.

If the group has students who present signs of having a difficult time coping with individual narratives, we make use of questions in the foreign language pertaining to the first lesson, which we have written on the blackboard beforehand. The answers to such questions must result in a short story. The questions should be accessible to all students. The mere fact that students are able to answer such questions on the third or the fourth day of the course (while during the testing for input levels similar questions have remained largely unanswered) is a very efficient stimulus, and the impulse to connect the individual narratives occurs with ever-increasing motivation.

Here is a model list of such questions:

1. What is the name of your best friend?
2. Where does he/she live?
3. Whom does he/she live with?
4. Is he/she married?
5. Has he/she any children? How many?
6. Has he/she a sister (a brother)?
7. What is the name of his/her spouse?
8. How old is he/she?
9. Where was he/she born?
10. Where has he/she studied? What has he/she studied?
11. Do you like to travel?
12. How do you prefer to travel?
13. Have you been abroad? Where?
14. Have you many friends? What are their nationalities? What are their occupations?
15. Give us a short description of your birthplace.

As a matter of course, the questions are first translated by the students (individually or together), to secure ourselves against any errors slipping into these initial lessons. Afterward, a student who has expressed a willingness to make a narrative in connection with the questions is asked to speak. Gradually, the most shy or unwilling students are given the floor.

When dealing with the initial three or four lessons the teacher has the right to modify the exact duration of the elaborations in order to keep in line with the general progress of the students.

Lesson One of the Italian textbook includes about 800 lexical units, Lesson Two about 350, Lesson Three 440, Lesson Four 220, Lesson Five 250, Lesson Six 140, Lesson Seven 200, Lesson Eight 150.

The distribution in the other textbooks is similar.

Lesson Two: "Waking Up"

I. Introduction

After the day's break (30 minutes), the teacher carries the introduction into the new material with the song "I am Greeting the Day," with which Lesson Two begins. The teacher is assisted by the students. Doctor Walter, a main character of the play, wakes up in the hotel, makes his usual physical exercises, and sings a song. The text of the song is read aloud in chorus and then translated. Verbs are dealt with briefly as they appear in the text. The teacher rapidly conjugates together with the group: "salutare," "respirare," "pensare" (respectively, "to greet," "to breathe," "to think") of the first conjugation; "sorridere," "ridere" (respectively, "to smile," "to laugh") of the second conjugation, which are reflexive in Bulgarian, but not in Italian. The grammatical unit of the day is the theme "Reflexive Verbs." Next come the familiar verbs "vedere," "dovere" (respectively, "to see," "must") of the second conjugation, "costruire" ("to build") of the third conjugation, and "andare" ("to go," "to walk")—an irregular verb. This is the first time we have come across it. For the time being we leave it alone. Then comes the reflexive verb "svegliarsi"—"to wake up"—of the first conjugation. Each student asks his or her neighbor what time he or she wakes up. We add the reflexive particles. The teacher then reveals how to form verbal adverbs: pens*ando* ("pens*are*"—"to think"). The teacher begins to sing the song of Dr. Walter and makes the group rise and dance for a while. The students take one another's hands and form a circle and dance a waltz. The second part of the song is in a marching pace. The participants are let loose, turn about and take a couple of steps out of the circle. The third part of the song is in a waltz pace again: the students take one another's hands, making the waltz steps to the left and to the right. At the end they stamp their feet several times, in rhythm with the words "where there's no fear."

Il Dottore Walter: (canta)

Saluto il giorno,	*I'm greeting* the day,
saluto *il sole*,	I'm greeting *the sun*,
saluto la grande città	I'm greeting the big city

che *a poco a poco*	which, *step by step*
si sveglia, respira—	*wakes up*, breathes—
sorride la vita.	*life is smiling.*
E vedo un uomo	And I see a man
andare tranquillo,	*walking* quietly,
pensando al mondo	*thinking* of the world,
che deve *costruir*;	that he must *build*;
un *mondo* nuovo,	a new *world*,
felice e puro,	happy and pure,
un mondo	a world
dove	where
non c'è *paura.*	there's no *fear.*

II. Active Concert Session

The teacher gives a 2–3 minute break. Meanwhile the room is aerated. The reading is analogous to that of the first lesson, but now the concert is different, the mood and thoughts it generates being different as well. One should never forget that italicized words are read by the teacher with a particular intonation, in order to stand out against the rest of the text. The reading is once more interspersed with short pauses of sufficient duration to allow a cursory glance at the grammatical instructions on the right-hand half of the page. It is in Lesson Two that the rest of the most important verbs of the first frequency (regular and irregular), the cardinal numbers, and the demonstrative pronouns make their appearance. During the reading in the active session these grammatical units are emphasized through intonational changes.

Since the volume of the material in this session is smaller, there is no need for breaks where the room is emptied. The teacher, however, may give a break, if he or she considers it proper to do so, after the first composition (J. Haydn: "Concerto for Violin and Orchestra No. 1 in C Major," nearly 5 minutes long).

The 5–7 minute break that follows the active session is never omitted.

III. Pseudopassive Concert Session

Here the music is also different, but the reading is basically the same as in Lesson One.

Saluto il giorno

Parole e musica: E. Gateva

Allegro

Saluto il giorno, saluto il sole, saluto la grande città che a poco a poco si sveglia, respira; sorride la vita. E

Andante

vedo un uomo andare tranquillo, pensando al mondo che deve costruir; un

Allegro

mondo nuovo, felice e puro, un mondo dove non c'è paura!

The ritual of the sessions is observed in the same way as in Lesson One. At the end we wait for the music to die away; then the teacher and the students leave in silence.

IV. Elaborations

First Elaborations

On the next day, much like the previous elaborations, work begins with questions from the teacher to each student: "How do you feel today?," "Is there anything new in business?" (this question relates to the new occupation). Things go fast, with the teacher cutting into the conversation with short phrases to add something, to bring about animation and playfulness, and to counter to some extent the early activation of the initial days, namely, at the beginning of the classes, when a certain "getting out" (returning to the mother tongue) of the language is observed.

Through this frequent, brief, and lively cutting in, the students obtain in the first days of the course an increased opportunity to listen to correct speech and to accumulate passive vocabulary and grammar which, in the days to come, will be activated spontaneously, without anxiety, without urging. These moments of the educational process should not be stressed too strongly. The teacher's conduct should be very flexible; he or she must keep his or her eyes wide open. His or her sense of tactfulness and diplomacy should be very subtle, lest not a single point of importance to the suggestopedic teaching and learning processes be skipped. When the forerunners of spontaneous activation in the students begin to appear, the teacher should skillfully direct this process until it becomes fully developed. Usually true activation makes its first appearance after the third or fourth lesson, that is, about the tenth day. Until that point the teacher should be very active and inventive to direct and oversee everything in a very subtle, very delicate way. And when this crucial moment—the spontaneous activation—finally occurs, the teacher should begin to gradually withdraw (a process where tactfulness is again of primary importance) and let the students monitor their own progress, not intervening except in cases of obvious mistakes and awkward situations. Generally speaking, the teacher's role should be gradually restricted to that of a consultant.

We are laying stress on these details here, before it is time to discuss them in full, so as to emphasize the importance of those moments which are to be taken into account from the very beginning.

After having kindly inquired after the students' good spirits (his or her own being always high!), the teacher proceeds to the elaboration of Lesson Two. The class listens to a professional record of the song, "I'm Greeting the Day." They study the song. The teacher asks whether some of the students would like to accompany the record on the piano (or the accordian, or the guitar, depending on what is available). If nobody is willing, the teacher may accompany him- or herself. Everybody sings and dances, as they did during the deciphering. At the end, mimicking Dr. Walter, the class performs a couple of easy physical exercises, counting up to 50. All the students, standing in a circle, turn around, relax, and then rise to tiptoe. Then they rest their weight on their heels. This exercise has a good physiological basis, and we make use of it to count up to 50 in the foreign tongue.

Lesson Two is divided into three parts. The teacher gives the students a free choice of the roles. They may also make use of the props, if they wish. The roles of Emilio and Francesco may be assumed by women as well. The reading proceeds at a moderate speed to enable the students to keep an eye on the translation. As already mentioned, the teacher corrects the reading mistakes in a soft voice and very mildly. If necessary, the teacher also reminds the class once more of the phonetic rules by means of examples. Part of the text is translated to assure the students that the material has been completely mastered at the translation level.

At the time of translation the teacher pauses at the underlined items of the vocabulary, including the familiar verbs and—the pauses becoming a little longer—the most important verbs of first frequency appearing in the lesson: "andare," "venire," "uscire," "dare," "fare," "stare," "sapere," "dire," "proporre" (respectively "to go," "to come," "to go out," "to give," "to make," "to stand," "to know," "to say," "to propose"). By means of a large toy clock the teacher demonstrates the different hours, noting what the class might do at the respective time of day. Each student addresses his or her neighbor with a question about the other's breakfast: where he or she takes it and what he or she has.

As for the reflexive verbs that pop up throughout the text, they are elaborated with the help of the doll Pipi, which performs in a comical and peculiar manner the morning ritual of getting up, exercising, washing one's face, having breakfast, going to school, etc.

The teacher takes advantage of the verb "stare" ("to stand," "to be situated") to mention the formation of continuous tenses. During the deciphering we have already spoken about the verbal adverb. The present continuous tense is easy to understand, but, for the time being, we shall refrain from making much use of it. The problem of continuous tenses in English and in Spanish, where their use is rather common, may be elaborated in a similar way, imperceptibly, without linking them with the notion of the native tongue (where such tenses may not exist), since such explanations serve to inhibit the learning of these tenses. As a matter of fact, however, neither their understanding nor their use is really difficult.

The second part of Lesson Two begins with the action in the Bank (page 29 of the Italian textbook). The class proceeds with reading roles. Then the parts are translated. The teacher focuses on the cardinal numbers. In order to consolidate the numbers and the simple arithmetical operations associated with them, the teacher supplies a card game. On the cards are marked the numbers from 0 to 20 in four colors: red, blue, green, yellow. There are also four cards with, respectively, the marks of multiplication (×), a red one; of addition (+), a blue one; of subtraction (−), a green one; and of division (÷), a yellow one. The names of the students, the winning numbers, and the premiums are written on the blackboard as follows:

Red Numbers: (×)
The card with the number 20 wins 2,000,000 lire
The card with the number 18 wins 1,000,000 lire
The card with the number 16 wins   900,000 lire
The card with the number 15 wins   800,000 lire
The card with the number 14 wins   700,000 lire
The card with the number 12 wins   600,000 lire
The card with the number 10 wins   500,000 lire

Blue Numbers: (+)
The card with the number 19 wins   400,000 lire
The card with the number 17 wins   300,000 lire
The card with the number 13 wins   200,000 lire
The card with the number 11 wins   100,000 lire

Green Numbers: (−)
The card with the number 9 wins 90,000 lire
The card with the number 8 wins 80,000 lire
The card with the number 7 wins 70,000 lire
The card with the number 6 wins 60,000 lire

Yellow Numbers: (÷)
The card with the number 5 wins 50,000 lire
The card with the number 4 wins 40,000 lire
The card with the number 3 wins 30,000 lire
The card with the number 2 wins 20,000 lire
The card with the number 1 wins 10,000 lire

    The four cards bearing the marks of arithmetical operations are taken out of the pack and put on the floor face down. The remaining cards are dealt. One of the students turns one of the four cards on the floor face up. This card defines the color and the operation through which the premiums will be realized. For instance, if the student has turned the card with the red multiplication mark (×), premiums will be won by the red numbers, figuring at the table through multiplication. Each player inspects his or her cards, and if in possession of some of the abovementioned numbers in red, he or she looks for a way to make combinations of the other cards in his or her hand (regardless of the color) which will—using multiplication—result in obtaining the winning red number. For instance, one of the students has *a red card with the number 18*, winning 1,000,000 lire. He or she also has a yellow card with the number 2 and a green one with the number 9. He or she announces aloud in Italian: "Two times nine makes eighteen!," and he displays the combination. The final result must be in any case a red number. If the combination is correct, the player wins; if not, he or she is out till the end of the whole game (he or she doesn't take part in any of the combinations with the remaining colors).

    When everybody has checked his or her cards and announced their combinations, and when all the premiums are written on the blackboard, the game proceeds to the other colors and operations. The red card with the multiplication mark is discarded. Another student turns over one of the three remaining cards on the floor, thus defining the color and the operation in the second part of the game. And so on. The cards are redealt and the game goes on. It is possible to make use of the zero card in combinations. Each student can have more than one winning combination. The premiums are summed up. By the end of the game each player should think up a way to "invest" the money he or she has earned to the profit of the course.

We keep translating the text until the end of the second part (up to the story about Michelangelo), paying attention to the underlined vocabulary and grammar. By the end of the day the class should have read the last (third) part. Its elaboration is left for the next day.

Second Elaborations

The Second Day after the Second Session

As usual, the day begins with the teacher inquiring after the students' good spirits. At an opportune moment one of the songs is sung. The story about Michelangelo is translated. The students are divided into two teams. Each student translates the sentence, then substitutes words from another sentence for the underlined ones, paying attention not to obtain nonsense. Every correct substitution earns 10 points.

The two teams pursue the competition. Twenty art reproductions (ten for each team) are hung on the blackboard. They are numbered in such a way that the figures are clearly seen by everyone. These are reproductions of sculptures by Italian masters, among which there are eight (four in each set) by Michelangelo, but not the most popular ones. They must be recognized. A correct answer earns 10 points.

The teacher reads aloud the extra text: "Patrizia," Part 2. Then the students read it sentence by sentence and translate. The teacher produces a small bag, full of various knick-knacks: a small mirror, a vial of perfume, a car, a motorbike, a ring, a piece of cloth, a pocketknife, an elephant, a horse, etc. The students are asked to close their eyes, and each one takes an item from the bag. This item is then brought home. The students from the first team should think up a very short personal story (with the new name and occupation) on the analogy of the story about Patrizia (Part 2), making use of the vocabulary found in the latter. This personal story, however, should be much shorter and should include in an adequate manner the item taken from the bag. Nothing should be written at home; the students should simply think about and *figure to themselves in the most vivid possible way* the things they could narrate, trying to find the necessary words in the foreign tongue in the story about Patrizia or in the past two lessons. The story should be interesting and very short, in order to enable everyone to tell their own.

The students from the second team should imagine a situation and should try to find the necessary vocabulary in Lesson One. The situation they should imagine is the following: they have just arrived at the station in some Italian town (they choose the town), where they have not been for many years, but where a close friend of theirs lives, whose address they possess. They call the friend by phone and they find he has moved to a new house. They dial his new phone number. The friend answers. They have not met for ages and speak about their families, their business, their plans for the week. The host asks his friends where they have put up for the night. The guests still have not found a hotel and want to know where they can find good lodging, listing their preferences with regard to meals. The host breaks off and invites them home, speaking about his lodging and the surroundings. The items from the bag are included in the dialogue in an appropriate manner. Almost all the vocabulary comes from the first lesson. The students pick up partners and choose their roles. In the evening they should look through the first lesson. We emphasize that writing is unnecessary. The situation should be mentally "seen," and the phrases that will be used in the personal story should be found in the lessons. The story should be very brief. This is a prerequisite of utmost importance.

Third Elaborations

The Third Day after the Second Session
Strictly observing the Methodological Instructions for the Suggestopedic Teaching of Foreign Languages, the teacher should carry out the monologic and dialogic speech very skilfully. (The speech in question has been planned on the previous day and is "worked out" by the students from the psychological and linguistic standpoints.) The teacher creates a cheerful and unstrained atmosphere, in which no special attention is paid to errors and the student is allowed to speak the foreign language (being made aware, of course, of his or her mistakes—the grammatical problems are being elaborated both at the conscious and still more at the paraconscious level quite seriously). When monologues and dialogues are directed with sufficient skill, the transition between them occurs in a very natural manner: dialogues become monologues, and vice versa. As already men-

tioned, our theoretical background and practical experience makes us prefer short monologic speech for the initial stages. This avoids the effect of "stress," provoked by some questions, when the students still have audio-articulative problems both with the teacher and—to a much greater extent—with their fellow students. The short story, assigned to the student as a task to be thought over in his mother tongue, that is, with psychological preparation, without any element of surprise and/or pressure, is in the beginning something the student lacks confidence in, but then gradually the student grows more confident and more eagerly expects the challenge. The moment comes when the students realize—as suddenly as an explosion—how much knowledge they have acquired and how well they can succeed in constructing their thought into phrases in the foreign language. (We have had very rare cases of single students not willing to join in. They should be let alone until the appearance of a spontaneous desire to do so.)

As already stated, the teacher should keep a close watch on the storytellers: at the appropriate moment he or she may insert a word into the narrative in an unobtrusive manner, in order to further stimulate the teller's capacities. The teacher's patients and kindness are important here. If a student speaks with too many mistakes (in the beginning), the teacher does not correct him or her. Rather, the teacher breaks mildly into the monologue in order to clarify the situation in question, to suggest that everything is all right, so that the discourse is easily followed. Encouraged in such a way, the student promptly "catches up." A similar situation (with quite a different background from the standpoint of psychology) occurs when an infant beginning to speak is understood only by his parents who, with the provision of patience, love, and care, stimulate the child to overcome his or her shortcomings. They never scold the child, never pass pedantic and sage remarks founded on grammatical rules and intended to make the child begin speaking at once without mistakes. That is why in the similar but not identical case of suggestopedic teaching of foreign languages, the psychological mastery of the teacher can solve the problem to a significant degree or, on the contrary, the lack of such mastery can result in a deepening of the conflict.

We pay attention at the last elaboration to reviewing each new lesson more than once, because it is of a particular importance to the suggestopedic teaching and learning process.

At the other stages of this process work is carried out more or less as a group, first reading in chorus and then translating in chorus. This approach serves to overcome any psychological and audio-articulative problems. For example, in asking a question taken from the text as part of the immediate elaboration of the latter, it is easier for the students to answer in chorus. In asking a similar, direct, easy question with the answer being present in the text, or in asking questions that are derived from these two types by means of gradual individual transformation, the answers are easier if given in chorus.

The last elaboration is characterized by offering each student the opportunity of manifesting more widely his or her individual capacities: monologues of personal design under the teacher's control; dialogues displaying features of independent narratives (i.e., of monologues); gradual development of monologues into discourses and spontaneous conversations on some subject drawn from life. The organization should favor maximum adherence to everyday activities and situations. This last elaboration, preceding the new lesson, is the clearest expression of the psychohygienic objectives of suggestopedy: first, an individual approach within the group and a promotion, by means of the teaching and learning processes, of overcoming the students' antisuggestive barriers, taking into account the psychological core of each individual; and, second, cultivating mutual respect and mutual tolerance of different temperaments and characters, to allow maximum profit from the educational process to be obtained by every one of the students.

The problem of antisuggestive barriers is formulated and dealt with in G. Lozanov's work *Suggestology and Foundations of Suggestopedy*. This basic topic of suggestopedy will not be considered in more detail in this Manual. In the very beginning we mentioned that the first encounter between teacher and student constitutes the initial psychological investigation of the former. A well-trained teacher does not need more than a week to get oriented and to organize his or her approach both to each student and to the group, as a whole, in its capacity as an intricate entity of different types, temperaments, and characters. Overenthusiasm at this stage smacks of amateurishness and is inadmissible. Bearing in mind that each human being is a combination of elements pertaining to the four types of temperaments and the two types of thinking (logical and artistic)—this complexity being linked with biological, genetic, and mental prerequisites—a simplified mechanical understanding of and dealing with the intricate maze of man's structures could result in quite the opposite suggestopedic effect. Given the complexity of the problem, the teacher should be extremely conscious and tactful during the last elaboration preceding the new lesson. His or her delicate introduction to the monologues is an example of unobtrusive intervention to be followed by the audience.

Step by step the remaining students break into their colleague's narrative with polite remarks or questions, thus turning monologues into lively and friendly conversations, seasoned from time to time with a personal view upon some problem or another. All these activities should take place under the teacher's supervision: the teacher should ease one student's aggressiveness and assuage another's excessive sensitivity.

Gradually, the students become fully confident of their learning. They cope successfully with the subject matter, both their self-confidence and their respect for fellow students increases, and these elaborations become one of the most pleasant experiences in suggestopedic practice.

The last elaboration preceding a new lesson is the right moment to introduce to the students a visitor from the respective country. In the majority of cases this is a teacher from the Institute who "acts" a visit. The "visitor" is introduced in a very natural way, speaking about him- or herself, about his or her homeland, etc., rousing the students' interest, and thus smoothly shifting to the subject having been assigned for the monologues. In a more advanced phase of the course such development results in a general conversation. The effect of such "visits" is excellent. They take place every two weeks, thus creating a state of pleasant expectation. Sometimes, when the Institute receives visitors from abroad, they are asked to be involved in the lessons in such a way. As a rule, they kindly agree.

Here follows an excerpt from an article by the Italian professor E. Zola, who visited the Insititute and was invited to assist at some of the lessons several years ago:

"Lozanov took me to the lesson.

"The lesson was in English. It exhibited the transformation of a group of Sofiots into Englishmen. They simulated a party in a London house, then they sang: Bring back my Bonny to me. I note a rather important detail: the teacher who is above all the inspirer of the group asks: 'What time did we say it was, six, wasn't it?' 'No, seven,' answered the lady who played the role of the host.

"In the symbology of numbers 'six' expresses the lack of harmony, while 'seven' is the number of completeness, of solved problems. At seven months the foetus has reached maturity. The preference for seven, which is so strong as to be expressed, suggests the degree of involvement of the woman's subconsciousness. Thus, after the initial perplexed smiles of the students, the teacher asks them to throw and catch a ball while answering questions; now the hands become nimble, preoccupied as the hands of playing children. These psychological fluctuations open the way for the information stream.

"I move on to the lesson in Italian. The students were in easy chairs, relaxed. One by one, making use of the vocabulary learned from the first lesson, they introduced themselves. As a matter of fact, they called themselves by Italian names and with fabricated Italian biographies. All of a sudden I penetrated those concocted worlds, those secret wishes of Sofia, noting how consistent was the correspondence between the students' faces and their intimate fantasies. Actually, a young girl by the name of Svetlana said nothing but that she was called Jilda and lived in Paris with a group of friends. A young man with a slouchy, but hearty appearance stated gravely that he is an Italian producer and lives in Rome with his girl. An elderly woman called herself Beatrice, and said she lived in Moscow where she is a university professor in Italian and shares her flat with her husband and his mother. A young man with a pensive face, with a hint of Turkish appearance, who might be met in some confraternity 'sufi,' pretended being born in Geneva in 1878 but having a young man's outlook because he was a Yogi; he had a lot of children, lived as a peasant, spoke Japanese and Hindi.

"A cheerful soprano said here name was Adelina Patti, she studied in the Conservatoire at Milan, she took after her mother, and she had ten children. There was also a reticent, gloomy face: he said he was Lucifer, born in Hades, and that he used to visit ancient lands and human hearts, as in Bulgakov's novel.

"After a thirty-minute break the second lesson in Italian began."*

---

*From the article, "In Only Three Days, at Sofia, after a Method Based on Suggestion" by Elèmire Zola; *Corriere della Sera*, 10 October 1978, Rome.

Figs. 17–18 - During an elaboration in English, March 1981, Sofia.

Fig. 18

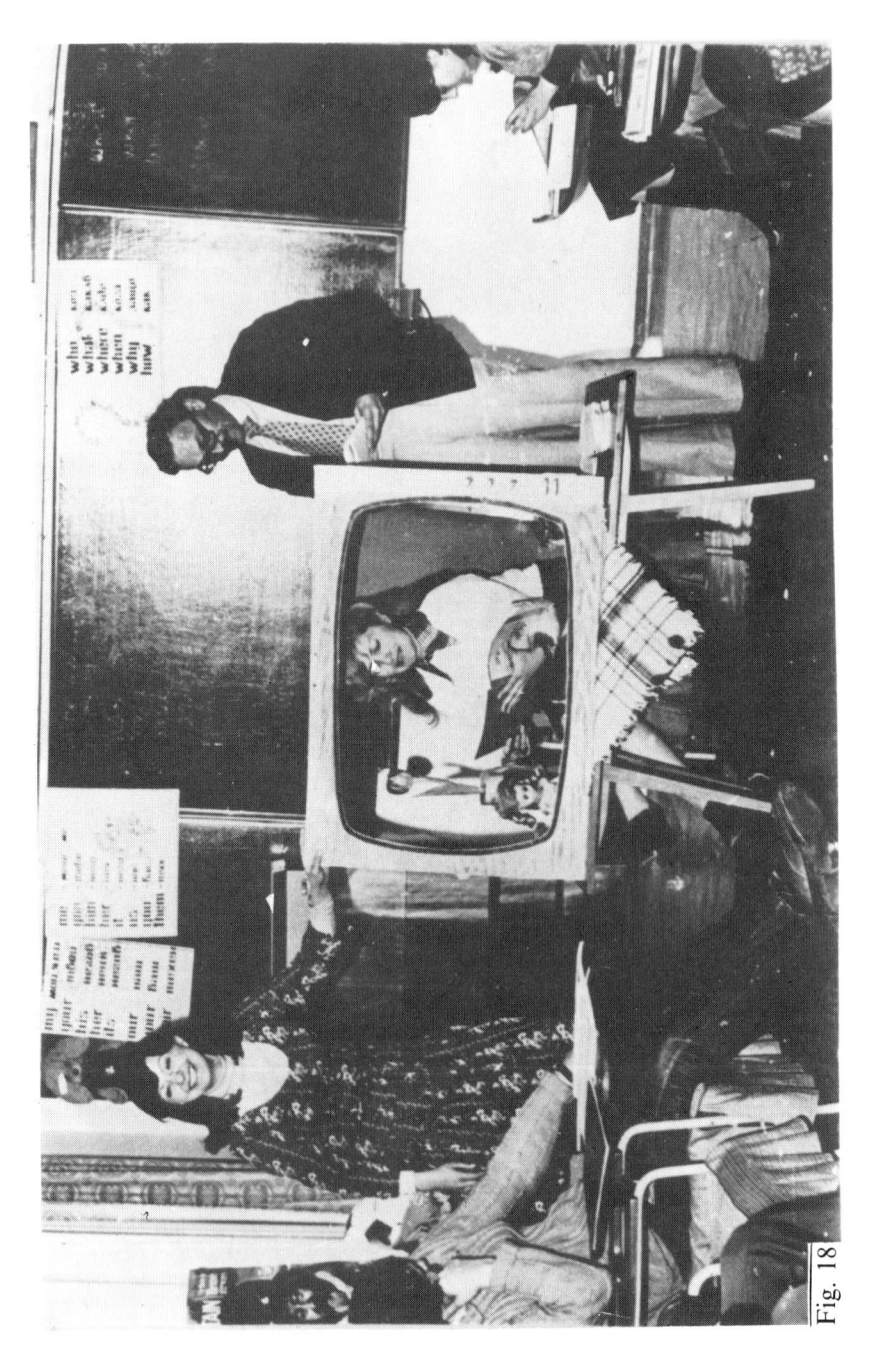

Lesson Three: "The Eternal City"

The prevailing subject is "Touring the City," that is touring Rome, the Eternal City. The teacher gives in a few sentences some of the most important and most interesting facts from the history of Rome: the Rome of the Emperors and the Republic; the Rome of the Christians; the Rome of the Middle Ages and of the Italian Renaissance; Michelangelo's and Raphael's Rome and the Vatican; the Rome of the Counter Reformation; Palestrina's Rome; the Rome of the Italian Risorgimento, the unification of Italy; the Rome of the Academy Santa Cecilia; the Rome of Moravia and Mellini. The talk is illustrated with slides and souvenirs. More often than not we make use of Passato prossimo (recent past perfect tense), which is readily used in Italian colloquial speech.

The reading during the *sessions* is carried out according to the already familiar ritual. When using the word "ritual" we feel bound to make a stipulation. We have in mind, of course, the kind of ritual that is related to the riches of positive experience: the solemn sequence in the organization of events which is not easily forgotten; an organization that stimulates and tranquilizes, inspires and fills with creative enthusiasm; an organization that becomes at the same time a symbol in and of itself a condensed "placebo."

In the first *elaboration* the reading of the first part of Lesson Three is performed by the students, who have assumed the respective roles and have been given the suitable props. Figaro gets a guitar, some towels, a tray with combs, a modern safety-razor, scissors, etc. The students translate the text of Figaro's "La ran la lera." The text being already intelligible, the students' motivation increases: they succeed in understanding the original text of an Italian aria. The class then listens to the aria. All the recordings have been made by professional performers, according to the requirements and the aims of suggestopedy. During the translation of the first part of Lesson Three relating to the museums in the Vatican, the basic moments are illustrated by means of slides and captivating explanations about the Basilica of St. Peter's, and the Sistine Chapel.

The first part is characterized by a concentrated use of the recent past (present) tense, formed by the present tense of "to be" or "to have" and the past participle of the conjugated verb. The teacher explains to the students that they already have a good grasp of the present tense. The abovementioned past tense will be used to express actions that are begun and accomplished in the past. There is another past perfect tense, but we shall come across it mainly in texts from literary works and from the press; at the present stage we shall use the recent past perfect tense for colloquial speech. The meaning of this tense is translated into Bulgarian, where some analogy can be found.

Theoretical explanations concerning this tense in its relations to transitive and intransitive verbs are not given. If some of the students express studiousness and special interests in grammar, we fix a time (a couple of minutes before or after lessons, by mutual consent) when the teacher is at the disposal of those interested. Instead of theoretical explanations, we try to create something that will be of greater benefit. The teacher recalls the joke about Rossini from Lesson One. Now this joke seems quite easy to the students. At the time of the first reading of this joke we spoke briefly of the past perfect tense and got acquainted with the way it is formed, but did not elaborate upon it. It was a similar case with some forms of the future tense and of the past imperfect tense. These tenses have made their appearance in the dialogue in quite a natural manner ever since the first lesson, but we paid little attention to them. Now we are going to go back and throw additional light on the problems. *We sing the song "A Beautiful Flower."* It also includes some forms of the tense. We turn the students' attention to the fact that the verbs they have already learned by heart in the present (*"to go," "to come back," "to leave," "to arrive," "to go out," "to come in," "to stay," "to start"*) are always conjugated with the auxiliary verb "to be." These pairs of verbs are quite easy to memorize. The same auxiliary verb ("to be") is used in conjugating the reflexive verbs, for example, in the anecdote about Rossini in the Italian textbook, page 21. "Dove *ci siamo visti?*" [Where *have we met (each other)*?]. The auxiliary verb "to be" serves to form the passive mood (as in the native tongue). A great many verbs, on the other hand, are conjugated with "to have."

On pages 104 and 105 of the Italian textbook are listed the irregularly formed past participles of some of the most important verbs. (The way of forming regular participles has been learned since the first lesson.) We make a rapid translation of the participles, the majority of which are familiar.

ac*cend*ere—acce*s*o: to light—lit	difendere—difeso: to defend
prendere—presò: to take	scendere—sceso: to descend

chiu*d*ere—chiu*s*o: to close
ridere—riso: to laugh
decidere—deciso: to decide
spar*g*ere—spar*s*o: to disperse
correre—corso: to run
perdere—perso, perduto: to lose
vin*cere*—vin*t*o: to win
dipin*gere*—dipin*t*o: to paint
spingere—spinto: to push
sce*gli*ere—sce*l*to: to choose
togl iere—tolto: to take off
cogliere—colto: to pick
risolvere—risolto: to resolve
chiedere—chiesto: to ask
rimanere—rimasto: to stay
nascondere—nascosto: to hide
rispondere—risposto: to answer
porre—posto: to place
trarre—tratto: to pull out
dire—detto: to say

leggere—letto: to read
scrivere—scritto: to write
corregerre—corretto: to correct
dirigere—diretto: to direct
condurre—condotto: to conduct
produrre—prodotte: to produce
esprimere—espresso: to express
concedere—concesso: to concede
succedere—successo: to occur
muovere—mosso: to move
vedere—visto, veduto: to see
fare—fatto: to make
mettere—messo: to put
vivere—vissuto: to live
costringere—costretto: to constraint
venire—venuto: to come
apparire—apparso: to appear
coprire—coperto: to cover
morire—morto: to die
soffrire—sofferto: to suffer

These participles, gathered in twos and threes, hang on the walls of the room, written on small signboards. The same artifice is made use of in the other languages.

In connection with the use of past perfect, we play the following game:

One by one, the students write on the blackboard all the verbs that can be found in the first part of Lesson Three, converting them into the infinitive. The group is divided into two teams. Each student (first one from team A, then one from team B) must make a sentence with a verb (in the succession they are written) in the past perfect tense. At the same time, if the verb requires the auxiliary "to be" the students must stand up. Those who fail to get up drop out. Those who confuse the auxiliaries "to be" and "to have" get no points. Those who manage well win 10 points for the team. By the end of the game the premiums are summed up. Next comes the second part of Lesson Three, after Figaro's "La ran la lera." The class reads with a "stop." The teacher starts reading, marking every stressed syllable by a stroke. The tempo is moderate. After having read aloud a few sentences, the teacher ceases speaking. The students must proceed with the reading in the same tempo. At a certain point, the teacher cries "stop." The students report on where they have come to. Reading is performed in this way until the end of the second part (i.e., the menu card in the restaurant). The second time the order "stop" is not given; the students who have come to the end begin translating for themselves, converting verbs into the past tense whenever possible. When everybody has read the whole text, those who are ready with the converting of the verbs begin (one by one) to translate, the text being already in the past tense.

The elaboration of the whole story of Mrs. Walter (pages 40 and 41 of the Italian textbook) is carried out in this way. The procedure is similar in the courses in English and Spanish. In the beginning, stress is placed on present tenses, but the other tenses make their appearance as well. In this way the students find their way in the verb system. In the next few lessons we make an active elaboration of the past perfect tense (the past simple tense: "My father *came* yesterday;" Pretérito indefinido: "Ayer *lei* un libro interesante"). Some of the didactic songs are of considerable help. In all foreign languages we spare time for the active elaboration of other tenses as well; past imperfect, future simple, and present tense of the conditional mood. The other tenses remain at the passive level.

Let us return to Lesson Three from the textbook in Italian.

After the sightseeing of Rome we drop in at a small restaurant, famous for its genuine Roman cuisine and, along with the Walters, make our choice from the menu. The role of the waiter is immediately assumed by a student and, more often than not, the "landlord" also appears, shepherding us politely to the unreserved tables. Each student orders a dinner to his or her taste. Quite naturally, the talk at the table centers on meals, on the specifity of national cuisines, on tastes, and preferences. At the end of the meal the students go to play in the gaming room.

The cards that are dealt this time illustrate various foodstuffs and household goods. Four cards with pictures of kindred items, numbered from 1 to 4, form a "suit." The first player leads a card. Everybody having a card of the same suit plays it. In such a way is formed a group of students, who invite to dinner the rest of their colleagues for the next day. The "hosts" are to provide some of the foods shown on the cards. For instance, on the cards there are sugar products: the group of "hosts" provides the "guests" with sugar, coffee, and sweets for the next day's dinner. The game is pursued by another student, who leads another card.

Ich bin allein gegangen

Text: R. Vratscheva
Musik: E. Gateva

Allegro

Ich bin allein gegangen und hab' nen Schwan ge-sehen. Er ist umhergeschwommen im Glanz des einsamen Sees. Ich bin allein gegangen an diesem schönen Morgen. Zwei Tauben hab'n gegirrt. Mein Herz hat sich verwirrt.

The remaining three cards of the suit are played. For instance: dairy products; the group provides butter and cheese for sandwiches; etc. A third group becomes responsible for entertainment (games), etc.

The working day is completed by the reading and translation of the last part of the story "Patrizia."

On the following day a snack is arranged. While tasting the light meals, everybody should speak about a town or city having impressed them. Picture postcards, slides, and souvenirs are shown. Some games are played, riddles in the foreign language are propounded, for example, "Musical Mosaic" and "Watch your Route, Drivers" (after A. Mouradian), etc.

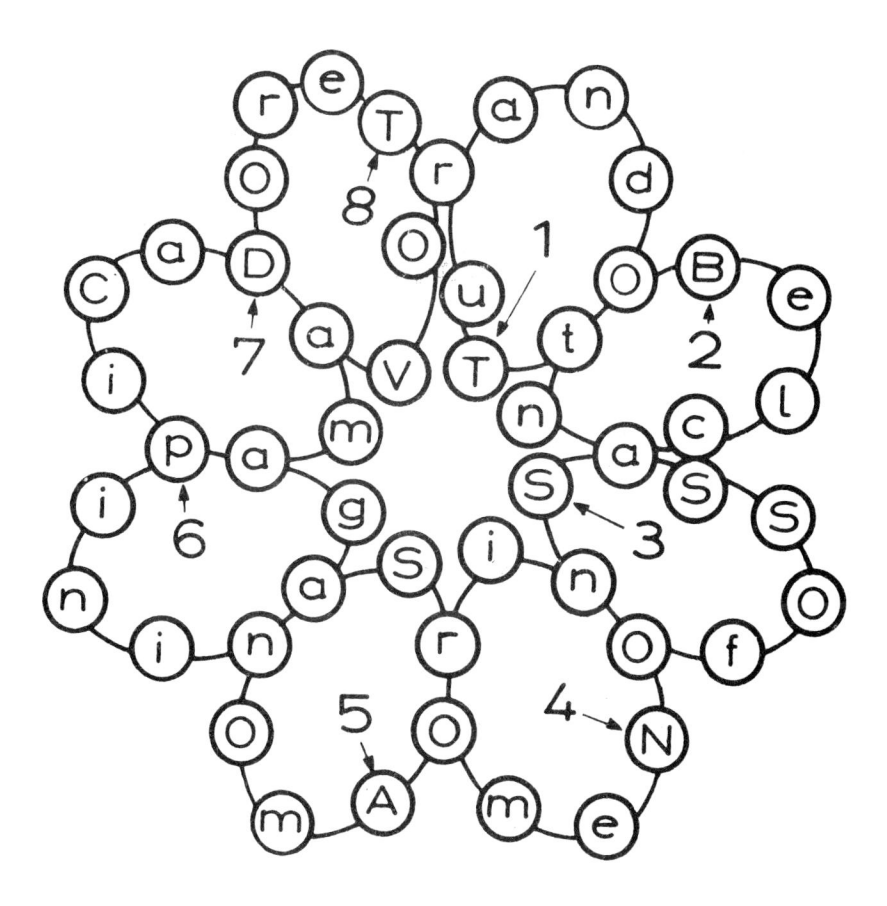

Fill in (clockwise):
(1) Pucini's opera; (2) Vocal performers' style in the Italian tradition of singing; (3) A wind instrument; (4) A character from the opera *Elixir of Love*; (5) A character from the opera *Aïda*; (6) A famous Italian violin virtuoso and composer; (7) Tchaikovsky's opera; (8) Verdi's opera.

Follow the route of a driver who must cross the quarter from West to East sticking to road signs and neither turning about nor shifting into reverse. Tell us about your birthplace.

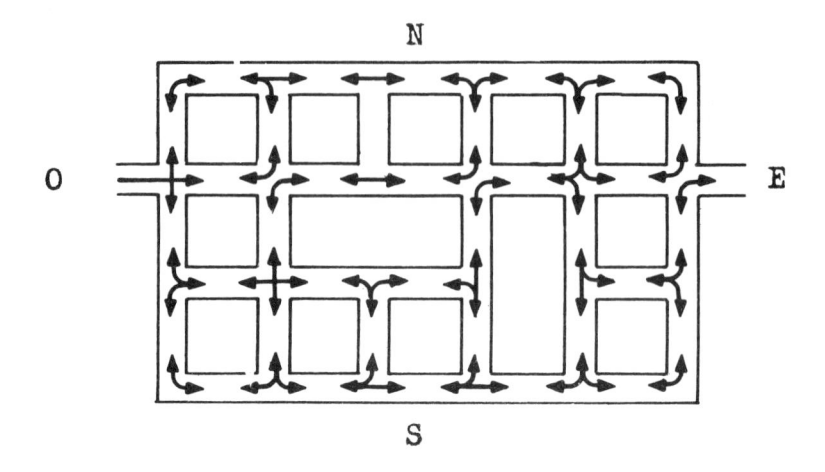

Some of the students are offered art reproductions treating the subject "Way of Life." For example: "Still Life" by the Spanish master Pereda; "Still Life" by the Italian master Morandi; "Fruits" by the French artist Cézanne; etc. The students bring the reproductions home and use them to create short stories for the next day.

Lesson Four: "The Seasons"

Prior to the introduction in Lesson Four we spare enough time for a test paper (aimed at providing feedback on the class' progress). If we are short of time, some students can postpone the narratives they have prepared for the next day. The test paper consists of the translation of the second or the third part of the story "Patrizia" into the mother tongue. Each part of the story comprises approximatively 250 words. The story has been translated only once. As a matter of course, all the words have been met (in another context) throughout the material of the past sessions.

Close to 100 percent of the students attain excellent results on the test. Similar test papers, *aimed at heightening the students' self-confidence* in mastering the material at the translational level, are given more than once. (Other excerpts from the textbook are also suitable.)

After the day's pause we make a short introduction into the new lesson (Lesson Four). It concerns the seasons. We listen to the song "Spring Forever," with which the lesson begins. This romantic song is slightly beyond the abilities of nonmusicians, that is why it is studied by the whole group. Nevertheless, it is quite appropriate as a basic theme for a discourse "Which is my most beloved season and why."

LA SIGNORA WALTER (canta):

Nella primavera	In spring
tutto fiorisce:	Everything blooms:
alberi e prati,	Trees and fields,
pieni di fiori,	Full of flowers,
spargono profumo,	Give off scent,
spargono bellezza,	Exhale beauty,
nel cuore stretto	In the sinking heart
nasce la speranza.	Hope arises
Ricca, trionfante,	Rich, triumphant,
calda, abbondante	Hot, abundant
seague l'estate.	Follows the summer.
Tutto ciò che ama	Anything that loves
non vuol'bruciarlo;	Does not want to burn;
sa che giorni d'oro,	It knows that golden days,
giorni d'autunno	Days of autumn
tra poco verranno,	are coming in a while,
portando freschezza,	bringing freshness,
portando salvezza,	bringing salvation,
pioggia,	rains,
poi neve,	and then snows,
il sole invernale	the winter sun,
il primo bucaneve.	the first snowflake.
Sempre primavera!	Spring forever!

The teacher talks with the students about the subject "Which is my most beloved season and why." Next follow the *concert sessions*.

Sempre primavera

Andante — Parole e musica: E. Gateva

Nella primavera tutto fiorisce!

Alberi e prati, pieni di fiori,

spargono profumo, spargono bellezza;

nel cuore stretto nasce la speranza.

Ricca, trionfante, calda, abbondante

rit.

segue l'estate.

a tempo

Tutto ciò che ama non vuol bruciarlo;

sa che giorni d'oro, giorni d'autunno tra poco verranno, portando salvezza, portando freschezza, pioggia, poi neve, il sole invernale, il primo bucaneve. Sempre primavera!

Elaborations

The first elaboration begins with Mrs. Walter's performance. In the morning, up and about, she sings the song "Spring Forever." The class reads and translates the text, then sings the song. The text of the lesson is divided into several parts and read once more. This reading is performed by different students having assumed different roles. The text is no longer translated. We emphasize some of the most important topics of grammar (e.g., the future tense). The original fragment by E. de Amicis, incorporated in this act is in the future tense. We convert it into present. When reading some of the parts, we deliberately allow "mistakes" to slip in. The teacher reads, adding unfamiliar phrases. The phrases may be felicitous, comical, unfelicitous. The students proceed with the reading in the same way. The fragment relating to the sightseeing may be read more hastily. There are almost no unfamiliar words in it and its main use is to serve as a background for the individual stories left untold.

An alternative is to create the following situation: one of the students is in Bulgaria for the first time. He or she carries a guidebook and asks the passersby about the location of some of the sights of the town. Everybody is helpful. Comical and confusing situations may arise. The psychological climate is already suitable to such a game, provided that it is organized with goodwill.

The story of Garibaldi is converted, whenever possible, into the past perfect tense. In doing this, we stick to the rule of the previous elaborations: the grammatical units from the Contents are not accorded explanations with the exception of those of particular importance. The remaining are merely marked during the reading and the translation. For instance, the most important grammatical unit in Lesson Four is the formation of the future tense. The explanation we give is intended to make the audience understand the simplicity of the topic: the respective endings are added to the infinitive of the verbs from the three conjugations. We pronounce the "r," characteristic of the infinitive, in a still more clear-ringing manner, in order to emphasize its presence in the future tense. The procedure is similar in French and in Spanish.

In English we give preference to the contracted forms ("I'll go...," "You'll go...") whenever possible. The formation of the future tense in German is still easier. The auxiliary verb "werden" is met in the very first lessons. The problem of syncopating in the future tense in Italian and Spanish is avoided: instead of explanations, the students are reminded of the numerous forms we have already come across in the previous lessons ("andrò," "andremo"—"I shall go," "we shall go"; "ci vedremo"—"we shall see each other"; "avrò"—"I shall have," etc.). They are mastered at the audio-articulative level. At present we add the forms of the most commonly used verbs in the way they are listed in the grammatical section at the end of the textbook.

II coniugazione

credere—creder-ò (I shall believe)
    creder-ai
    creder-à
    creder-emo
    creder-ete
    creder-anno

III coniugazione

aprire—aprir-o (I shall open)
    aprir-ai
    aprir-à
    aprir-emo
    aprir-ete
    aprir-anno

I coniugazione

parlare—parler-ò (I shall speak)
    parler-ai
    parler-à
    parler-emo
    parler-ete
    parler-anno

Particolarità del futuro semplice

avere (to have)
  avrò (I shall have) avremo
  avrai avrete
  avrà avrànno

essere (to be)
  sarò (I shall be) saremo
  sarai sarete
  sarà saranno

andare—andrò (to go—I shall go)
potere—potrò (can)
dovere—dovrò (must)
vivere—vivrò (to live)
vedere—vedrò (to see)
bere—berrò (to drink)
volere—vorrò (to want)
tenere—terrò (to hold)

fare—farò (to do—I shall do)
stare—staro (to stand—to be present)
dare-darò (to give)
tradurre—tradurrò (to translate)
porre—porrò (to place)
trarre—trarrò (to pull out)
dire—dirò (to say)
venire—verrò (to come)

Spanish Language

Futuro imperfecto

El infinitivo + -é
    -ás
    -á
    -emos
    -éis
    -án

hab<u>l</u>ar, cr<u>e</u>er, escrib<u>ir</u>—hab<u>lar</u>é, cre<u>er</u>é, escrib<u>ir</u>é—(I shall speak, I shall believe, I shall write)

(a) formas irregulares:

decir—diré, dirás, . . .	to say—I shall say
haber—habré, habrás, habrá (hay)	to have
hacer—haré	to make
poder—podré	can
poner—pondré	to place
querer—querré	to want
saber—sabré	to know
salir—saldré	to go out
tener—tendré	to have
venir—vendré	to come

FREQUENT AND PRECISE REMINDERS OF GRAMMATICAL AND LEXICAL FORMS WHICH FIGURE IN THE PAST LESSONS BUT WHICH HAVE NOT BEEN ELABORATED, ARE PARTICULARLY USEFUL AND EFFECTIVE. THIS SHOULD BE DONE ON ANY OCCASION DURING THE ELABORATION OF THE NEW LESSON. BY IMPLICATION, THE TEACHER MUST KNOW THE TEXTS OF THE LESSONS BY HEART. THE SLIGHTEST HINT HE OR SHE GIVES SHOULD RESULT IN THE PROMPT AND SPONTANEOUS RECOLLECTION OF LARGE AMOUNTS OF BYGONE MATERIAL ON THE PART OF THE STUDENTS.

The subject "The Seasons" is a suitable occasion for painting a collective canvas. The teacher proposes to each student that he or she should depict in figures and colors his or her thoughts and feelings in relation to the different seasons. Large sheets of drawing paper are provided for that purpose. The painting may be abstract, according to the students' preferences. Songs that treat the same subject are an appropriate background to the act of painting. When the canvas is ready, the students explain their ideas in the foreign tongue. The canvases are hung on the wall and remain there until the end of the course. Painting may be made use of when treating other subjects as well; these canvases should also be hung on the walls.

During the last elaboration we can spare time for the reading aloud of some anecdotes. We think it preferable to let the students first read them at home. These anecdotes contain almost no unfamiliar words, except a few which the students can look up in the dictionary (they should have already begun referring to a dictionary). After this the time has come when the students are expected to tell short anecdotes about themselves. Telling anecdotes is not intended as entertainment, but as a means of teaching the students how to construct easy, concise, and witty sentences, loaded with a condensed body of information. Complicated anecdotes are to be avoided, lest the students come across unexpected difficulties of equivocal character.

When carrying out the elaboration of anecdotes, we may resort to games Nos. 10, 13, 16, 18, and 26. When assigning the task for the last day of the last elaboration of Lesson Four (the same holds good for Lesson Five as well), the teacher gives the students the opportunity to choose between telling an easy anecdote or preparing a short story inspired by art reproductions on the subject "Nature in Painting." For instance, one could use a reproduction of Roerich's "Sketch" intended for Stravinsky's ballet "The Rite of Spring," or else a reproduction of Constable's "A Cart with Hay," etc.

Lesson Five: "The Months"

One day prior to introducing the subject "The Months," the students are asked to remember some story they have been told about their birth or about the birth of a relative (or friend) of theirs. If a student does not feel like reporting about him- or herself the student may invent something.

So far, the stories have been told in the present tense, making use when necessary of the past perfect (passato prossimo)—mainly in direct speech. This stage of learning is characterized by the original quotation of direct speech, that is, it is not converted into indirect speech in order to avoid a sequence of tenses: knowledge that is reserved for a higher level of learning a foreign tongue. There are also advantages from the cummunicative standpoint: the discourse is more lively, more unaffected. Now we can afford to explain to the students that they are in the position to use another past tense: the past imperfect (imperfetto), which allows them to express incompleted actions in the past. We give a familiar text as an example (e.g., one of the familiar songs could be converted into the tense in question). We translate and compare the meaning with the past imperfect tense in the mother tongue. We mention in passing the ways of forming the tense. This is quite easy, much like the forming of the future tense. The ending for the infinitive is discarded, and the endings for the past imperfect are added to the stem. These endings are identical for all three conjugations.

I coniugazione   *II coniugazione*   *III coniugazione*

cant<u>are</u>—canta-<u>vo</u>   ved<u>ere</u>—vede-vo   sent<u>ire</u>—senti-vo
canta-<u>vi</u>
canta-<u>va</u>
canta-<u>vamo</u>
canta-<u>vate</u>
canta-<u>vano</u>

av<u>ere</u>—ave-vo

<u>essere</u>—ero   eravamo
         eri   eravate
         era   erano

The existence of the past imperfect tense and its meaning in Spanish and French is analogous.

In English and in German, to express both completed and uncompleted actions in the past, we use past simple tense, or imperfect (these tenses have already been studied as perfect ones). Explanations when teaching these languages are rather laconical, but a lot of examples are given, and comparison with the native tongue is extensive.

The subjects "The Seasons" and "The Months" are connected with studying the song "Canzone di Bacco" with words by L. dei Medici. This song can be used both in the introduction and in the elaborations. Its tune is suitable as an easy dance in the folk style.

CANZONE DI BACCO

1. Quant' è bella giovinezza,
   che *si fugge* tuttavia!
Rit. Chi vuol'esser'lieto, *sia*;
   di doman'non c'è certezza.
2. Queste ninfe ed altra gente
   son allegre tuttavia.
Rit. Chi vuol'esser'lieto, *sia*;
   di doman'non c'è certezza.
3. Or'da Bacco riscaldati,
   ballan', saltan', tuttavia.
Rit. Chi vuol'esser'lieto, sia;
   di doman'non c'è certezza.
4. Or'insieme mescolate
   suonan', cantan' tuttavia.
Rit. Chi vuol'esser'lieto, sia;
   di doman'non c'è certezza.

BACCHUS' SONG

How beautiful is youth
That *flies away*, however!
He who wants to be happy, *let him be*;
Tomorrow is not certain.
Those nymphs and other people
Are still merry.
He who wants to be happy, *let him be*;
Tomorrow is not certain.
Now, inflamed by Bacchus,
They still dance, they still jump.
He who wants to be happy, *let him be*;
Tomorrow is not certain.
Now, mingled with each other,
They still play, they still sing.
He who wants to be happy, *let him be*;
Tomorrow is not certain...

Canzone di Bacco
Poesia: L. dei Medici
Musica: E. Gateva
Allegro

We include the entire class in the discourse "In which month was I born." Next follows the musical sessions.

During the elaborations the text of the Lesson Five is read with members of the class assuming roles. At the beginning of Lesson Five we listen to a recording of *La Bohème*: Rodolfo's and Mimi's arias. The few unfamiliar words in these arias should be specified beforehand. The students should understand the text, and listening to Italian opera classics gives them aesthetic gratification.

Similar experiences are being tried in the other foreign language courses, where we have also introduced original songs and classical opera fragments on the analogy of the course in Italian. The students listen to German songs by Schubert, Schumann, Brahms, Wolf, fragments from Mozart's *The Magic Flute* and *The Abduction from the Seraglio*, fragments from Bizet's *Carmen*, old-time French and English songs, Spanish and Ibero-American classical songs, and fragments of zarzuelas and folk music.

The last part of Lesson Five (Emilio's dream) is wholly converted from the past imperfect into the present tense, since it is also possible to narrate. Each student reads or translates that part of the text, which refers to the month he or she was born in. For the last elaboration we assign three subjects: "A Dream," "A Daydream," or the description of a literary hero: appearance, character, features—without his or her name being mentioned. On the next day the students try to identify this character.

The American student Mr. D. from the Training Course for suggestopedic teachers in Italian, held in San Francisco in 1979, has made a superb recording of his acting Dr. Faust, presenting his own translation of famous sentences of Goethe's. Suggestopedic practice abounds in similar examples. The subjects "A Dream" and "A Daydream" are equally blessed in contributing to the development of the students' creative fantasy, as well as to the spontaneous reproduction of the foreign language.

The elaboration of Lesson Five is the last time accorded to active grammar. By the end of the course the students will have mastered at the active level the present tenses, past perfect and past imperfect tense, future tense of the regular and irregular verbs of first frequency in the indicative and imperative mood and some of the most common forms in the subjunctive mood, as well as the present tense of the conditional mood. The rest of the grammar that figures in the textbook serves as a passive fund. It is mastered at the translational level and is further improved in the course of further studies.

After having brought this bulk of material to an end, we spare a day for review. As already mentioned, the material is made up of vocabulary and grammatical units of the first frequency, suitable to activation. The students are not told that the day is set apart for review.

We go back to the first pages of the textbook and make a collective translation of the original quotations heading the lessons. We give short but interesting explanations concerning those quotations. Each quotation is in symbolic relation to the respective lesson. For instance, the first quotation (page 6 of the Italian textbook) relates to the textbook as a whole: it treats the widespread interest in the Italian Renaissance, in the Italian way of thinking, in the Italian language which logically possesses the features of the languages that have not ceased to develop—namely, a strong tendency to music and to expressiveness. At the end of the textbook, when dwelling on Emilio's and Dr. Walter's letters, we devote another brief reiteration of this subject, thus definitely elucidating the problem of links. The discovery of symbolic links between quotations and the text in the following lessons is left to the students. The procedure is very similar when dealing with the last revised editions of the textbooks in other foreign languages.

Next comes a game of cards. The cards are marked with the following captions:

1. Looking for and putting up in a hotel. Money exchange. (The material is derived from Lesson One and Lesson Two).
2. A telephone call: calling a friend abroad (Lesson One, Lesson Two).
3. Looking for a snack-bar or a restaurant. Ordering breakfast, lunch, dinner (Lesson One, Lesson Two, Lesson Three).
4. Inquiring about various services of prime necessity; emergency calls. Looking for the main sights of the city (Lesson One, Lesson Two, Lesson Three, Lesson Four, Lesson Five).
5. Television and radio programs (Lesson One, Lesson Four).
6. Definite and indefinite articles. The noun.
7. The adjective. Numbers.
8. Pronouns.
9. The verb: present and future of the indicative, present of the conditional.
10. The verb: past perfect and past imperfect tense.
11. The adverb.
12. Prepositions, conjunctions, interjections.

The cards numbered 6, 7, 8, 9, 10, 11, and 12 have printed on them small tables with the most useful paradigms, for example, card No. 6 presents a table of the variants of the definite and indefinite articles, accompanying a given noun. Card No. 7 presents some of the most common qualitative adjectives presented as antonymic pairs (nice–ugly, young–old, white–black, high–low, etc.); possessive adjectives; demonstrative adjectives, indefinite adjectives, interrogative adjectives; numbers. Card No. 8 presents a table of the personal pronouns, and of the demonstrative, indefinite, relative and interrogative pronouns. Card No. 9 presents a table of the most common verbs in the present and future tenses. Card No. 10 presents a table of the most common verbs in the past perfect and past imperfect tenses. Card No. 11 presents the most common adverbs of time, place, etc. Card No. 12 comprises the most common prepositions, conjunctions, and interjections. As a matter of course, the tables are presented in a simplified form, that is, sometimes only one person of the verb is enough to suggest the way of forming all the persons.

The game is opened by the student holding card No. 1. When speaking about the subject of the card, he or she includes now and then the students holding cards Nos. 2–5. The students holding cards Nos. 6–12 are the "buttons" of the robot. They are in permanent readiness to offer a card from No. 6 to No. 12 to the speaker, as well as to immediately correct any gross communicative mistake that has slipped into the conversation. After the first subject is over, the floor is taken by the student holding card No. 2. And so on, until the subjects of cards Nos. 1–5 are exhausted.

Lessons One–Five present a vocabulary within the framework of approximatively 2,000 words, mostly of high (very common) frequency. By the end of the course this number will increase by about 500. After Lesson Five the words in the textbook are not underlined. During the active session the students underline for themselves those words that are of some interest according to their own judgment. The teacher also has underlined in his or her copy the words that are of importance. When reading aloud, he or she emphasizes them by means of extra intonation.

The translation, presented in active sessions, is not omitted until the end of the course.

Lesson Six: "At the Concert"

During the introduction to Lesson Six the teacher narrates in a very concise form some reminiscence of his or her first visit to the theater, or concert, opera, exhibition. The teacher may illustrate his or her narrative by photographs, recordings, or other suitable materials. The overall translation that used to be made is no longer attempted. Some passages are elucidated by means of synonyms, in accordance with the teacher's decision. The reading of the new lesson is carried out by the students assuming roles or engaging in some other kind of games. After the text is read, the teacher elaborates some grammatical and lexical items of particular importance, met for the first time in this part. His or her explanations of the new grammar should be quite cursory. He or she does not activate it. If the students tend to use it spontaneously, he or she encourages them. During the last elaboration we include all the students in a general conversation treating problems of the arts, preferences and tastes, reminiscences of one's first visit to the theater, a concert, an opera performance, an exhibition. The students have brought art reproductions, favorite L.P. records, collections, etc. Sports themes are also discussed.

Lesson Seven: "Friendship"

The translation of Lesson Seven is distributed among the students beforehand and they are asked to read the whole text at home. We recommend that the reading be performed, if possible, the way the teacher does it: with adequate intonation and clear-cut diction, against the background of classical music. Each student must previously underline the words of particular interest to him or her and, when reading aloud, those words should stand in relief due to a play of intonation. On the following day we rapidly check the words the students have chosen to underline and give the floor over to a simple retelling of the subject matter by the greatest possible number of candidates. For the following day we assign as a subject for individual stories, "An Interesting Scene of My Life," which must be elaborated by analogy with the original fragment, incorporated in Lesson Seven. The students' narratives should contain verbs in the past tenses.

Lesson Eight: "Goodbye, Rome"

During the introduction we go on "a shopping tour." We work out a plan of what to buy for whom. Additional ideas are provided by textbooks, magazines, and other suitable aids. A "trip" to Florence is forthcoming. We plan the program.

The last *session* is given with a particular solemnity.

During the *elaborations* the teacher gives some of the history and cultural patrimony of Florence as it relates to the role this city played in the European Renaissance. The teacher speaks about the role of the Republic of Venice as well. A couple of slides enliven these cursory remarks and take us to Florence, to a small hotel near the Arno. The end of the textbook is "concentrated" in the song "Silence."

On the following day we bring the elaboration of the last lesson to an end. We play game No. 25 in connection with the subject "Shopping." The studies are completed with the story, "Elsa and Giovanni Civinini in Vienna."

The teacher congratulates the students on their successful work throughout the course and announces that preparation of the shooting of the motion picture for the course has begun. Each student should appear before the microphone for a little test, prior to the definite distribution of the roles.

Output Level

This is when the testing for output level (final proficiency) begins. The questions are those from the input level test. The student is allowed sufficient time to compose an unworried, comprehensive answer and the whole procedure is tape-recorded.

The remaining students are gathered in another room where, in the presence of officials of the Institute, they are given the text from the input level test and asked to translate. Measuring the output level is usually performed during the last two days, together with other activities. The very last day of the course is organized both by the students and the teacher. The intention is to leave the most durable and pleasant memories with all the participants. Finally, the teahcer bids farewell to each student in turn, in the way he or she greeted each one at the first encounter.

After the course is over, the teacher decodes the data from the input and output levels (both written and oral—from the tapes), converts them

Silenzio

Andante — Parole e musica: E. Gateva

Scende la notte incoronata di stelle.
Luce di luna abbraccia il mondo.
Tutti abbiamo trovato la calma. Silenzio...
Dopo un giorno pieno di moto,
rit...
l'alma agitata vuole riposo...

into the working forms of the Institute, and delivers all the materials (including the tapes) to the archives of the Institute for further statistical processing and storage.

We include here three exemplary forms: first, the blank that is filled in using the data from the decoding, and then the blanks (Nos. 1 and 2) which are filled in with data for further statistical analysis. The forms are used both for the oral and written tests.

SAMPLE COURSE FORMS

SUGGESTOLOGY RESEARCH INSTITUTE

File Card for Decoding Input and Output Level in Suggestopedic Foreign Language Courses

Name of student ....
Course in .... language; .... grade
Start date .... End date ....
Name of the teacher ....

Note: The decoding of the student's answers, tape-recorded for input and output levels, is performed by the teacher in writing, in the exact manner the answers are uttered by the student.

INDEX CARD No. 1

For the Level of Communicativeness Attained by the Students in Suggestopedic Foreign Language Courses

Name of the student ....
Course in .... Teacher ....
Input level (date)
Output level (date)
  I. Answers to 28 questions.
  II. Translation into the mother tongue. Number of sentences (phrases) in the text ....

I. Answers	1. Communicatively correct		2. With mistakes, but the idea is understandable	3. Communicatively wrong (the idea is lost)
	(a) Fully correct	(b) With insignificant mistakes		
			(for the foreigner)	

II. Translation No. of sentences (phrases)	(a)	(b)	2.	3.

Explanatory Notes to Index Card No. 1:
1a. Sentences and phrases that are fully correct are underlined with two green lines.
1b. Sentences and phrases with insignificant mistakes are underlined with a single green line.
2. Sentences and phrases that have mistakes are underlined with a single blue line.
3. Sentences and phrases that are wrong are underlined with a single red line.
   Note 1: Sentences and phrases that are exactly the same are counted only once.
   Note 2: Sentences and phrases are "communicatively correct with insignificant mistakes" (1b) when containing fortuitous errors: definite and indefinite article, declensional endings, verb endings (if the pronoun is correctly used), prepositions.
   Note 3: Sentences and phrases are "communicatively correct, with mistakes but the idea is understandable" (2) when a part of the sentence is missing: the verb, the subject, the object, an adverbial modifier.

INDEX CARD No. 2

For the Morphemes Used by the Students in the Suggestopedic Foreign Language Courses

Name of the student ....
Course in .... Teacher ....
Input level (date)
Output level (date)
  I. Answers to 28 questions.
 II. Translation into the mother tongue. Number of parts of speech in the text ....

No. of parts of speech used	1a Correct	1b With few mistakes	2. Wrong
1. Definite and indefinite article			
2. Nouns			
3. Adjectives			
4. Pronouns			
5. Numbers			
6. Verbs			
7. Adverbs			
8. Prepositions			
9. Conjunctions			
10. Interjections			

Note 1: When filling in Index Card No. 2 one should use a glossary of the words from the textbook, taking into account the paradigms of the grammatical categories as well.

Note 2: In defining the degree of correctness, one should refer to the notes for Index Card No. 1.

FURTHER IMPROVEMENT IN THE FOREIGN LANGUAGE AFTER THE FIRST GRADE OF SUGGESTOPEDIC COURSES

It is known that the improvement of a foreign tongue (and even of the native one) is a practically lifelong process for a human being.

The first grade of suggestopedic courses lays the foundation necesssary for mastering a foreign tongue, the beginning being assisted by a teacher. Because of the organization of suggestopedic teaching and learning, the stage of self-education is rapidly reached.

Education may be pursued in courses designed in a more free-and-easy way, along "club" lines, with the participation of a teacher. The teacher's functions are only consultative. Discussions on subjects of interest to the majority of the students are organized, in addition to discourses on various themes, concerts, and recitals (in the respective foreign language).

The second part of the textbook in Italian (Sofia, 1975) is a methodological sequel of the first part. This second part is a kind of reader. There is no translation in the right-hand half of the page. Unfamiliar items are explained through synonyms and paraphrases during deciphering. The teacher and the students are equally active in such discussions. The number of sessions is reduced. The students' part in such club conferences is rather considerable.

The second part of the textbook begins with a brief historico-geographic survey of "the regions, towns and cities of Italy." This survey abounds in artistic visual aids. Literary fragments that are in notional relation to the subject are incorporated in a natural manner. This is the case of Grazia Deledda's short novel *Elias Portolu*, namely, the part treating the island of Sardinia. The style of this author, a Nobel prize winner for 1926, is both refined and accessible.

La Sardegna è tutta boschi e *pascoli*.
La città principale è Cagliari,
porto assai attivo.
Tra le altre città abbiamo

Sassari e Nuoro, patria della grande scrittrice
italiana Grazia Deledda (1875–1936,
premio Nobel 1926), autrice di una serie
di romanzi nei quali ci sono delle pagine
indimenticabili con *descrizioni* del paesaggio,
dei *costumi* e delle scene della vita sarda.
"Seduti che furono in cucina,
mentre zia Annedda *versava* da bere,
zio Portolu *s'impadroní* di jacu Farre,
un suo parente, un bell'uomo rosso e grasso
che respirava lentamente
e non lo lasciò piú in pace.
—Vedi, —gli gridava,
tirandogli la falda del cappotto,
e accennandogli i suoi figli,
—li vedi ora i figli miei?
Tre *colombi*!
E forti, eh, e sani, e belli!
Li vedi in fila, li vedi?
Ore che è tornato Elias,
saremo come quattro leoni;
Non ci toccherà neppure una mosca.
Anche io sai, anche io sono forte;
non guardarmi cosí, Jacu Farre,
io di te me ne infischio, intendi?
Mio figlio Mattia è la mano destra;
ora Elias, sarà la mia sinistra.
E Pietro, poi, il minore, Prededdu mio?
Non lo vedi? è un fiore!
Ha seminato dieci quarti *d'orzo*
e otto di frumento e due quarti di *fave*;
eh, se vuol sposarsi, può tenerla bene la moglie!
Non gli mancherà la raccolta.
E un fiore, Prededdu mio.
Ah, i miei figli!
Come i miei figli non ce ne sono altri a Nuoro.
—Eh! eh!—disse l'altro quasi *gemendo*.
—Eh! eh! Cosa vuoi dire col tuo eh! eh! Jacu Fà?

Dico bugie forse?
Mostrami altri tre giovani, migliori dei miei figli,
onesti, laboriosi, forti.
Uomini sono, essi, uomini sono!"

Elias Portolu, G. Deledda

The most important parts (forming a meaningful sequence) of Natalia Ginzburg's play *Ti ho Sposato per Allegria* are also included. The style and language of this play are situated on the boundaries of romanticism and realism, between fiction and theater. The language is elegant, accessible, colloquial. The idiomatic expressions are easy to catch.

Natalia Ginzburg

TI HO SPOSATO PER ALLEGRIA

Commedia in tre atti

Personaggi
Pietro
Giuliana, moglie di Pietro
Vittoria, donna di servizio
Madre di Pietro
Ginestra, sorella di Pietro

Atto primo

PIETRO:	Il mio cappello dov'è?
GIULIANA:	Hai un cappello?
PIETRO:	L'avevo. Adesso non lo trovo piú.
GIULIANA:	Io non me lo ricordo questo cappello.
PIETRO:	Forse non te lo puoi ricordare. Non lo metto da molto tempo. Noi è solo un mese che ci conosciamo.
GIULIANA:	Non dire cosí, "un mese che ci conosciamo" come seo non fossi tua moglie.

PIETRO: Sei mia moglie da una settimana.
In questa settimana,
e in tutto il mese passato,
non ho mai messo il cappello.
Lo metto solo quando piove forte,
oppure quando vado ai *funerali*.
Oggi piove, e devo andare a un funerale.
E un cappello marrone, *moscio*.
Un buon cappello.
GIULIANA: Forse l'avrai a casa di tua madre.
PIETRO: Forse. Tu non è che l'hai visto per caso,
in mezzo a tutta la mia roba,
un cappello?
GIULIANA: No. Però tutta la tua roba
l'ho fatta mettere in naftalina.
Può darsi che ci fosse anche questo cappello.
Vai a un funerale? Chi è morto?
PIETRO: E morto uno.
Da quanti giorni l'abbiamo, Vittoria?
GIULIANA: Da mercoledi. Tre giorni.
PIETRO: E tu subito le hai fatto riporre in naftalina
la nostra roba da inverno?
GIULIANA: La tua. Io di roba da inverno non ne ho.
Ho una gonna, una maglia, e l'*impermeabile*.
PIETRO: Hai fatto mettere in naftalina
tutta la mia roba da inverno? Subito?
GIULIANA: Subito.
PIETRO: Geniale. Genialissimo.
Però ora facciamo *pescar fuori*
il mio cappello.
Devo andare a questo funerale.
Con mia madre.
GIULIANA: Dimmi chi è morto.
PIETRO: E morto uno che si chiamava
Lamberto Genova.
Era un amico dei miei.
E morto l'altro ieri,
all'improvviso, nella stanza da bagno,
mentre si faceva la barba.

GIULIANA: Lambero Genova? Io lo conoscevo.
Lo conoscevo benissimo! È morto?
PIETRO: Si.
GIULIANA: Nella stanza da bagno?
Lamberto Genova!
Io lo conoscevo, ti dico!
Lo conoscevo benissimo!
Una volta mi ha anche prestato dei soldi.
PIETRO: Impossibile. Era un uomo cosí *avaro*.
GIULIANA: Però mi ha prestato dei soldi.
Era molto innamorato di me.
PIETRO: Vittoria!
Guardi se riesce a trovare un cappelo!
Un cappello marrone, moscio, tutto *peloso*!
La signora dice che forse
l'ha messo in naftalina.
(Vittoria entrando.)
VITTORIA: Allora sarà nell'armadio
delle quattro stagioni.
PIETRO: Cos'è l'armadio delle quattro stagioni?
GIULIANA: E l'armadio, nel corridoio.
E in quattro scomparti.
Vittoria dice che si chiama cosí.
VITTORIA: Però ci vuole la scala.
Devo andarla a prendere in cantina.
E in alto, la roba da inverno,
e io solo con la *seggiola*
non ci arrivo.
PIETRO: Possibile che sia cosí difficile
riavere il proprio cappelo?
(Vittoria via.)
GIULIANA: Lo sai quando l'ho visto
l'ultima volta?
PIETRO: Ma tu forse non l'hai mai visto!
GIULIANA: Non dicevo del cappello.
Dicevo di Lamberto Genova.
Lo sai quando è stato

155

	che l'ho visto, Lamberto Genova,
	per l'ultima volta?
PIETRO:	Quando?
GIULIANA:	Pochi giorni prima d'incontrarti.
	Gennaio, era.

      (segue)

The book also contains the most popular arias and duets from Verdi's *Rigoletto*. The archaic and poetical terms are explained by simpler everyday words. The arias are illustrated by pictures that give an interpretation of the subject modernizing the libretto. These pictures provoke a state of surprise and expectation, thus favoring the easier memorization of the texts.

CORO:	Zitti, zitti moviamo
	a vendetta
	ne sia colto or
	che men l'aspetta.
	Derisore sì audace, costante
	a sua volta schernito sarà!
	Cheti, cheti, rubiamgli l'amante,
	e la Corte doman riderà.
	Zitti, cheti,
	attenti all'opra!

(s'internano nella casa e trascinano Gilda la quale avrà la bocca chiusa da un fazzoletto. Nel traversare la scena ella perde una sciarpa.)

      Giuseppe Verdi, *Rigoletto*, Act One

RIGOLETTO:	Parla . . . siam soli . . .
GILDA:	(Ciel! dammi coraggio!)
	Tutte le feste al tempio
	mentre pregava Iddio,
	bello e fatale un giovine
	offriasi al guardo mio,
	se i labbri nostri tacquero,
	dagl'occhi il cor,
	il cor parlò.

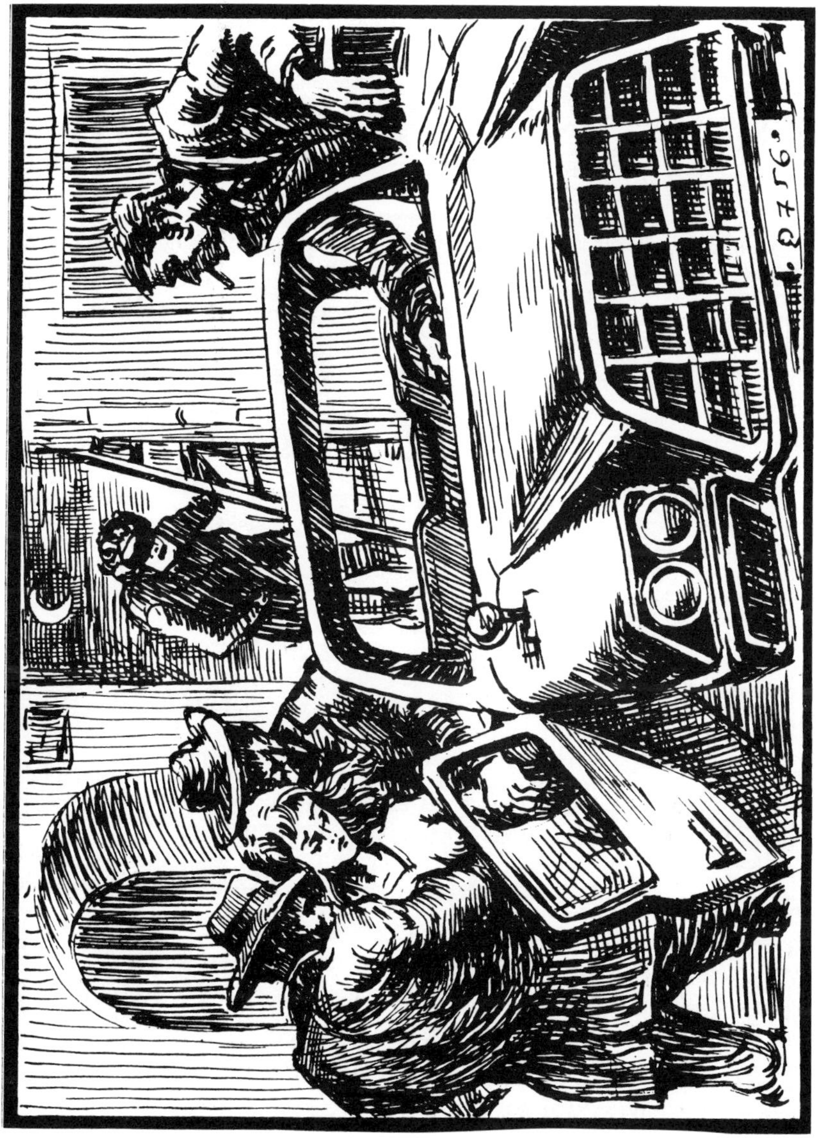

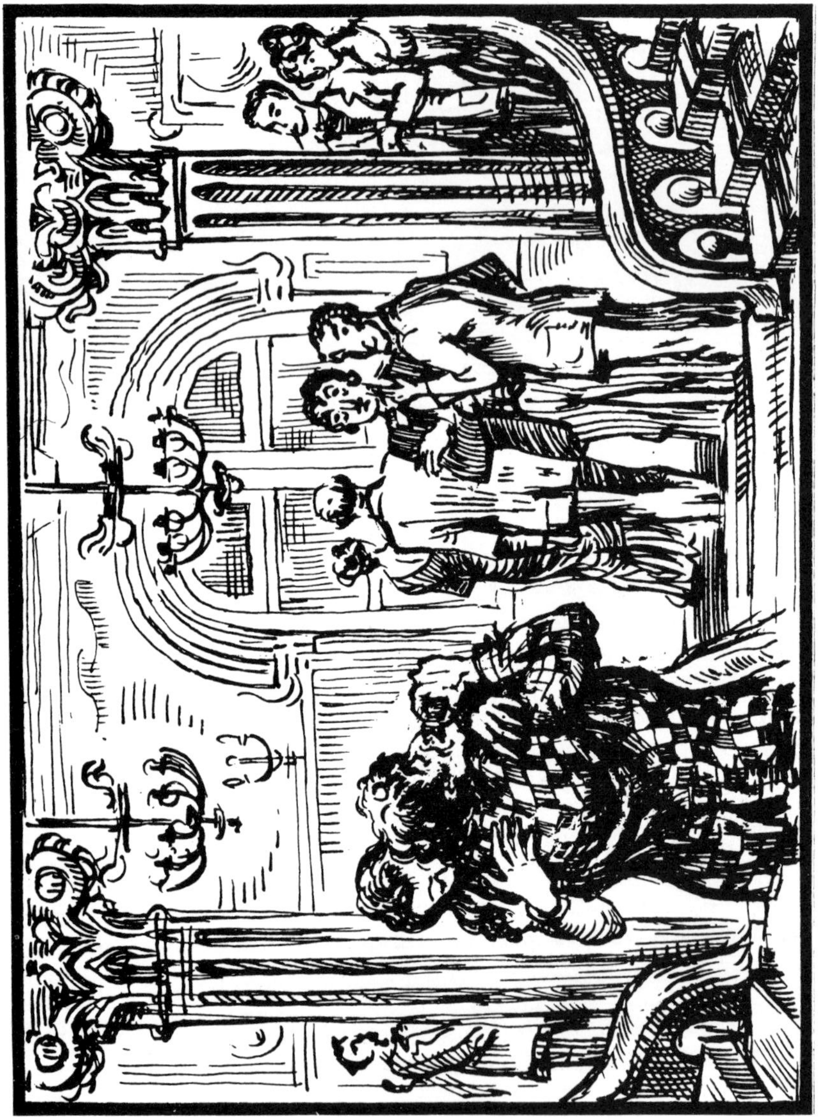

> Furtivo fra le tenebre
> sol ieri a me giungeva.
> "Sono studente, povero,"
> commosso mi diceva
> con ardente, palpito amor
> mi protestò.
> Partì... partì...
> il mio core aprivasi
> a speme piú gradita,
> quando improvvisi apparvero
> color che m'han rapita,
> e a forza qui m'addussero
> nell'ansia piú crudel.

Giuseppe Verdi, *Rigoletto*, Act Two

The grammar provided for elaboration is almost identical to that in the first part of the textbook. It is, however, extended to embrace certain particularities and is amalgamated, so that there are two global themes. The first theme comprises: The noun. Substantive, adjective. The pronouns. The definite, indefinite, and partitive article. Prepositions and conjunctions. The second theme comprises: The verb. Conjugations, tenses, aspect, mood, voice. The adverb. Some of the grammatical units that have remained at the passive level in the first part of the textbook, are now coming to the fore. For example: the remote past tense (passato remoto), the imperative, conditional, and subjunctive moods, some continuous tenses, the sequence of tenses.

The grammar is elaborated during the initial ten days both on the basis of literary and other texts from the reader as well as on the basis of texts selected by the students themselves according to their personal interests. At the same time the attention is turned to writing, which has almost been mastered at the paraconscious level. Coping with the copious reading material (from both parts of the textbook) has contributed to the largest extent to the mastering of writing without undue loss of time.

The same principles of organization relate to the suggestopedic courses intended for students having studied the foreign language in some other school or course and who have come to the Suggestology Research Institute with the hope of improving their knowledge.

PART 2

SUGGESTOPEDIC TEACHING OF FOREIGN LANGUAGES TO SCHOOL-AGE CHILDREN

The suggestopedic teaching of foreign languages to children and adolescents from the 1st to the 11th grades is organized in accordance with the three basic principles of suggestology and with the principles and means of suggestopedy. (For more details and formulations, see G. Lozanov, op. cit.).

The teachers should have passed through special training in suggestopedic theory and practice. They should be aware of the basic suggestopedic requirements in adapting the methodology to the respective age brackets. They should also be acquainted with the program for suggestopedic teaching of all subjects to school-age children in order to succeed in applying the suggestopedic global approach to the intersubject relations. In this connection, it is imperative that they have mastered the theory and practice of the suggestopedic globality, in order to discriminate it from educational complexity and encyclopedism—a penchant they should keep well clear of.

The teaching of foreign languages to school-age children is distributed as follows:

1st Grade (1st year): Duplicating teaching with artistic performances and worked-out lessons. (This type of teaching can be applied not only in duplicating schoolhours.)

2nd Grade (2nd and 3nd years): Intensive teaching (10 days, 2 schoolhours each), followed by supporting lessons (1 schoolhour weekly), on the basis of a textbook in two parts.

(4th year): Review and improvement of the creative automation of the subject matter from the 2nd and 3rd years on the basis of a reader (1 school hour weekly).

3rd Grade (5th and 6th years): Intensive teaching (10 days, 2 schoolhours each) followed by supporting lessons (1 schoolhour weekly) on the basis of a textbook in two parts.

4th Grade (7th and 8th years): Intensive teaching in the 7th year (10 days, 2 schoolhours each) and supporting lessons on the basis of a chrestomathy in the 8th year.

5th Grade (9th, 10th and 11th years): Intensive teaching and supporting lessons on the basis of the textbooks for adults of the Suggestology Research Institute, revised in view of each student's particular needs. Review and supporting lessons in the 11th year.

Figs. 21–26 - Sets in the classroom designed for the duplicating teaching with performances in English ("Friends" and "Where Are Horse and Dog?") and in Russian ("Doctor Aybolit").

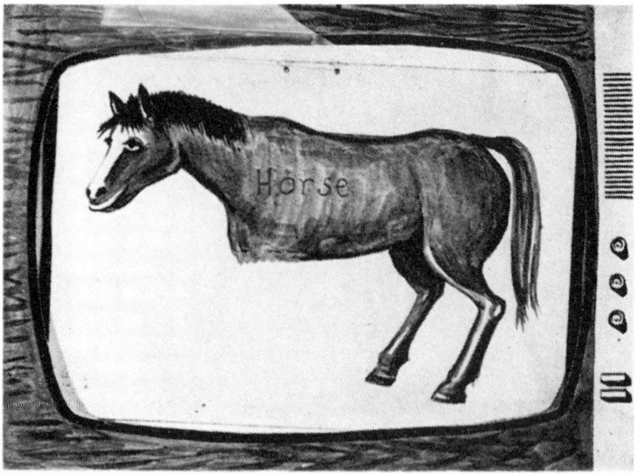
Horse

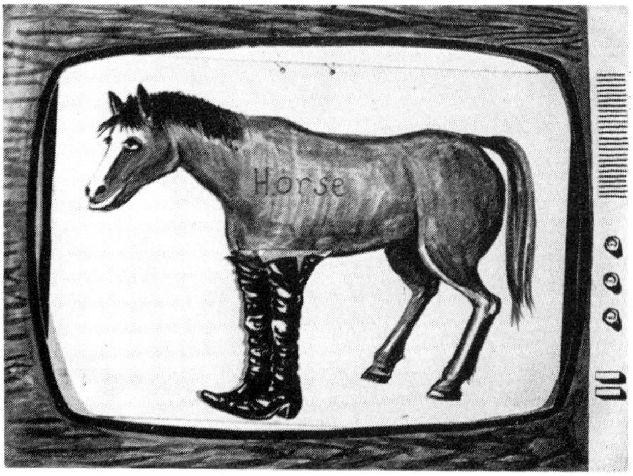
Horse

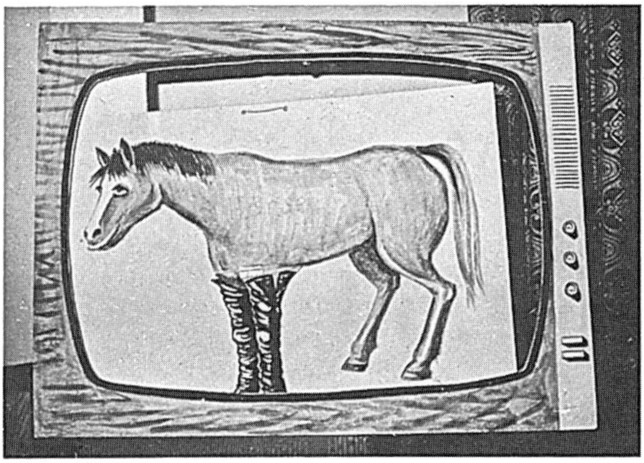

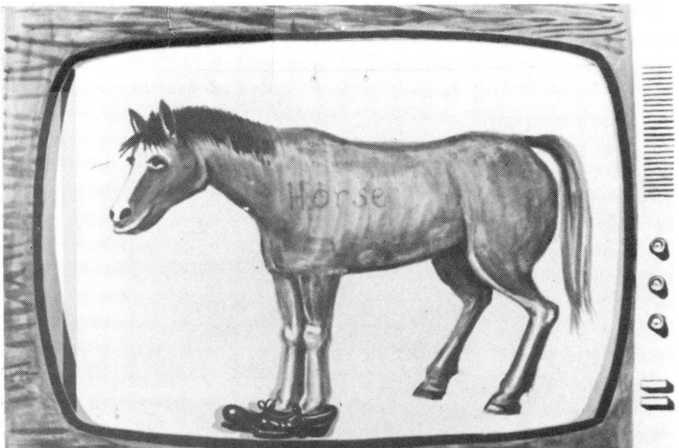
Horse

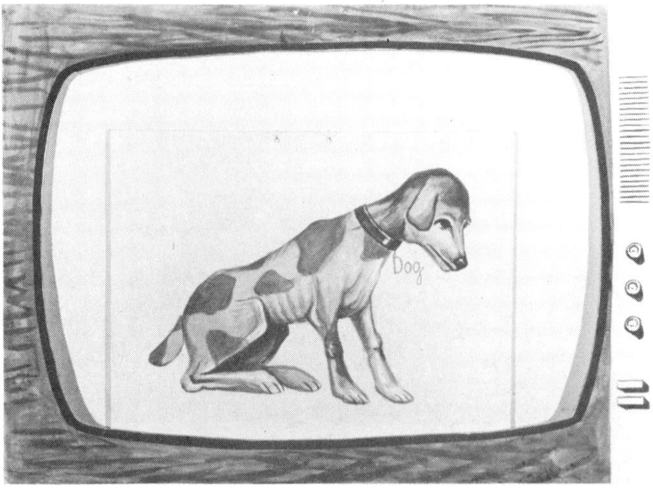
Dog

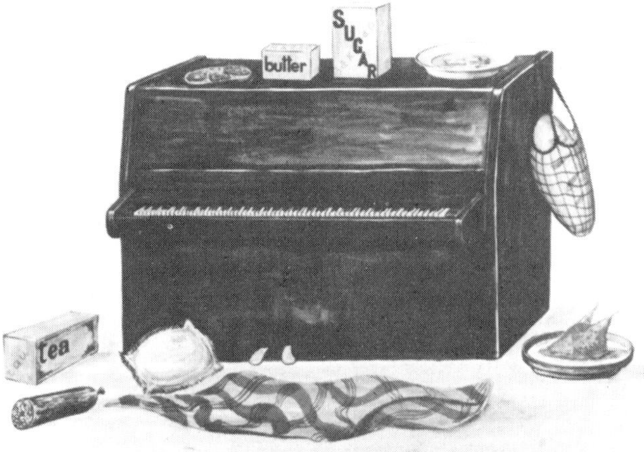
SUGAR
butter
tea

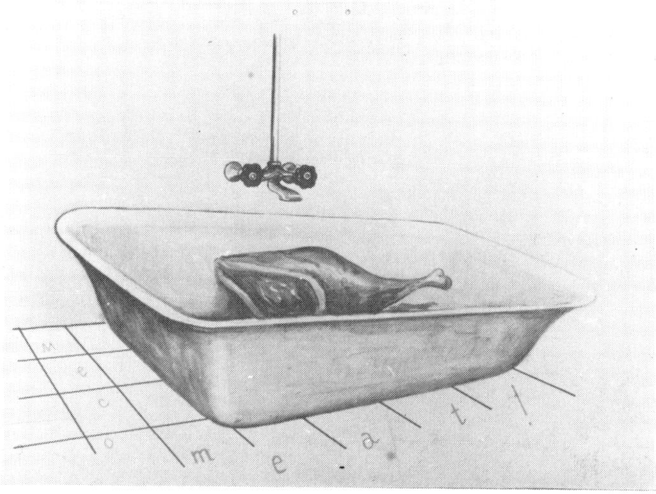
M e c o m e a t !

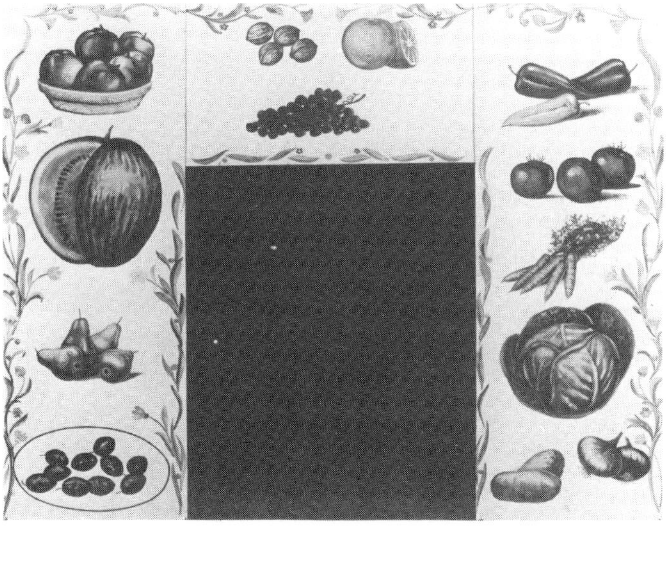

Доктор Айболит
Открылась больница
для птиц и зверей.
Идите лечиться
туда поскорей!

FIRST GRADE

Globalized Teaching of Foreign Languages in the First Year of the Suggestopedic School, with Artistic Performances and Elaborated Lessons

The teaching process begins much like the course for adults with a motivating encounter of teacher and children, followed by a testing of the preliminary level of knowledge in the tongue to be studied. The testing procedures should be (a) nontraumatic, and (b) conducive to increasing the children's motivation to study foreign tongues. This is attained first of all through the organization of the work as a whole as well as through the behavior of the teacher.

The testing is drafted at the communicative level, according to suggestopedic theory. It is similar to the testing used for adults with the necessary adaptation. Here follows the *Questionnaire* for testing children at the 1st grade of education:

Questionnaire

For Input-Output Level of Schoolchildren from the Classes with Integrated Lessons in Foreign Languages

1. What is your name?
2. Where is your home? (How far is it from the school? On which Street?)
3. Whom do you live with? (*Note*: The posing of questions Nos. 5, 6, and 7 depends on this answer.)
4. Have you a sister/brother?
5. What is the name of your mother (father, grandmother, grandfather)?
6. How old is your: father, mother, grandfather, grandmother, brother, sister?
7. What are your parents' occupations?
8. Where were you born? When were your born? How old are you?
9. Where do you study?

10. How did you come to school (alone, with whom, by what)?
11. What kind of fruit and vegetables do you like most?
12. What animals do you like most?
13. What song or poem in ─────── (language) do you like most? Do you want to sing it/to recite it?
14. What do you carry in your bag?
15. What does your house look like?

The integrated teaching of foreign languages is carried out during the lessons in manual training, singing, and drawing in the 1st schoolgrade, simultaneously with the regular work of the respective teacher. The foreign language teacher is the second one in the classroom. He or she makes use of the utterances from the teaching of his or her colleague, and skillfully introduces the foreign tongue, applying at the same time the suggestopedic global approach in the intra-subject relations.

The next section of the foreign language subject matter begins with a *suggestopedic play* in the classroom. The play itself, as well as its performance and subsequent elaboration, the scenery, etc., are subjected to numerous requirements.

Requirements for the Foreign Language Suggestopedic Play Used for Globalized Teaching

1. First of all, the play should be written at a professional level, with due knowledge of childrens' psychology, and of the suggestopedic requirements to set tasks near the upper limit of the children's capacities (and even slightly above this limit).

2. The play should synthesize the greatest possible number of arts: theater, music, ballet, pictorial, and plastic arts.

3. The play should bring about the appropriate conditions for the children to join in during the performance itself.

4. In accordance with suggestopedic theory, the play should integrate the subject matter of several disciplines.

5. The foreign language should be presented in a globalized way—both the lexical and grammatical units. The subject matter should be of sufficient scope; it has to be communicative and to outline the structural models in an unobstructive manner.

A number of other requirements, for example, the features of the songs, the games, the characters, the implied meaning, etc., are developed elsewhere.

Requirements for the Performance of the Foreign Language Suggestopedic Play Used for Integrated Teaching

1. The performance is not just a theatrical one—the included topics of didactic importance are stressed, but *mildly, indirectly*.

2. The actors (who are most often, but not always, foreign language teachers) have been trained in clear-cut suggestopedic diction with intonational accentuations.

3. The translation is either obtained via visual aids (a rich set of props and scenes), or is given verbally—in a very concentrated form, only at previously well-defined moments. Here, also, preliminary training is necessary.

4. The actors have already received suggestopedic training at the rehearsals, which are devoted more to the suggestopedic preparation than to the purely theatrical one.

We shall abstain from more details about the suggestopedic staging, for this is another section of the suggestopedic theory and practice.

The following pages contain the first two plays created for the purpose of teaching the English language with subsequent elaboration. We also include the first play for teaching Russian. It is not necessary to go into details concerning every single language, because this would interfere with the creative lines of the suggestopedic teacher. The only short requirement is to observe the foundations of suggestology and the principles and means of suggestology, and to adhere to the given models.

FIRST GLOBAL THEME

E. GATEVA

Friends

(*First Play*)

A suggestopedic play for the first global theme with elaborations for duplicating teaching foreign languages in the first grade of the suggestopedic schools.

English translation: S. Petrunova
Under the methodological guidance of G. Lozanov, M.D., Med. Sci. D.

Scenario and staging plan for conducting the first suggestopedic lesson in English with first-graders, use being made of intersubject relations in the first global theme, namely:

Mathematics: Quantity. Natural numbers 1 to 10. Zero. Operations within the multitude to 10.

Bulgarian (Native) Language: Leárning to read by means of posters. Reading aloud: "I like to read."

Homeland Knowledge: Natural environment, plants and animals.

Pictorial Arts: Watercolors—acquainting. Drawing from nature—fruit. Illustration of fairy tales, etc.

Manual Training: Working with natural materials.

Physical Education: Harmonious and plastic body. Ballet.

ENGLISH LANGUAGE:

Lexis: Introduction, School, Fruit, Vegetables, Flowers, Colors.
Animals.
Numbers 1 to 10.
Elementary questions on the themes.

Grammar: The verbs: to be, to have, can, to speak, to write, to read, to live, etc., from the play. Present tense.
Noun and adjective
Personal pronouns
Possessive pronouns

CHARACTERS

The Interpreter
A Hindu
A Russian (male or female)
A German (male or female)
A French Man
An English Woman
An American Woman
A Flower Clerk
A Greengrocery Sales Clerk
A Ballerina (a girl from the choreographic school)
Children

Time: The present. Place: The classroom, during a lesson in singing, drawing, or manual training in the 1st school year.

ACT ONE

(A group of foreigners, guests of the country. In fact, they are foreign language teachers.)

Preliminary instructions for the teacher:

1. Do not forget that you are taking part in a suggestopedic lesson, not in a theatrical performance. Suggestopedy makes use of certain aspects of theater in view of the reinforcement of motivation and interest toward the school subjects.

2. During the whole suggestopedic lesson, which resembles at first sight a show, teachers are interested in the childrens' reactions in connection with the didactic material, and govern them.

3. Tactfully, and with a flexible suggestopedic approach, the teacher includes the whole class and speaks to every child, including him or her in the play in a more or less cursory way.

4. The teacher skillfully sets the shifts in tempo—fast and slow—as well as the dynamic nuances of the emotional intonation.

THE INTERPRETER:
(In Bulgarian, addressing the children)
> Hello, children! You don't know me, but quickly we'll get acquainted and be friends. I must let you know something very important. You have guests from abroad. Are you children speaking foreign languages? You certainly understand Russian which is quite easy for you Bulgarians. As for me, my name is Eva and I am Italian. I learned Bulgarian from my friend Gianni. Here he is!

(She produces out of her bag Gianni—a doll).

> This is Gianni Manolo Juan Rodriguez de Prado. What a long name! That is so, because his father and his grandfather were Spaniards, and Spaniards bear the names of all their great-grandparents. His mother is Italian. The story of Gianni's learning Bulgarian is very very long, but here are the highlights: Gianni was born in England. He was living there when he met a Bulgarian boy by the name of Ivancho. Ivancho spoke fluent English. Gianni asked him where he had studied English to know it so well, and Ivancho proudly answered that he had learned it at the 122nd School 'Chr. Kurpatchev' in Sofia. Ivancho told Gianni wonderful things about Bulgaria. Later on I learned Bulgarian from Gianni; we both came to Bulgaria. I liked it very much and remained to work as a translator.
> Do you hear? Gianni is speaking to you. Do you hear? He doesn't speak, he sings. He is very considerate and very eccentric. Another time I'll tell you more about my friend, if you like. And now the guests, who are Gianni's friends, want to meet you and to learn Bulgarian quickly. They all speak English also, but I think, children, that you're going to win the contest and learn English sooner than they will learn Bulgarian. Let's see! Now, children, this is Mr. Gupta, from India head of the delegation.
> *Do you speak* Bulgarian, Mr. Gupta?

(The same question is repeated in English. From now on, when an English text is placed in the right half of the page, that means an identical Bulgarian text is on the left half of the original.)
> *Do you speak* Bulgarian?

THE HINDU:
(Wearing a turban and carrying a camera and a notebook where he keeps writing down Bulgarian words.)

> (In broken Bulgarian.) I understands a bit Bulgarian. I wanted to learn to read Bulgarian. I know not read. How children here learned to read so fast? I want too. I speak English perfectly well. I studied English for twenty years.

(Further on, the Hindu translates only the italicized words.)

> *My name is* Asvagosha Gupta.
> *I am* a journalist.
> *I write* for newspapers.

(He produces a newspaper from his pocket.)

> *I speak* English very well.
> *I live* in Bombay.
> *I want to* speak Bulgarian.
> I want to *read* Bulgarian.
> *Can you understand* me?

A CHILD:
(In English.) Yes, we can, *of course*.

THE RUSSIAN WOMEN:
(In broken Bulgarian.)
> Well done!
> And we understand each other easily, don't we, children?
> My name is Olga Nikolaevna.
> I am from Moscow.
> All my colleagues here speak only English.
> I also speak fluently English, and French, and German, and Italian, and Spanish, and Bulgarian, of course.
> And this is Mrs. Helga Schmidt from Germany.
> She is my friend.

THE GERMAN WOMAN:
(The interpreter translates on the spot.)

> Ich kann nicht Bulgarisch sprechen! I cannot speak Bulgarian!

> Ich kann nur "molja" sagen.　　I can only say "please."
> Ich spreche aber fliessend Englisch.　　But I speak English very well.
> 　　Do you speak Bulgarian?

THE INTERPRETER:
And this is Mme Ronet from France.

THE FRENCH WOMEN:
(In French.)

> Moi aussi je ne parle pas bulgare.　　I cannot speak Bulgarian too.
> Je ne comprends rien.　　I don't understand anything.
> Je ne parle que l'anglais.　　I speak only English.

THE INTERPRETER:
Look, children, this is Mrs. Daisy from England.

THE ENGLISH WOMAN:
(She translates from English to Bulgarian, and vice versa, only the underlined words. All the rest is illustrated by means of props.)

> I know a couple of
> Bulgarian words.
> *My name is Daisy.*
> *What is your name?*

(She addresses 3 to 4 children, helping them find the answer.)

> *I live in England.*
> *You live in Bulgaria.*
> *I live in London.*
> *I have* a large family:
> a *husband*, two *daughters*,

(She counts with the fingers—one, two.)

> three *sons*.

(She counts—one, two, three.)

> I have *mother* and *father*,
> *brother* and sister,
> a grandmother and a grandfather.
> Here are *all together*.

(She counts to ten together with the children.)

> *Look!*

(She presents several pictures of the members of her family to some children.)

> Look at their *pictures*!

(She addresses some of the children.)

> *Have you a sister?*

(She addresses other children.)

> *Have you a brother?*
> I have a pretty *house*.
> I have a *garden with many flowers*.
> This is my house.

(She presents a photograph or a drawing.)

> My *little* daughther *has*
> many *toys*:
> a doll,
> a poodle, a cat,
> a monkey, a bear.

(In Bulgarian.)

> What does the monkey do?

(She points at the posters for learning to read in Bulgarian, which hang on the wall, and the children read in Bulgarian.)

> a ball, a car.

(The children have been previously instructed to bring a favorite toy from home for this lesson and the English lady points to some of the children's toys and asks:)

> *Have you a doll?*
> *Have you a ball?*
> This is *my friend* Pamela.
> *She is from* America.

177

Fig. 27 - The suggestopedic plays "Friends" and "This is the Doll."

THE AMERICAN LADY:
(The underlined words are translated *by the English lady*.)

>My name is Pamela.
>I live in a *big city*.
>I am a *teacher*.
>I teach music.
>I sing with *the children*.
>This is a lovely *song*.
>Listen to it!

(The English woman translates the words phrase by phrase after the American woman has sung them. The American lady sings the song twice: the first time slowly, with clear-cut diction, the second time faster.)

>I am, I am a *happy man*.
>You are, you are my *good old* friend.
>*He* is my friend,
>*She* is my friend,
>*We are* good friends,
>All happy friends.
>*Let us sing* together
>and dance!

(Everybody sings and dances.)

>Here is *another* song.
>My schoolchildren *greet* me with it.
>*Everybody sing*!
>Good morning to you! (twice)
>Good morning, dear teacher,
>Good morning to you!

(The words are translated in the same way.)

>*What is this*?

(She opens a parcel. There is a nice doll.)

>This is Doll.
>*She goes* to school.
>She has a *schoolbag*.

I Am a Happy Man

Words by L. Kozhuharova
Music by E. Gateva

Allegretto

I am, I am a happy man. You are, you are my good, old friend. He is my friend, she is my friend, we are good friends, all happy friends.

Популярна песен

Good morning to you good morning to you good morning dear teacher good morning to you.

(The American woman shows the bag.)

> What has she in the bag?
> She has many *things*.
> Look!
> What is this?
> This is my bag,
> *full* of many things:
> *books* and *pencils*,
> *pens* and *sweets*.

(The American woman displays the items. The English woman translates on the spot, according to the children's reactions.)

> My friends and Doll are *hungry*.
> *They love* fruit and vegetables.
> *Let us go* to the market.
> It is autumn.

(The song "Autumn" from the opera *Fairy World* is heard in Bulgarian and in English. A ballerina dances a pantomime, related to the words and the music. She wears a classical tutu in tender autumnal colors and holds a basket full of fruits and flowers. The change of scenery is done during this dance.)

END OF ACT ONE

Note: The tempo of Act One is faster till the appearance of THE ENGLISH WOMAN and THE AMERICAN WOMAN. Pauses should be avoided.

Andante

The earth is spread with golden leaves now and autumn has come all in beauty, preparing her nectars delicious to drink in her honour then. In soft, loving whispers she's urging the song bird to make for the south. While

autumn herself is to linger un-

til the first white snow drifts down.

ACT TWO

(At the marketplace. Two arches decorated with painted fruits, vegetables, and flowers on them, are hung during the interlude—a ballet—onto opposite walls of the classroom. In front of one of the arches sits the Greengrocer's Sales Clerk, wearing clothes in very gay colors and knitting a fluffy shawl. At her feet there are a pannier of particolored woollen yarn and a basket full of apples. In front of the arch with the flowers stands the Flower Clerk, arranging the flowerpots. The scenery illustrates the theme in mathematics: multitudes of fruits, vegetables, and flowers; natural numbers up to ten. The fruits and vegetables that are to be pointed at are painted on the panels.)

THE ENGLISH WOMAN:
(In Bulgarian.)

    Please, we want fruits and vegetables.

THE SALES CLERK:
(She sings and points at the vegetables. A translation, if needed, is given by the English Woman, in a very cursory way.)

    "*Peppers*, peppers, peppers,
    Red and *green* and *yellow*!
    With *tomatoes* mellow!"
    Choose, please!

THE ENGLISH WOMAN:
    Oh! All Bulgarians speak English!

THE AMERICAN WOMAN:
    Farmer, have you apples to *sell*?
    Hey diddle diddle. (2)

THE SALES CLERK:
    Yes, I have *some* apples to sell.
    Hey diddle diddle, apples to sell.

THE AMERICAN WOMAN:
    Farmer, have you *pears* to sell?
    Hey diddle diddle. (2)

Peppers, Peppers!

Peppers, peppers, peppers!
Red and green and yellow,
how I like to eat them
with tomatoes mellow!

Farmer, Farmer have you apples to sell?
Hi diddle diddle hi diddle du do?
Yes, I have some apples to sell.
He diddle diddle apples to sell!

THE SALES CLERK:
>   Yes, I have some pears to sell.
>   Hey diddle diddle. (2)

THE AMERICAN WOMAN:
>   Farmer, have you *plums* to sell?

THE SALES CLERK:
>   Yes, I have some plums to sell.
>   Hey diddle plums to sell.

(The dialogue is sung and illustrated with the fruits.)

THE AMERICAN WOMAN:
>   *How much it?*

(The English Woman translates.)

THE SALES CLERK:
(Together with the children.)

>   One and one is two.
>   Oh, this is me and you.
>   One and two is three.
>   We are gay and free.
>   Two and two is four.
>   Never say "No more!"

(She gives her the apple as a present. The Flower Clerk intervenes. She counts up ten roses and offers them as a present.)

THE FLOWER CLERK:
(Together with the children.)

>   "One, two, three. Look at me!
>   Four, five, six. Look at Nick!
>   Seven, eight, nine. Ann is fine.
>   Ten, ten, ten. Sing it again!"

(Everybody sings "Good Morning!")

THE ENGLISH WOMAN AND THE AMERICAN WOMAN:
>   Oh, thank you!
>   What lovely flowers!
>   What beautiful colors!

THE FLOWER CLERK:
(Addressing the children. She recites the words in a sing-song manner, linking them with the scenery, which represents their meaning.)

> What is *pink*?
> A rose is pink
> By the fountain brink.
>
> What is *red*?
> A poppy's red
> in its barley bed.
>
> What is *blue*?
> The sky is blue
> Where the clouds float through.
>
> What is *white*?
> A swan is white
> Sailing in the light.
>
> What is yellow?
> Pears are yellow
> *Rich* and *ripe* and mellow.
>
> What is green?
> The grass is green
> With small flowers between.
>
> What is violet?
> *Clouds* are violet
> In the summer twilight.
>
> What is *orange*?
> Why, an orange,
> Just an orange!

—CH. G. ROSSETTI

THE ENGLISH WOMAN:
> *Dear children, see you again!*
> *It is pleasant here!*
> *So long!*
> *Goodbye!*

(Every child is given an apple, the "guests" a flower each. Against the background of the song "What is Pink?", the Little Ballerina performs a pantomime.)

THE TEACHER:
And now, children, let us choose the best fruit and draw it. Which fruit are we choosing? We are going to draw next hour.

Elaborations in the English Language of the Play *Friends*

1. In the respective hours (singing, drawing, and manual training) the teacher in English language always bears in mind the global themes of the suggestopedic program for teaching the Bulgarian language, mathematics, homeland knowledge, singing, drawing, manual training, and eventually physical education.

2. The regular teachers of the classes also have the plans of the English language elaborations, in order to be able to prepare or to continue the work in the respective lesson, duplicating the English one.

First Elaboration

Lexis: Acquainting, Fruits, Vegetables, Colors. Elementary questions on the lexical themes.
Grammar: The verbs "to be," "to have," "to sing," "to like," "to draw."

Plan of the Lesson
Fifteen minutes in the first lesson and fifteen minutes in the second lesson.
1. Entrance of the teacher with the greeting "Good morning," singing of the song "Good Morning" by the children (the song from the play).
2. Acquainting with the song "I Am a Happy Man" from the play. The children introduce themselves to one another in English. The verb "to be." Elaboration of the song. Use is made of the toys: a doll, a poodle, a monkey, etc. Singing the song and an attempt to dance it.
3. Introducing the theme "Fruits" (apples, pears, plums, oranges). "Vegetables" (peppers and tomatoes), "Flowers" (a rose, a poppy, violets), and "Colors" (yellow, green, red, blue, white, black, orange),

through the paintings, the props from the play and the colored sheets from the drawing block, used in manual training. The verbs "to have," "to draw."

Note: In a special notebook, the teacher writes down by the end of each lesson the vocabulary and the grammar, presented in the play, *Friends*.

Second Elaboration

Fifteen minutes in the lesson of singing.

First theme of the subject (singing): conceiving the melody in its melodious and metrical nuances.

    (a) Identifying a learned song out of a couple of its initial tones.
    (b) Identifying songs with the same metrics.
    (c) Discriminating between low and high tones.

Plan of the Lesson

1. Identifying a learned song out of a couple of its initial tones.
Identifying songs with the same metrics.

(a) The teacher starts singing (without words) the opening tones of the song "Good Morning." Which is this song? The children go on (with the words).

What is Your Name

Allegro

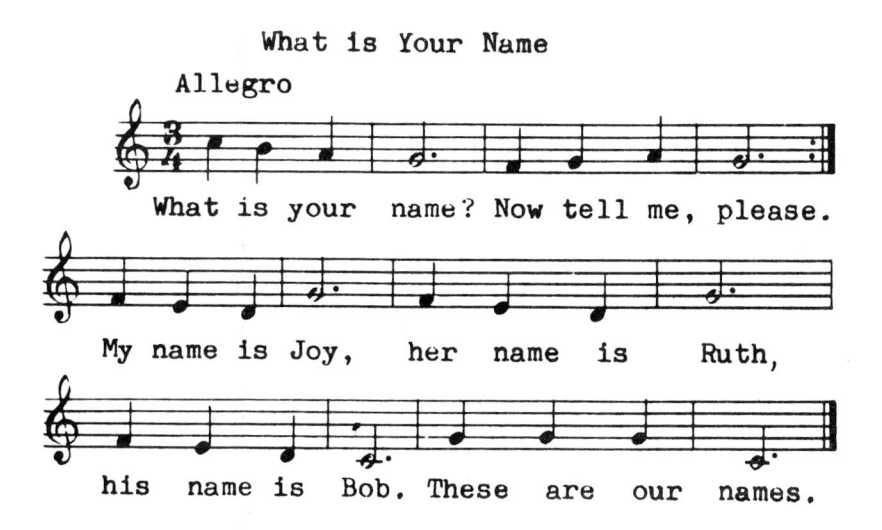

What is your name? Now tell me, please.
My name is Joy, her name is Ruth,
his name is Bob. These are our names.

(b) The teacher makes slight waltz steps under the opening tones of the song "I Am a Happy Man." Which is this song? The children identify it and with slight waltz steps, gracefully, like the ballerina from the performance, dance it as a waltz. The teacher counts: 1, 2, 3. Then the teacher counts: *1* 2 3 *4* 5 6 *7* 8 9 (10). Every first beat is stressed as being stronger than the other two.

(c) Studying the song "What Is Your Name?" by means of toys: a doll, a poodle, a fox, etc. (from the play). The children are activated to take part in the game, to "replay" the song.

Note: Different groups of children, previously specified, are activated during different hours.

Comparison of the three songs. They have the same metrics: three-four time. The first beat is stressed (strong). The second and third beats are weaker. Theoretical details are not given; metrical times are marked intonationally.

2. Discriminating between low and high tones. The opening tone, connected with the question (What?) is high. The tone connected with the name Bob is the lowest. The last tone is the same as the one for "Bob," but they all are similar to one another. The first one is simply twice as high as the last one (and as the one for "Bob," of course). The tones for "Joy" and "Ruth" are equal and of medium height.

3. Vocabulary, grammar: consolidating of the subject matter from the first elaboration.

Slightly broadening the notions on the possessive pronouns. Elementary questions.

Third Elaboration

Plan of the Lesson
Each lesson takes fifteen minutes in the hours of manual training—continuing the work with the colored drawing block.
 1. Greeting with the song "Good Morning."
 2. Elaborating the theme "The School."
    (a) Where does the child live? (near the school, far away from school).
    (b) How does the child come to school? (alone, with a companion, on foot, by some vehicle).

(c) What does the child carry in his or her schoolbag? What has the child? (the verb "to have"). Questions.

Note: The teacher makes use of a doll or an "animal," which is his or her "friend," in order to act out the above-mentioned questions before addressing the children.

Revision of the colors connected with the colored drawing block. The most important colors are counted. Review of the counting up to ten.

3. Elaborating the theme "The Family." Has the child a brother, a sister, a grandfather, a grandmother? Where do they live? What is their occupation? (the verb "to be"). Occupations. The children should bring along family pictures (snapshots) for the next lesson.

4. The lesson ends with a song: "Peppers, Peppers" or "I Am a Happy Man." Vocabulary: elaborating the themes "The School," "The Family," "Occupations." Questions. The cardinal numbers to ten. Colors—a review. Grammar: consolidating the verbs "to be" and "to have." Elaboration of the verb "can." Elaboration of the verbs "to live," "to work."

Fourth Elaboration

Plan of the Lesson
Fifteen minutes in the hour of singing.
1. Greeting with one of the songs having been studied.
2. Consolidating the three-four time metrics and measure. Waltz. The song–dialogue "Farmer, Have You Apples to Sell?." Translation of the dialogue. Studying it. Further activation through "other goods." Mathematics: cardinal numbers to 10 and simple arithmetical operations within the framework of addition and subtraction up to ten.
3. Consolidating the verbs "to be," "to have," and other simple verbs from the play.
4. Questions about familiar vocabulary.

Fifth Elaboration

Plan of the Lesson
Each lesson takes fifteen minutes in the hours of singing and drawing.
1. Singing all the songs from the play.
2. Consolidating the song "Farmer, Have You Apples to Sell?." Drawing after the theme of the song. Review of the colors. The song–dialogue

should be performed after having divided the children into two groups.

3. Activating the verses, connected with simple arithmetical operations: addition and subtraction up to ten, in the way they are given in the play.

Sixth Elaboration

Plan of the Lesson

Each lesson takes fifteen minutes in the hours of manual training.

1. The children have previously made a "frame" in brown paper. For several lessons the children will draw, in connection with Rosseti's verses (from the play), the basic things: a rose, a red poppy, blue sky, violet clouds, a tree with yellow pears, grass with small flowers, an orange-like sun.

2. This work will be done against the background of the verses, which are to be presented as a song (couplets one to four)—via a tape-recorder or a live performance of the teacher.

3. The children will be given a Bulgarian translation of the first and second couplet in broad form, and will be reading the translation in Bulgarian, assisted by the teacher.

4. Gradually the children learn by heart all the verses in English beginning with the first couplet in the first lesson.

5. All colors mentioned in the play will be referred to by pointing at objects that are those colors.

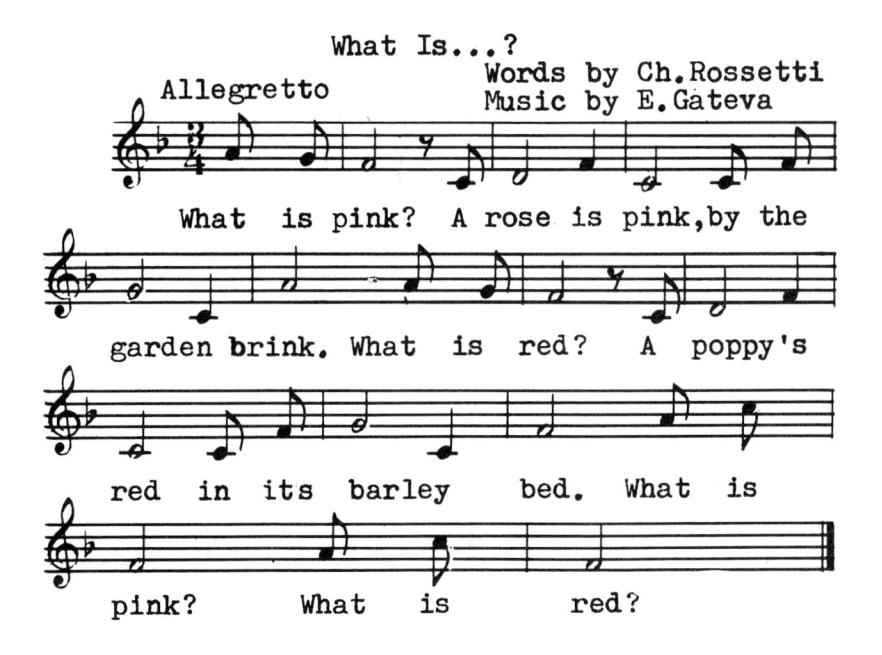

What Is...?

Words by Ch. Rossetti
Music by E. Gateva

Allegretto

What is pink? A rose is pink, by the garden brink. What is red? A poppy's red in its barley bed. What is pink? What is red?

What is . . .?

1. What is pink?
   A rose is pink
   By the fountain brink.

2. What is red?
   A poppy's red
   In its barley bed.

3. What is blue?
   The sky is blue
   Where the clouds float through.

4. What is yellow?
   Pears are yellow
   Rich and ripe and mellow.

Seventh Elaboration

Plan of the Lesson
Each lesson takes fifteen minutes in the hours of singing and drawing.
1. Beginning with a familiar song.
2. Consolidating the verb "to have" in all the persons, the mathematical operations, and the taught vocabulary using a story with a short plot (e.g., "Dog's Family"). The teacher tells a short story about a dog named Dog, and each child narrates a very short story concerning a pet animal.
3. Drawing at will in connection with the themes: "The Family," "The House," "The Garden," "Domestic Animals," specifying the vocabulary in English.
4. Ending the lesson with a song.

Eighth Elaboration

Plan of the Lesson
Each lesson takes fifteen minutes in the hours of manual training.
1. The song "What is Pink?": listening to it and singing aloud of the first and second couplet. The singing should also take place in the form of a dialogue between two groups or two individuals.
2. Working out a translation of the third couplet in Bulgarian. Studying the third couplet in English (with the melody). Linking it to the first and the second couplet. Singing should be performed in the form of a dialogue as well. The vocabulary is to be memorized.
3. Continuing the work with the colored drawing block: The picture after Rossetti's rhymes. The children cut a regular band of light blue paper: the "sky." The teacher draws clouds on the blackboard. The children copy them on the backside of a sheet of white, light blue, dark blue, or violet paper, then cut them out and carefully stick them on the sheet, representing the sky.
4. Consolidating the verbs "to be" and "to have," the numbers and the simple arithmetical operations (in between).
5. Ending with a song.

Ninth Elaboration

Plan of the Lesson
Fifteen minutes in the hour of singing.
1. Further studying the song "What is Pink?": Fifth couplet.
   (a) Translation and reading aloud.
   (b) Which is the highest tone in the melody? (The tone of the question "What?").
   (c) Which is the lowest tone? (The tone of the indefinite article: "*a* rose," "*a* poppy").
   (d) Is the melody over after having sung "What is pink? A rose . . ." And after having sung: "By the fountain brink" ("No"). How does the end of the song sound? (Quietly. As if there were a full stop.) Let us sing the end.

Tenth Elaboration

Plan of the Lesson
In the hours of drawing and singing.
1. The regular teacher has previously written on the blackboard the following (in Bulgarian):
   (a) My name is _____.
   (b) I want to be _____.
   (c) I live at _____.
   (d) I live with _____.
   (e) I have _____.
   (f) I like _____.
2. Singing aloud the song " What Is Your Name?"
3. Reading (in chorus) the text on the blackboard.
4. The teacher speaks about himself (herself) in English, adhering to the points 1–6 (i.e., filling the blanks orally). The whole narration should be both brief and captivating.

All children are activated in the course of several lessons, so that every child can make up a short autobiography (in English).

As a matter of course, the children doing best receive a slightly expanded treatment. All should remain, however, within the framework of the vocabulary and grammar, presented as the subject matter of the first global theme.

Eleventh Elaboration

Plan of the Lesson
Fifteen minutes in the hour of singing.
Bringing the work on the six questions to an end.

Twelfth Elaboration

Each lesson takes fifteen minutes in the hours of singing, drawing, and manual training.

Plan of the Lesson
1. Preparation for replaying the play. Choosing the actors and distributing the roles for Act One. The content is abridged and reduced to its essentials from the children's standpoint.
2. Act Two is performed by all the children. They are salesmen at the marketplace.
3. Inviting guests.
4. Preparing the children's drawings (in the colored drawing blocks) for the competition held in Act Two of the play.
5. Preparing props.

SECOND GLOBAL THEME

Preliminary Introduction

To the Second Performance for the Integrated Lessons in the First Grade of Suggestopedic Schools

Fifteen minutes in the hours of singing, drawing, and manual training.
1. The highlights of the lexical and grammatical matter in the play "Where are Horse and Dog?" are introduced in situations, differing from those in the play.
2. The children are mildly activated in that part of the vocabulary (of the play) which has not been illustrated during the performance itself.
3. Activation is needed for the prepositions, the adverbs of place and of time, the interrogative form with "do" (by analogy with the already

familiar form with "can"), the impersonal forms "there is," "there are" (with the respective negations), the verbs of the first frequency (cf. the Manual in Italian: grammar to Lesson One). All this subject matter should be extracted from the performances (One and Two).

4. Games of the kind "Where is...?" and so on can be adopted successfully.

Something is hidden from the children. In the process of seeking it, it is possible to activate in the foreign language prepositions and adverbs, question forms, qualitative adjectives, verbs of first frequency, etc.

E. GATEVA

Where are Horse and Dog?

(*Second Play*)

A suggestopedic play for the second lesson with deciphering for the integrated teaching of foreign languages in the first grade of the suggestopedic schools.

English translation: S. Petrunova
Under the methodological guidance of G. Lozanov, M.D., Med. Sci. D.

Scenario and staging plan for conducting the second suggestopedic lesson in English with first-graders, with use being made of intersubject relations in accordance with the global themes, namely:

Mathematics: Third global theme: Natural numbers up to 1,000; addition and subtraction of numbers up to 1,000; without carryovers.

Bulgarian (Native) Language: Reading easy texts (the ABC book for the first grade).

Homeland Knowledge: Social and natural environment. Foodstuffs and clothing. The winter.

Pictorial Arts: Graphic drawing. Molding of animals: a cat, a dog, a horse.

Manual Training: Working with natural materials. Making of New Year ornaments.

Singing: Development of a musical ear and of a metrorhythmical sense.

ENGLISH LANGUAGE:

Lexis: Parts of the human body.
Environment and what we do in it. The room.
Clothing.
Foodstuffs.
Grammar: Present continuous tense.
Imperative mood.
The negative form of "to have," "to do," and "to be."
The interrogative form of the verbs with "do."

The impersonal forms "there is," "there is not" in singular and plural.
The verb "must."
The basic prepositions.
The case forms of personal pronouns.
Some adverbs of time and place.
The adjective.

CHARACTERS

PAMELA (the American woman from the first play *Friends*)
A SAILOR, A SOLDIER, A MUSICIAN (it is possible to assign these three roles to a single performer)

Time: The present. Place: The classroom, during a lesson in singing, drawing, or manual training in the first school grade.

WHERE ARE HORSE AND DOG?

(Enter Pamela. She greets the children naturally in English with the song "Good Morning, Dear Children.')

PAMELA:
    Good morning, dear children!
(All start singing with her.)
    How are you?
    Do you remember me?
    You see,
    I can
    speak a little Bulgarian.
    I am Pamela,
    the American lady.
    I remained
    to live
    in your *country*.
    Bulgaria is a *beautiful* country.

> But *I* often *think*
> of my friends.
> They are in America.
> They are *merry*.
> Now *I'll tell you*
> something
> *about them*.
> *They can do*
> *strange* things.
> *Listen*!
> *Look*!

(A knock at the door. A man with tousled hair sticks his neck out. This is Jim, the sailor. He opens the door wide, smiling at Pamela and the children. He comes in and shakes hands soundly with Pamela and some of the children. Jim wears a sailor's T-shirt, blue-jeans, one of the legs being rolled up to the knee. His socks are red; his shoes are worn out. He wears a pirate's bandage, covering one of his eyes, which are both normal. The bandage keeps slipping down; he keeps taking it up, confused, lest the children be aware of its aimlessness.)

JIM:
> Hallo, children!
> I am Jim, *the sailor*.
> *I'm looking for* Pamela.
> I see *her* here,
> *with you*.
> *Who are you*?

PAMELA:
> Jim, they are my friends.
> Children, Jim lives near *the sea*.
> He has *a boat*.

(Out of his traveling bag, Jim produces a large toy boat.)

JIM:
> Pamela, here is my boat.

PAMELA:
> Children, his boat can *fly*.

JIM:
> Pamela, *where are*
> your *fat* cat
> and your *thin,*
> *sick* dog?
> *You know,*
> they are looking for you *too.*
> Oh, *here they are!*
> See them on the screen.

(Jim makes for the TV set. The latter is made of cardboard and its screen represents an empty space, where the cheerful animals appear. The animals are painted on masked cardboard sheets. Some parts of their bodies are missing, and Jim produced them out of his bag. These parts are painted on separate cardboard sheets. Jim puts them on the right place.)

PAMELA:
> Oh dear!
> Cat, where is your *head*?
> Dog, where is your *tail*?
> Horse, where are your *legs*?

JIM:
> Oh, *they've lost them*!
> *It's all right.* All right!
> I have . . .
> I have *some* heads,
> some tails and some legs.

(Jim fumbles in his bag and produces a cat's head with a hat. The head is too small for the cat's body. At this moment the bandage slips once and for all from his eye and Jim takes it away, winking joyfully at the children as if they were his accomplices.)

PAMELA:
> But, Jim, this head is very *small.*
> And my Cat has not *a hat.*

JIM:
> *Well*, this head is good, too.

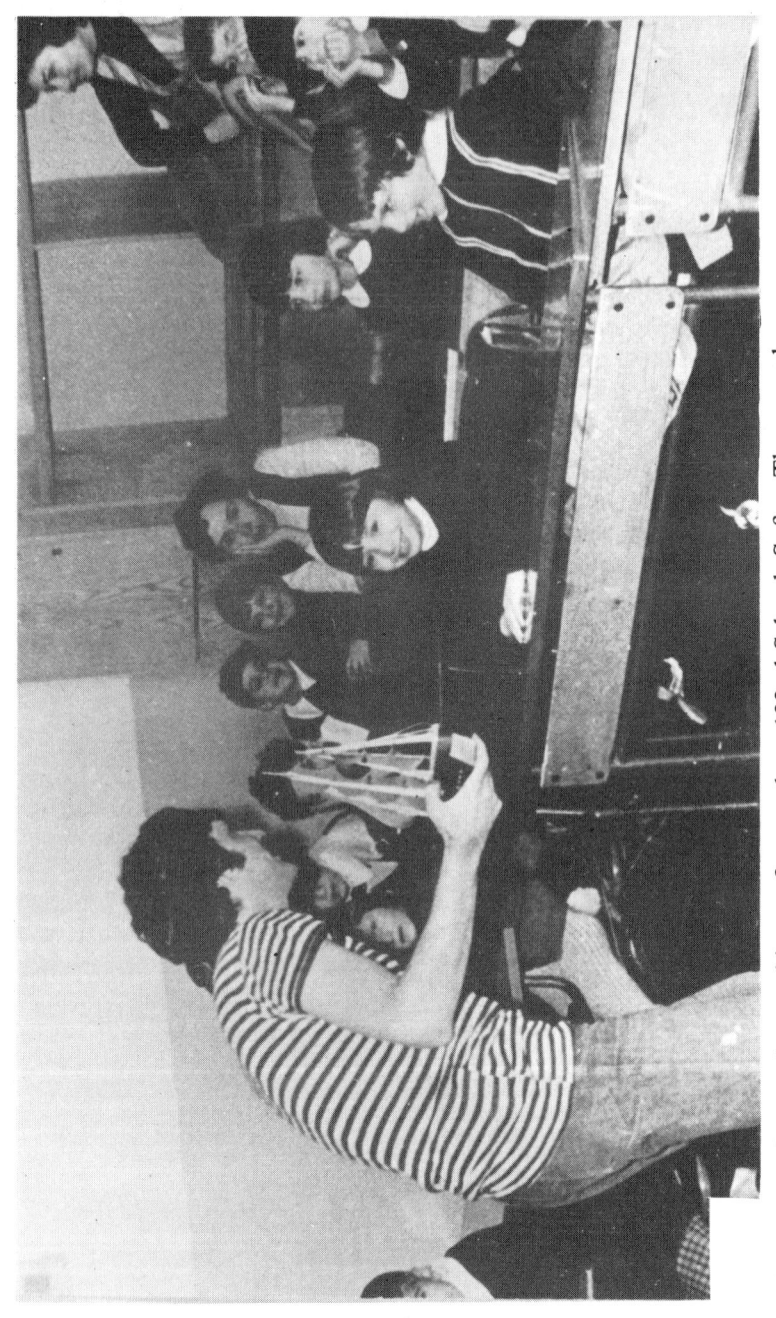

Figs. 28–29 - Integrative teaching to first-graders, 122nd School, Sofia. The second suggestopedic play "Where Are Horse and Dog?" (in English).

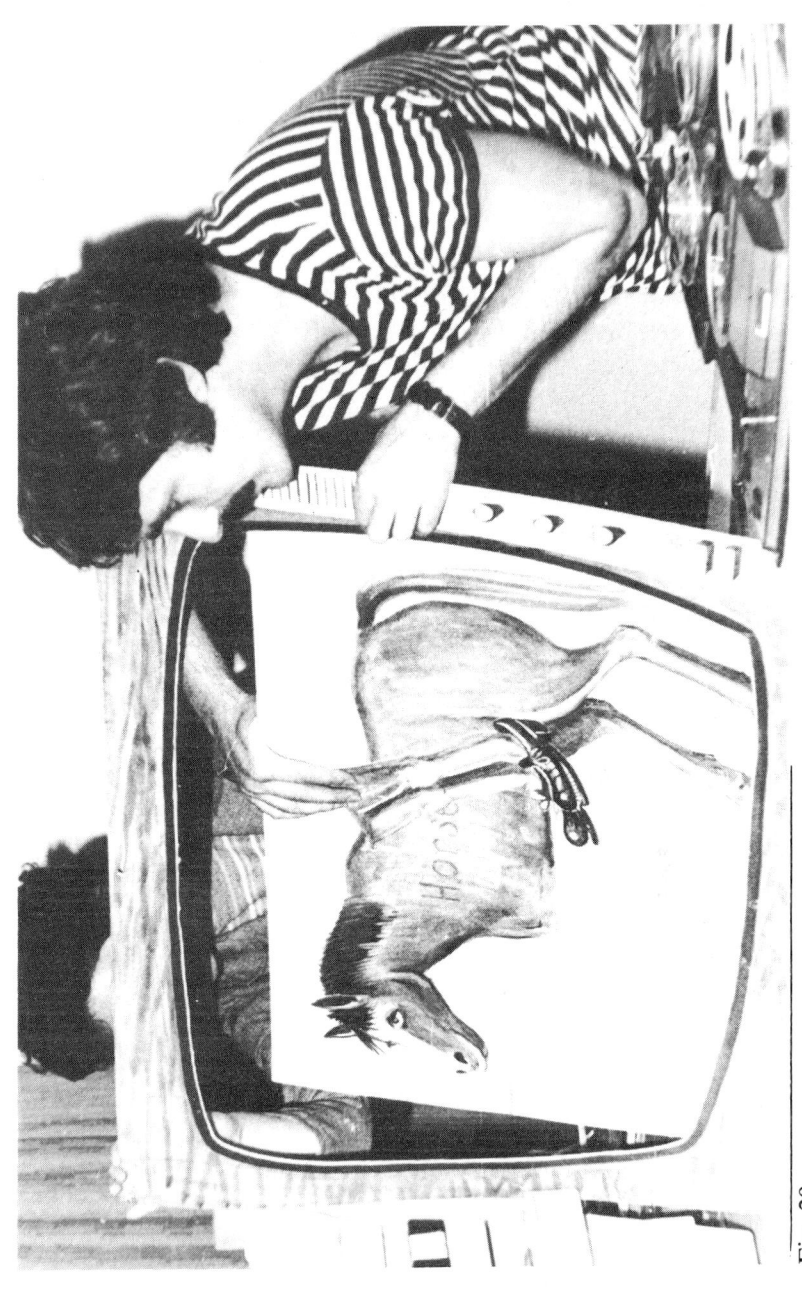

Fig. 29

(In the screen appears the horse without forelegs. Jim produces two forelegs in boots and puts them in place.)

PAMELA:
> But, Jim, Horse *has no boots*.
> Horse has *shoes*.
> Where are the shoes?
> Cat has boots.

(While Jim is fumbling in his bag, Pamela makes the round of the classroom, asking the children how they are shod. They display their boots and shoes. Some of them answer her questions.)

JIM:
> Pamela, look!

PAMELA:
> Oh, these shoes are *torn*!
> These shoes are *old*.

JIM:
> These shoes are very good.
> Here is the tail of Dog.

PAMELA:
> But, Jim,
> Dog has not a *long* tail.
> Dog has a *short* tail.
> This one is good.
> Jim, *put* the boots
> on Cat!
> But where is Cat?
> Are you *in the sock*, Cat?
> Are you *behind* the boot, Cat?
> Are you *under* the hat, Cat?

(Pamela takes out everything from Jim's bag: a sock, a boot, a hat. She looks for the cat. The children join in. Meanwhile, Jim disappears.)

> But where is Jim?
> Are you *far away*, Jim?
> Are you *near by*, Jim?
> Jim, where are you?

[The song "Summer" (seasons from the Appendix) is heard (tape-recorded). Pamela translates here and there into Bulgarian, with an accent, the most interesting moments of the song. Meanwhile, the male performer has changed clothes and is ready to reappear as a Soldier.]

>Little boy blue, where are you?
>come, blow your horn,
>the sheep in the meadow,
>the cows in the corn.
>Where is the boy,
>Who tends to the sheep?
>He's under the haystack
>fast asleep.
>Little boy blue.

PAMELA:
Children, Jim *is sleeping!*
Look! Look!
The brave soldier is coming.
He is opening the door.
He is coming in.

(Enter the Soldier. He wears a soldier's beret, a tunic, boots. His gestures are cowardly. Everything he makes is very slow. He is looking for something. His eyes are frightened. Pamela names everyone of his moves in a slow, and clear-cut manner.)

He is closing the door.
He is sitting down.
He is thinking.
He is going to the window.
He is looking for something.
He wants to open the *window.*
The milk is under the window.
Soldier, *don't open* the window!
Here is Cat!

(The Soldier hastily opens the window. The Cat is at the windowsill. She falls down. But there is also a large stick of chocolate at the windowsill. The Soldier grabs it and runs away.)

You see,
Cat is in the milk!

(Pamela lifts a white plastic bucket, where the toy cat has fallen.)

Cat likes *to drink*
milk,
milk with *chocolate*.
We are hungry, too.
Let us go to the house
of my friend
the Musician.
There are many things
to eat here: salami, sandwiches,
soup,
roast chicken,
tasty bread.
Butter, cheese, sugar,
tea.

(While the Soldier is changing clothes, the performance leader or a teacher sets up the scenery for the Musician's house. This consists of:

(1) A panel, with a piano painted on it. The Musician's bed is near the pedals of the piano. Pillows and blankets are topsy-turvy. On the top of the piano there are various foodstuffs, labeled—in English—butter, cheese, sugar, tea. A loaf of bread in a net hangs at the side of the piano. The floor around the "bed" is interspersed with: a soup tureen, sandwiches, cups.

(2) Another panel has an electric cooker painted on it. The door of the cooker can be opened (it is made of a second piece of cardboard). In the empty space behind that door there is a telephone and some bottles of juice.

(3) A third panel has the bathroom painted on it: a bath tub and a shower. There is a smoked leg of ham in the bath-tub.

(4) On the wall hangs a toy diningroom.

Pamela makes use of the pause to activate the themes: "What meal do you like most?," "The room," "How much does it cost?" (foodstuffs, furniture)—all in connection with the mathematical theme. The activation is rapid and short.

Enter the Musician, making stormy conductor's gestures. He sits down on the floor, writes something on music paper, hums, tears the paper to pieces, and throws them off, displeased. Then he begins to write again. He is blind and deaf to everything around. He wears a dark jacket, partly unbuttoned, under which a waistcoat is seen. He has tied a gaily-colored shawl around his neck, but there is no shirt under his waistcoat. His headdress consists of a battered-in, old, collapsible, hat, which he keeps putting on and taking off nervously. During all this time the songs "Riddle" and "Snowflakes" (or some other from "Seasons") are heard very remotely. The songs are either tape-recorded or sung by the performance leader with an accompaniment that suits the circumstances.

All of a sudden the Musician catches sight of Pamela and the children. He looks at them, surprised. Then he kisses Pamela's hand.)

THE MUSICIAN:
Come in,
come in!
Sit down, please!
Oh, yes, sit down,
sit down *on the floor*!

(He quickly takes off his jacket, inviting Pamela to sit on it, but Pamela seems surprised at his not wearing a shirt. The Musician feels ashamed; he puts the jacket on in a hurry, inside out. In order to provide Pamela with something to sit on, he takes off his hat and offers it to her. Pamela hesitates for a while, then sits down on the floor, over the hat.)

Yes, I have no *chairs.*
I have no *bed.*
I sleep under the piano.
Excuse me, please!
My telephone *is ringing.*
But where is my telephone?
Oh, yes, my telephone is in *the cooker.*

(He opens the door of the cooker and takes out the telephone.)

Hallo, hallo, . . . , *nobody*!
Pamela, do you want a drink?
A juice?
The juice is in the cooker, too.
Help yourself!

(The Musician passes the bottle to Pamela. She realizes that the bottle is empty and makes a gesture of despair.)

PAMELA:
   Oh, this Musician!

THE MUSICIAN:
   Pamela, are you hungry?
   The roast meat is in *the bathroom.*

PAMELA:
   In the bathroom?

THE MUSICIAN:
   Oh yes.
   And *the bread*?
   Where is the bread?
   Here it is, Pamela,
   a piece of bread.

(He produces a piece of bread out of the pocket of his jacket. Pamela takes it and realizes that it is stone-hard.)

   Oh, yes, the bread is
   in the shopping bag.
   And the milk is in *the clock.*
   The cat and the *mouse* are
   in the clock too.

(He takes the cat and the mouse out of the clock—or from behind the clock—and hands them to Pamela. She embraces the cat, and throws the toy mouse on the floor.)

   What is the time?
   It is . . .
   Pamela, children,
   listen to my songs!
   Do you like them?

(He gives the music sheets with the songs "Riddle" and "Snowflakes" to Pamela. She turns to the performance leader, and they both begin to study the songs in quite a comical fashion. But they end by loving the songs. Their singing engages the children too. Everybody sings. Three little girls, in "snowflake" garments, made in advance, perform a dance–pantomime to the tune of the song "Snowflakes," (or some other from "Seasons") while the rest of the children are singing. Suddenly, the Musician takes a look at the clock. Something comes to his mind.)

But, children, where are
Horse and Dog
Let us look for them!
Let us look for them!

(He begins to search, in the children's schoolbags, under the desks, then takes Pamela's hand and both of them leave.)

Good bye!

Riddle

Allegretto

Music by E. Gateva

26.

1. We are the twelve little men,
who make the year go,
Starting over again,
we are the little men.

2. Do you remember them?
Making sunshine and snow.
We are the twelve little men
Who make the year go. (12 months)

Snowflakes

Lightly

Snowflakes fall on trees and walk. Snowflakes fall as white as chalk. Snowflakes fall into my hand. Snowflakes brighten up our land.

Notes to the Elaborations of the Second Global Theme "Where Are Horse and Dog?" for the Globalized Lessons in the First Grade of the Suggestopedic Schools

1. The elaborations, which follow the second play, are analogous to those of the first play. That is why the foreign language teachers should prepare a plan of the lesson prior to each hour. This plan should contain several items and should be in written form. Providing all the props, needed for the lesson—tapes, records, and so on—is also part of the teachers' duties.

2. The preparation for a New Year's gala day in the hours of singing, drawing, and manual training should be made the best use of in order to consolidate the basic lexico-grammatical units from both plays, completed with units from the New Year's and winter themes.

3. Particular attention should be paid to consolidating the verbs of first frequency, the specificity of asking questions in English, the affirmative and negative answer, the present continuous tense, and the most important prepositions and adverbs. There is the possibility of obtaining successful elaborations in connection with the question "What are we doing for the gala day?," with the songs "Riddle," "Snowflakes," and other tape-recorded songs, as well as by means of other materials, judged to be suitable for the children.

4. Small cards with words in the foreign language written on them should be placed appropriately in the classroom. Thus, the words can be assimilated peripherally by the children. For instance, such cards could be hung on the neck of the poodle, the cat, the doll, the teddybear. On the cardboard poster of foodstuffs could be seen the captions: butter, tea, sugar, etc.

Small round pieces of cardboard should be made, bearing English names for the children, all phonetical particularities being included and marked with different colors. The children should choose English names, under which they will participate in various games. Gradually, the games will proceed into reading.

5. The opportunity to make the best use of the other school subjects should always be kept in mind. This should be done in accordance with the Program for the Suggestopedic Schools and with the instructions, given in the staging plans, where the headlines of the global themes are listed (in mathematics, the Bulgarian language, homeland knowledge, manual training, drawing, and singing).

6. The plan of the lesson should be brought into line with the regular teachers of the class, in order to obtain a satisfactory synchronization.

7. Until the end of the schoolyear the elaborations in the English language, performed solely on the basis of songs, verses, and games should include both the past simple and the future tenses. Examples should be found in the songs and poems thereafter (see the Appendix), as well as in other suitable materials.

8. The basic suggestopedic requirements should always be kept in mind:

(a) Strictly avoid giving theoretical (grammatical) explanations and definitions to small children; use should be made of imitation, translation, analogies.

(b) Strictly avoid tedious and senseless iterations; search and find the natural variability by means of games and absorbing plots.

(c) If the moment has come to proceed to a new section of the subject matter, strictly avoid aiming at an absolute mastering of the old one.

Suggestopedic Integrative Teaching of the Russian Language to First-Graders

Scenario, staging plan, and intersubject relations, based on *Doctor Aybolit* (K. Tchoukovski)—E. Gateva.

Linguistic adaptation: R. Vracheva
Under the methodological guidance of G. Lozanov, M.D., Med. Sci. D.

DOCTOR AYBOLIT

(After K. Tchoukovski)

CHARACTERS

THE NARRATOR
DOCTOR AYBOLIT
BARBARA, his sister
A MONKEY OWNER
A SINGER
VOICES, from backstage
   (1) A HORSE, A DOG, A CROCODILE (male voice);
   (2) A MONKEY and A BUTTERFLY (female voice).

Place: the classroom.

Картина 1, ДОКТОР И ЕГО ЗВЕРИ   (Act 1: Doctor and His Animals)

(Doctor Aybolit's quarters: a table and a chair. On the table: a candlestick, some books—Сказки, жизнь животных, лесная газета, etc. A chest of drawers with some medicines on it—йол, рыбий жир, мазь, мел, etc. Animals (toys) everywhere. A painted scenery: intermingled pine twigs and a name plate "Доктор Айболит".

The doctor is writing at the table. He is in no hurry. He wears a white overall and a gay-colored shawl around his neck. He is surrounded by animals (toys). A couple of living parrots in a cage.

THE NARRATOR (a woman in national Russian dress) opens K. Tchoukovski's book and begins reading the story of Dr. Aybolit. She swiftly translates the underlined words in all the characters' parts.)

THE NARRATOR:

Живет на свете доктор добрый.	There lives in the world a good-natured doctor.
Зовут его Айболит.	His name is Aybolit.
У него есть злая сестра.	He has a wicked sister.
Сестру зовут Варвара.	Her name is Barbara.
А меня зовут Оля.	And my name is Olja.
А тебя как зовут?	And what is your name?

(She addresses the children.)

Больше всего на свете доктор любит зверей.	Best in the world the doctor loves animals.
Я тоже люблю зверей.	I love animals too.
А ты любишь зверей?	Do you love animals?

(She asks some of the children which animals they love.)

Вы видите:	You can see:
в комнате у него живут зайцы.	in his room live rabbits.
В шкафу у него живет белка.	In his cupboard lives a squirrel.
На диване живет колючий еж.	On the sofa lives a thorny hedgehog.
Но из всех своих зверей доктор Айболит любит больше всего утку Кику,	But from all his animals Doctor Aybolit loves best the duck Cicka,
собаку Авву,	the dog Avva,
маленькую свинку Хрю-Хрю,	the little guinea-pig Hru-Hru,
попугая Карудо и сову Бумбу.	the parrot Carudo, and the screech owl Bumba.

(While the Narrator points at Dr. Aybolit's pet animals, he examines them with his stethoscope, checks their teeth with a dentist's mirror, and examines their throats, ears, and eyes.

Meanwhile, Barbara keeps going in and out, making dusty clouds with her broom. She wears several colored necklaces. She looks disheveled and irritated. When she is scolding the Doctor and the animals, a pair of huge blue earrings shake in her ears and the many bracelets on her arms make a ringing sound.)

BARBARA:
(Addressing the children.)

А я Варвара - сестра доктора.	And I am Barbara, the doctor's sister.
У тебя есть сестра, есть брат?	Do you have a sister, do you have a brother?
Я не люблю зверей!	I don't love animals!

(She is very polite when speaking to the children, then brusquely turns angry and jumps upon the animals.)

Прогони их сию же минуту.	Kick them out immediately.
Они только мешают.	They only stand in my way.
Не желаю жить	I don't want to live
с этими	with these
зверями и птицами!	animals and birds!

THE DOCTOR:

Нет, Варвара, они не плохие!	No, Barbara, they are not bad!
Я очень рад,	I am very glad,
что они живут у меня.	that they live with me.

(The Doctor pushes Barbara away to the door, as if casually.)

THE NARRATOR:

Со всех сторон	From all parts the ill come to the doctor to be cured
к доктору приходят лечиться больные.	
И каждый сразу становится здоров.	And everyone gets well immediately
Если какой-нибудь мальчишка	If a boy
ушибет себе руку	hurts his hand
или нос,	or nose,
он сейчас же бежит	he runs right away
к Айболиту - и, смотришь,	to Aybolit—and, you see,
через десят минут	after ten minutes
он уже здоровый, веселый,	he is already healthy, cheerful,
играет в прятки	playing hide-and-seek with
с попугаем Карудо,	the parrot Carudo,
а сова Бумбу угощает его	and the screech-owl Bumba treats
конфетами и яблоками.	him to sweets and apples.

(She goes to some child of the class, who has been hurt and hands him or her an apple or a candy.)

| Однажды к доктору приходит... | Once to the doctor comes... |

(Enter Barbara who throws in a "sick horse.")

THE VOICE OF THE HORSE:
| Лама, воной, фифи, куку! | lama, vono, fifi, cucu! |

THE DOCTOR:
(Addressing the children, with a funny wink:)

Да, да. Она сказала:	Yes, yes. She said:
У меня болят глаза.	My eyes hurt me.
Дайте мне, пожалуйста,	Give me please
очки.	a pair of spectacles.

THE VOICE OF THE HORSE:
| Капуки, кануки! | Capuci, canuci! |

THE DOCTOR:
| Она сказала: | She said: |
| Садитесь, пожалуйста! | Sit down, please! |

(He puts a pair of spectacles on the horse.)

THE VOICE OF THE HORSE:
| Чака! | Chaca! |

THE DOCTOR:
(Addressing the children:)
| Это значит: Спасибо! | This means: Thank you! |

THE NARRATOR:
Скоро все звери,	Soon, all the animals,
у которых плохие глаза,	who feel badly in the eyes,
получают от доктора Айболита	receive from doctor Aybolit
очки.	a pair of spectacles.
И коровы - в очках,	The cow has spectacles,
и кошки и собаки - в очках.	and the cat and the dog have spectacles.
Даже старые вороны	Even the old crows
не вылетают из гнезда	don't fly off their nests
без очков.	without spectacles.

Figs. 30–31 - Integrative teaching to first-graders, 122nd School, Sofia. The first suggestopedic play "Doctor Aybolit" (in Russian).

(The Narrator points at the animals with spectacles, painted on cardboard. Enter Barbara. She angrily carries some animals inside and throws them at the Doctor's feet. The Doctor wags his finger at nasty Barbara and gives the newcomers a pat.)

BARBARA:

| Всех лечишь, | You cure all, |
| но денег не берешь! | but don't take money! |

THE DOCTOR:

| Но какие же <u>деньги</u> | What kind of <u>money</u> |
| у черепах и орлов! | with tortoises and eagles! |

(The Doctor hangs up a notice. He reads it aloud slowly and the children follow him. A song with the words of the notice is heard at once. Everybody sing.)

A SINGER:

Открыта больница	A hospital is opened
Для птиц и зверей.	for animals and birds.
Идите лечиться	Go to be cured
<u>Туда</u> поскорей!	<u>There</u> quickly!

Картина 2: ОВЕЗЬЯНА ЧИЧИ   (Act 2: The Monkey Chi-chi)

THE NARRATOR:

Наступает ночь. Все звери спят. Night falls. All the animals are sleeping.

(Doctor Aybolit lights the candle. He gently strokes each animal to wish it "Good night." The Russian folk-song "Ах ты, ноченька" is heard. A ballerina in classical tutu dances in tune.)

A SINGER:

Ах ты, ноченька,	Eh, you sweet night,
ночка темная,	dark night,
ночка темная,	dark night,
ночь осенняя.	autumn night.

Али нет у тебя ясна месяца, Али нет у тебя Ярких звездочек?	I wonder if you really don't have a clear moon, if you really don't have bright stars?

(Everybody sings the first couplet.)

THE NARRATOR:

И вдруг...	And suddenly ...

(The song suddenly stops. An anxious knock at the door.)

THE DOCTOR:
(Addressing the children:)

Кто там?	Who is there?

(He urges the children to ask in their turn "Кто там?")

THE VOICE OF THE MONKEY:

Это я.	It is me.

(The Doctor picks up a child and they both open the door. They fetch inside a monkey. The monkey's neck is bandaged.)

THE DOCTOR:

Что у тебя болит?	What ails you?

THE VOICE OF THE MONKEY:
(Plaintively:)

Шея. Я убежала от злого хозяина. Хозяин злой человек. Он бьет меня. Он мучит меня.	It's my neck. I escaped from a wicked master. The master is a wicked man. He beats me. He tortures me.

(The Doctor unrolls the bandage. There is a leather strap at the neck of the monkey.)

THE DOCTOR:

Живи у меня, обезьяна. Я не хочу, чтобы тебя обижали. Кушай, Чичи! Ах, какая ты милая, хорошая!	Live with me, monkey. I don't want, so that you are offended. Eat, Chi-chi! Ah, how sweet and good you are!

Fig. 31

(The Doctor offers some nuts to the monkey. At that moment a loud knock at the door is produced.)

The Monkey Owner:
Отдай мне обезьяну! Give me the monkey, back!
Эта обезьяна моя! This monkey is mine!

The Doctor:
Не отдам! I won't give it back!
Ни за что не отдам! I won't give it back on any terms!
Я не хочу, I don't want,
чтобы ты мучил <u>ее</u>. for you to torment <u>her</u>.

(The churl makes efforts to grab Dr. Aybolit's neck. The Doctor speaks to him in a calm voice.)

Убирайся сию же минуту! Get out of here, right away!
А если <u>ты будешь драться</u>, And if <u>you want to have a fight</u>,
я позову собаку Авву, I will call the dog Avva,
и она искусает тебя. and she will bite you all over.

(The dog's snarl is heard from backstage.)

ДОКТОР АЙВОЛИТ ЗА РАВОТОЙ (Act 3: Doctor Aybolit Works)

The Narrator:
Каждый день к доктору Айболиту Every day to Doctor Aybolit
приходят звери лечиться. come animals to be cured.
У кого болит <u>живот</u>, Some have a <u>stomach</u> ache,
у кого зуб. some a toothache.
Однажды пришла к Айболиту One day to Aybolit came
<u>бесхвостая лисица</u>. a tailless fox.
Доктор пришил ей <u>хвост</u>. The Doctor stitched a tail
 to the fox.

(Addressing the children:)

А у тебя есть лисица? Do you have a fox?
А у тебя есть Миша? Do you have a Teddy-bear?
А заяц? what about, rabbit?

(She shows the children the tailless fox. The Doctor "stitches" the tail.)

А потом из далекого <u>леса</u> пришла <u>медведица</u>. Она жалобно стонала. У нее болела лапа. Доктор промыл рану и смазал ее своей чудесной мазью.	And after that from a remote forest came a <u>she-bear</u>. She was groaning plaintively. Her paw hurt. The Doctor bathed the wound and he smeared it with his wonderful ointment.

(The Narrator displays the Teddy-bear with the sore pad. The Doctor takes the bowl with the ointment and smears some of it over the pad.)

Потом пришел больной заяц и так далее. Давайте посмотрим сколько животны пришли.	After that came an ill rabbit, and so on. Let's <u>see</u> how <u>many</u> animals came.

(The Narrator writes on the blackboard the numbers from 1 to 10, associating them with the names of animals. She goes on counting tens and hundreds, up to 1,000. Another knock at the door.)

THE DOCTOR:

Come in!

(He walks to the door and picks something up from the floor. This is a multi-colored butterfly.)

THE VOICE OF THE BUTTERFLY:

Я на <u>свечке</u> себе крылышко <u>обжег</u>. Помогите мне, помогите мне, Айболит. Мое раненое крылышко болит!	I <u>singed</u> my winglet on the candle. Help me, help me, Aybolit! My wounded winglet hurts!

[The Doctor lifts the butterfly (made of paper), woefully observes it for a couple of seconds in the palm of his hand, then he smiles and begins to sing.]

THE DOCTOR:

Не печалься, <u>мотылек</u>! Ты ложися на <u>бочок</u>: Я пришью тебе другое, Шелковое, голубое, Новое, Хорошее Крылышко!	Don't be sad little <u>butterfly</u>! You lay on your <u>flank</u>: I will stitch to you another, <u>silken</u>, blue, New, Better, Winglet!

(The Doctor opens a box, containing various colored pieces of cloth: green, red, yellow, and so on. He ends by finding the previously prepared wing; bright blue with red dots. While searching, he has named the different colors. The Doctor sticks the wing up and hangs the butterfly on the wall.)

"Ладно, ладно, веселись, Только свечки берегись!"

O.K., O.K., be gay, only from candles keep away!

(Doctor Aybolit blows the candle out.)

Картин 4. КРОКОДИЛ (Act 4: The Crocodile.)

(The Doctor is yawning. Part of the song "Ах, ты, ноченька" sounds again from backstage. A new knock at the door. Immediately the song dies away. The Doctor opens the door and fetches inside a crocodile.)

THE DOCTOR:

Бедный крокодил!
У него заболели зубы.

My poor crocodile!
He has a toothache.

(He examines the crocodile's teeth. Then he gives him some medicine.)

Пей, это чудесное лекарство.
Ты уже здоров.
Правда?
Он уже здоров.

Sing, this is a wonderful medicine.
You are well, already.
Is it true?
He is well, already.

THE VOICE OF THE CROCODILE:

Как у вас хорошо!
Сколько у вас зайчиков,
птичек, мышей!
И все они такие жирные,
вкусные!
Позвольте мне остаться
у вас навсегда.
Я живу в цирке.
Но я не хочу возаращаться
к хозяину цирка.
Он плохо кормит меня,
бьет, обижает.

How well it is here!
How many rabbits,
birds, and mice you have!
And all of them are so fat,
delicious!
Let me stay
with you forever.
I live in the circus.
But I don't want to go back,
to the circus's owner.
He feeds me badly,
beats me and offends me.

223

THE DOCTOR:

Оставайся! Пожалуйста!	You can stay! Please!
Только чур:	Only, be careful:
если ты съешь хоть одного зайчишку,	if you eat up even one rabbit,
хоть одного воробья,	even one sparrow,
я прогоню тебя вон.	I will kick you out of here.

THE VOICE OF THE CROCODILE:

Ладно.	O.K.
Обещаю вам, доктор:	I promise you, doctor:
Не буду есть ни зайцев,	I will not eat neither rabbits,
ни птиц.	nor birds.

(The Doctor places the crocodile under the table. Enter Barbara, screaming.)

BARBARA:

Видеть его не желаю!	I don't want to see him!
Он такой противный,	He is so repulsive,
зубастый.	large-toothed.
Пусть живет далеко,	Let him live far away,
в жаркой Африке.	in the great heats of Africa.
Почему он с нами?	Why is he with us?
Он все портит.	He spoils everything.
Вчера съел	Yesterday he ate up
мою зеленую юбку.	my green skirt.
Она лежала у меня	It was by my side
на окошке.	on the little window.

(She furiously brandishes a torn skirt.)

THE DOCTOR:

И хорошо сделал.	And he did well.
Платье надо прятать в шкаф,	The clothes must be kept in the cupboard,
а не бросать на окошко.	and not thrown on the little window.

(He picks up the skirt and some other garment and puts them into the chest.)

BARBARA:

Из-за этого противного Крокодила многие люди боятся приходить к нам.	Because of that repugnant Crocodile many people are afraid to come to us.
Приходят одни бедняки, а ты не берешь у них денег,	Here come only poor people, and you don't take money from them,
и мы теперь так обеднели, что мы не сможем купить себе хлеба.	and we now became so poor, that we can't buy bread.

(The Doctor inserts phrases into Barbara's speech, which she repeats without being aware. He knows her rebukes by heart.)

Не нужно мне денег.	I don't need money.
Мне и без денег отлично.	I feel perfectly without it.
Звери накормят и меня и тебя.	The animals will feed me and you.

(The Doctor fumbles in his pockets in search of some money. He turns them inside out, searches on the table, under the books, but finds nothing. Then he begins singing a merry song and dancing around his angry sister Barbara. The ballerina, in Russian national dress, dances to the sounds of the following song.)

THE SINGER:

Во поле береза стояла, Во поле кудрявая стояла, Люли, люли, стояла.	There was a birch in the field it was tufty and branchy, Luli, luli, there it was.
Как пойду я в лес, погуляю, Белую березу заломаю, Люли, люли, заломаю.	When I go in the woods, for a walk the white birch I'll be snapping, Luli, luli, I'll be snapping.
Вот тебе башмачки, обуйся, Вот тебе кафтанчик, оденься. Люли, люли, оденься.	Here are shoes for you, put them on, Here is a caftan for you, put it on. Luli, luli, put it on.

(The ballerina presents Barbara with gaily colored puppy's slippers and with a sleeveless jacket. Barbara is pleased. She displays her acquisitions to the children. The Doctor, the Narrator, and Barbara take the hands of some children, dance and sing the song "Во поле береза стояла". Suddenly is heard another knock at the door. Everybody asks "Кто там?". The Doctor opens the door. Nobody there.)

THE DOCTOR:

Я должен искать за дверью.	I must search for the door.
Мы снова встретимся.	We will meet again.
До свидания, ребята.	Goodbye, children.

КРАЙ   The End

Due canzoni dello spettacolo
"Dottor Aibolit"

Parole: K. Ciukovski
Musica: E. Gateva

Allegro

Открыта больница для птиц и зверей. Идите лечиться туда поскорей. Открыта больница для птиц и зверей. Идите лечиться туда поскорей.

Не печалься, мотылёк!
Ты ложися на бочок!
Я пришью тебе другое,
шелковое, голубое,
новое, хорошее крылышко!

Ах ты, ноченька
Canzone popolare russa

Moderato

Ах ты, но-чень-ка,
ноч-ка тем-на-я,
ноч-ка тем-на-я,
да ночь о-сен-ня-я,
ноч-ка тем-на-я,
ночь о-сен-ня-я.

Во поле береза стояла

Allegretto 　　　　　　　　Canzone popolare russa

Во по-ле бе-ре-за сто-я-ла,
во по-ле ку-дря-ва-я сто-я-ла,
лю-ли, лю-ли сто-я-ла,
лю-ли, лю-ли сто-я-ла.

GRADUAL TEACHING FROM THE SECOND YEAR ON

The teachers who work with schoolchildren from the second grade on should have a thorough knowledge of the theoretical requirements and the recommended practice, the extensive treatment of which has been the subject of the first part of the present Manual (Part 1: Suggestopedic Foreign Language Courses for Adults). They must also abide by the textbooks in the gradual teaching of schoolchildren, published under our supervision.

The Methodological Instructions for the suggestopedic teaching of foreign languages to schoolchildren, adduced below, are a supplement to the basic Instructions for the teaching to adults and are intended to facilitate the teacher's everyday work.

A list of the musical compositions selected for the purposes of suggestopedic sessions with schoolchildren is also adduced.

METHODOLOGICAL INSTRUCTIONS

For the Teaching of Foreign Languages in the Suggestopedic Intensive Courses with Schoolchildren (a Supplement to the Instructions for the Teaching to Adults)

The methodological instructions for the suggestopedic teaching of foreign languages to schoolchildren (first-graders not included) are a transformation of the methodological instructions for the suggestopedic teaching for foreign languages to adults, in view of the age-related specificities of the pupils. The subject matter, curricula, and programs are respectively modified, in conformity with the methodological requirements and the age-related specifics. The present document indicates the most important modifications that are to be taken into consideration when referring to the different sections.

I. Introduction

1. The children's *names* remain the same, the teacher modifying them slightly to make them sound properly in the respective foreign language.

2. Each child chooses a (future) *occupation*, according with his or her will. As the course progresses, occupations may change.

(*Note*: The introduction into the first lesson *takes about 10 to 15 minutes*, and of the next lessons *7 to 8 minutes*.)

II. Active Concert Session

The teacher reads aloud the first globalized lesson against the background of the first part (or the first two parts) of the musical composition.

(*Note*: The children are given the textbook from the very first hour and follow the text in the foreign language, as well as the translation in the mother tongue. The tempo of the reading is controlled to conform to the children's capacities for following both sides of the pages without strain. The teacher does not read aloud the translation. Generally speaking, the teacher tends to minimize the translation from the very first encounter.)

III. Pseudopassive Concert Session

The teacher reads aloud the text in the foreign language against the background of the remaining part(s) of the same musical composition. *The children draw.* The subject of the drawing is chosen by the child. The drawings will be made use of in the hours of the elaborations. By the end of the intensive course the drawings are presented for a competition and an exhibition. The work on a half-finished drawing may be resumed in the next lessons.

(*Note*: FOR THE MANNER OF READING AND ITS CHARACTERISTICS, PLEASE REFER TO THE INSTRUCTIONS FOR THE TEACHING TO ADULTS.)

IV. Elaborations

The elaborations are carried out on the analogy of the elaborations with adult learners, making use of a wide choice of children's games, songs, plays, tales, toys, etc.

(*Note*: In the course of events the children are distributed into groups, thus allowing the activation of every one of them in the different hours.)

THE SPONTANEOUS ACTIVATION OF THE CHILDREN IS A MOMENT OF PARAMOUNT IMPORTANCE AND IS ENCOURAGED BY ALL POSSIBLE MEANS.

(*Note*: From mid-course on, writing is also included, and the part allowed to it in class gradually increases in higher grades.)

V. Input and Output Levels

Input and output levels are taken on the analogy of the courses for adult learners (and the teaching to first-graders), the tests being respectively modified to conform with the age-related characteristics of the pupils, the subject matter, and the program.

1. Oral test: questions to be answered; a short story in the foreign language.
2. Reading a text of suitable complexity.
3. Translation from the foreign into the native language of a story with a certain degree of learning.

1. THE PRESENT INSTRUCTIONS ARE INSEPARABLY LINKED WITH THEIR COUNTERPART FOR ADULT LEARNERS.
2. EACH TEACHER MUST PREPARE AN INDIVIDUAL PLAN–SYNOPSIS ON THE ELABORATION OF EACH GLOBALIZED LESSON, ON THE BASIS OF THE PRESENT INSTRUCTIONS. HE OR SHE MUST ALSO PROVIDE ALL THE ADDITIONAL VISUAL AIDS THAT ARE NEEDED FOR THE LESSONS FROM THE FUNDS OF THE INSTITUTE.

MUSICAL PROGRAM DESIGNED FOR LESSONS IN FOREIGN LANGUAGES IN SUGGESTOPEDIC SCHOOLS

A. *Vivaldi*
    1. The Four Seasons
G. F. *Händel*
    2. Wassermusik
L. *Mozart*
    3. Divertimento (Peasant's Wedding)
       Kindersymphonie
       Musikalische Schlittenfahrt
J. *Haydn*
    4. Symphony No. 82 in C Major "L'ours"
    5. Symphony No. 101 in D Major "L'Horloge"
W. A. *Mozart*
    6. Concerto for Violin and Orchestra No. 5 in A Major
    7. Eine kleine Nachtmusik
    8. Concerto for Piano and Orchestra in F Major
L. *von Beethoven*
    9. Romances for Violin and Orchestra in G Major
    10. Concerto for Piano and Orchestra No. 1 in C Major
P. I. *Tchaikovsky*
    11. Concert for Violin and Orchestra in D Major
    12. The Four Seasons: 12 Pieces for Piano

APPENDIX

Model Songs for the Suggestopedic Teaching and Learning Process

SEASONS - Music by E. Gateva

1. Winter

Allegretto

It's snowing it's snowing, it's snowing.

What a lot of snow!

Let us make some snowballs.

We all like to throw. It's

snowing, it's snowing, it's snowing.

Let us sledge and ski!

When I'm dashing downhill

Clear the way for me!

Allegro

Down came the snowflakes one winter's day.
I made a snow man when I went to play.
Out came the sunshine, dancing and gay;
But shy Mister Snow man ran softly away.

2. Spring

Allegro

I heard a cuckoo gaily sing, in springtime, in springtime. I heard a cuckoo gaily sing, and this is what he sang: "Cuckoo, cuckoo, cuckoo!"

I saw him singing as he flew
In springtime, in springtime.
I saw him singing as he flew,
And this is what he sang:
"Cuckoo, cuckoo!
Cuckoo, cuckoo!"

I heard his song from far away,
In springtime, in springtime.
I heard his song from far away,
And this is what he sang:
"Cuckoo, cuckoo!
Cuckoo, cuckoo, cuckoo!"

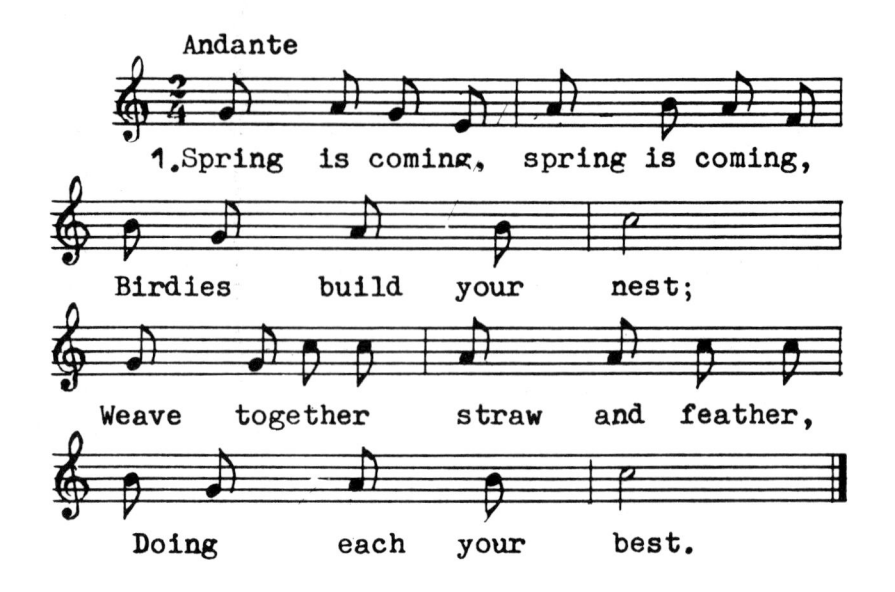

1. Spring is coming, spring is coming,
Birdies build your nest;
Weave together straw and feather,
Doing each your best.

2. Spring is coming, spring is coming,
All around is fair.
Shimmer, quiver on the river,
Joy is everywhere.

3. Summer

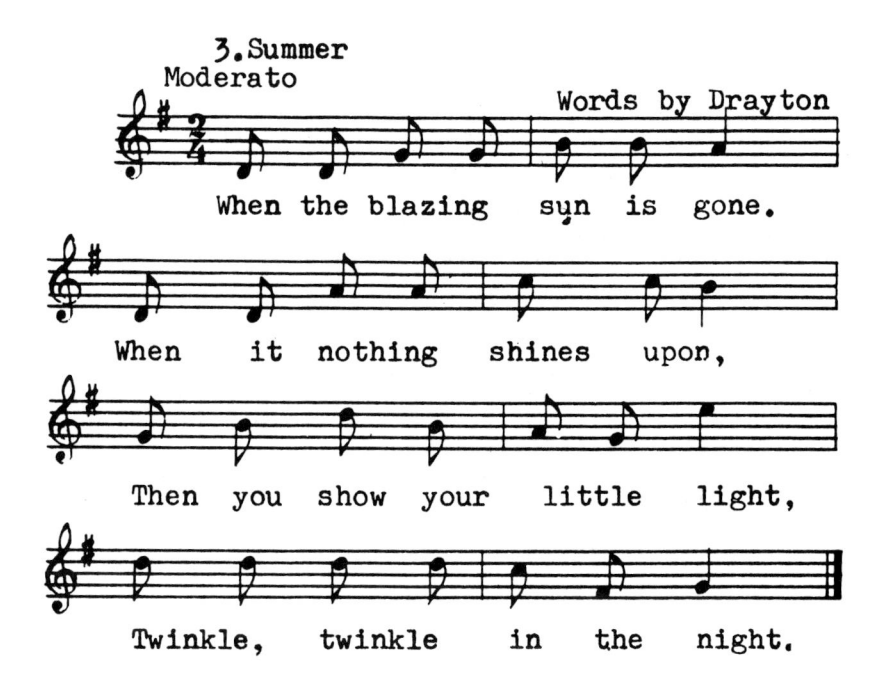

Moderato

Words by Drayton

When the blazing sun is gone.

When it nothing shines upon,

Then you show your little light,

Twinkle, twinkle in the night.

37 Allegretto

Sing a song, blackbird, sing me a song. The sunshine is brilliant, the daylight is long. The lilac is blooming; it's perfume is strong. Sing a song, blackbird, sing me a song.

4. Autumn

Allegretto

The summer is over, the trees are all bare, there's mist in the garden, and frost in the air. The meadows are empty and gathered the sheaves. But isn't it lovely, kicking up leaves?

John from the garden
Has taken the chairs;
It's dark in the evening
And cold on the stairs.
Winter is coming
And everyone grieves-
But isn't it lovely
Kicking up leaves?

A Question

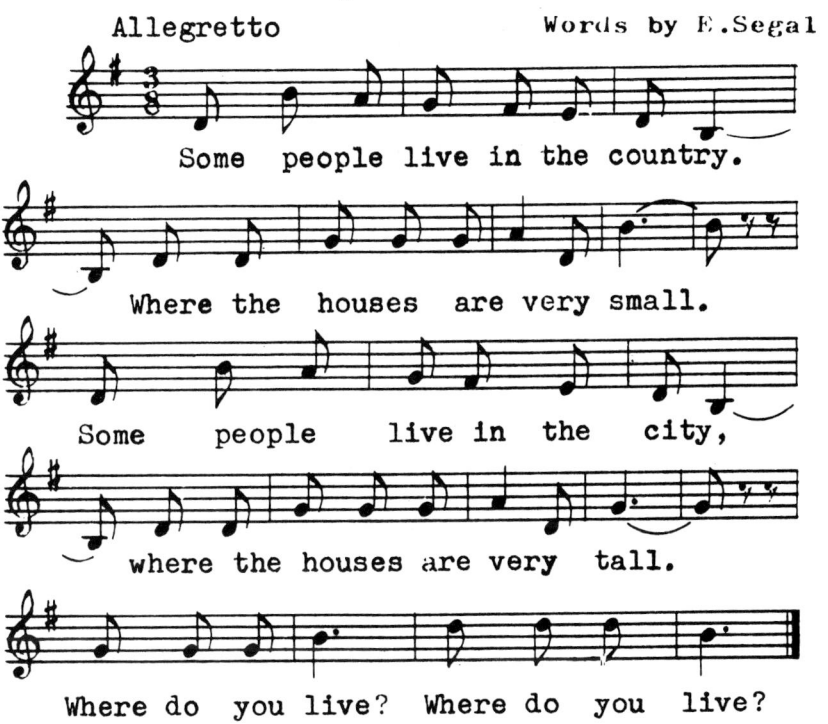

Allegretto Words by E. Segal

Some people live in the country.

Where the houses are very small.

Some people live in the city,

where the houses are very tall.

Where do you live? Where do you live?

Three Didactic Songs

Tre canzoni didattiche

Parole: R. Vraceva
Musica: E. Gateva

Я готовлю завтрак вкусный

Allegretto

Я готовлю завтрак вкусный,
ты за хлебом ходишь сам.
Он уроки быстро учит.
Он все может наш Иван.

Мы с Иваном крепко дружим.
А вы дружите ли, с кем?
Друг не только в счастье нужен.
Знают дети-насовсем.

Рано утром

Allegro

41.

Рано утром я встаю,
делаю зарядку.
Жучка видит сон в углу
и зевает сладко.
Я водой с мылом моюсь,
зубы чищу щеткой.
Полотенцем вытираюсь.
Жучка смотрит робко.// -сон.

Я причесываю Жучку,
Лапки вытираю.
Быстро морду вымываю.
Кушать приглашаю.

Я ем хлеб с вареньем сладким
Жучка-с колбасою.
Ай да вкусен ранний завтрак
с утренней расою.

Я люблю тебя, моя земля

Andante

42.

Я люблю тебя, моя березка! Я люблю тебя, моя земля! Как хочу твоей я доброй ласки, твоего ума и тепла.

Я люблю тебя, моя родная!
Для меня ты-радость, счастье, свет.
Ты дороже всех на свете, мама!
Ничего прекрасней в мире нет.

INDEX

activation, 27
Active Concert Session, 22, 69, 111
active session, 73
Ah, you right (song), 229
analytical–synthetical activity, 101
antisuggestive barriers, 120
application, 5, 6
artistic–didactic songs, 29
artistic songs, 21
Autumn (song), 182–183, 243–244

bank action, 115
bogus name, 21
bogus occupation 21
Bon anniversaire (song), 56

Ça me suffit (song), 84
Canzone di Bacco (song), 141
children
    input and output levels, 233
    musical program, 233
    tests, 233
choice of names and occupations, 61
collective canvas, 138
comparison of songs, 190
concentrated psychorelaxation, 3
"Concert, The," 145
conjugating verbs, 100
conjugation, 94
consonati, 90
continuous tenses, 115
    English, 115
    Spanish, 115
correcting mistakes, 24, 119

deciphering, 2
definite article, 103–104
De Tag (song), 59
dialogues, 120
didactic games, 78, 79
Die Blume (song), 58
Doctor Aybolit (play), 213–226
Doctor Aybolit (song), 227–228
dramaturgy, 68

Early in the Morning (song), 247–248
elaborations, 24, 78, 90, 94, 103, 113, 211
el acento, 92
Elias Portolu (novel), 151
English language, 92
Estoy muy contento (song), 53

Farmer (song), 185
file card, 148
final proficiency, 146
first day after session, 79
first elaborations, 24, 87
first encounter, 28
first grade, 169, 211
first year of suggestopedic school, 169
foreign language improvement, 151
foreign languages, teaching children, 161
"Four Seasons, The," 79
fourth day after first session, 105
Friends (play), 172–187
"Friendship," 145
future tense, 38, 137

game of cards, 143
German language, 93
Ginzburg's play, 153
globalized subject matter, 63
global themes, 159
Goodbye, Rome, 140
grammar, 83
grammar, synthetized, 68
Grazia Deledda, 151

I am a Happy Man (song), 54, 180
Ich bin allein gegangen (song), 129
I Love My Motherland (song), 249
indefinite article, 104
Index Card No. 1, 149
Index Card No. 2, 150
"infantilization," 89
input–output level, 10
inspiration, 3
instructions to students, 18
introductory notes, 1
I prepare breakfast (song), 246
irregular verbs, 41, 44
Italian language, 90
    consonati, 90
    l'accento, 91

l'accento, 91
Lâ famille heureuse (song), 55
Lession One, 90
    elaborations, 90, 94
Lession Two, 108
    elaborations, 113, 118
lexical themes, 89
loading, 1
Los marineros (song), 52

methodogical instructions, 21, 231
    introduction, 28
methodogical stages
    elaboration, 2

introduction, 2
session, 2
Michelangelo (story), 117
modal verbs, 47, 102
model list questions, 109
model scenario, 29
model songs, 235
monologues, 120
"Months, The," 139
"Musical Mosaic" (game), 130
Musical Program, 70, 73
    children, 234

Natalia Ginzburg's play, 153

Open Session, 17

paraconsciousness, 2
paraconscious psychological capacities, 63
past imperfect, 140
past participles, 126
past perfect, 127
"Patrizia" (story), 105
"Patrizia," Part 2 (story), 117
Peppers, Peppers! (song), 185
personal pronouns, 42
phonetical explanations, 108
    English, 108
    French, 108
    German, 108
    Spanish, 108
plays
    Doctor Aybolit, 213–226
    Friends, 172–187
    Ti Ho Sposato per Allergeria, 153–159
    Where are Horse and Dog?, 198–209
poor results, 88
prepositions, 106
pseudopassive concert session, 23, 72, 111

psychological atmosphere, 9
psychological loading, 3

Question, A (song), 245
questionnaire, 5, 7
  school children, 169

reading in chorus, 89, 120
recent past tense, 125
recent present tense, 125
reflexive verbs, 110
reserve capacities, 1
Riddle (song), 209
Rigoletto, 156
role of art, 70
Rome, the Eternal City, 125

Saluto il giorno (song), 112
schoolchildren, 231
schoolchildren questionnaire, 169
Seasons (song), 237–228
"Seasons, The," 138
second day after first session, 96
second day after second session, 117
second elaboration, 25, 96
second global themes, 196
Sempre primavera (song), 134
Silenzio (song), 147
Snowflakes (song), 210
songs
  Ah you, right, 229
  A Question, 248
  Bon anniversaire, 56
  Ça me suffit, 84
  Canzone di Bacco, 141
  Der Tag, 59
  Die Blume, 58
  Doctor Aybolit, 227–228
  Early in the Morning, 247
  Estoy muy contento, 53
  Farmer, 185
  I am a Happy Man, 54, 180
  Ich bin allein gegangen, 129
  I Love My Motherland, 249
  I Prepare Breakfast, 246
  Lâ famille heureuse, 55
  Los marineros, 52
  Peppers, Peppers!, 185
  Riddle, 209
  Saluto il giorno, 112
  Seasons, 237–238
  Sempre primavera, 134
  Silenzio, 147
  Snowflakes, 210
  Spring, 239–240
  Spring Time, 85
  Summer, 241–242
  Terra mia cara, 99
  There stood a birch tree, 230
  Ti voglio tanto bene, 98
  Un bel fiori, 33
  What Is . . . ?, 193
  What Is Your Name?, 189
  Where do you live?, 245
Spanish language, 91
  el acento, 92
"spontaneous" activation, 26
spontaneous dialogic speech, 107
Spring (song), 239–240
Spring Time (song), 85
stimulating students, 27
Storie (song), 31
Stories
  Michelangelo, 117
  "Patrizia," 105
  "Patrizia," Part 2, 117
suggestopedic play, requirement for, 170, 171
suggestopedic practice, 78
suggestopedic school, first year, 169
suggestopedic textbook, 64
Summer (song), 241–242
synthetized grammar, 68

teacher's delicacy, 21
teacher's dynamism, 21
teacher's easiness, 21
teaching foreign languages to children, 161
teaching second grade, 231
Terra mia cara (song), 99
testing, 9
testing output level, 146
testing phase, 8
tests, children, 233
There stood a birch tree (song), 230
third day after first session, 103
third day after second session, 118
third elaboration, 26
Ti ho Sposato per Allegria (play), 153
Ti voglio tanto bene (song), 98
training of teachers, 70

Un bel fiori (song), 33
underlined words, 67
underlining, 66

verbal system, 108
verbs, 38
 conjugating, 100
 future, 38, 137
 futuro, 43
 irregular, 41, 44
 past imperfect, 38, 140
 past perfect, 38, 127
 present, 38
 pretérito imperfecto, 43
 pretérito indefinido, 43
Verdi's *Rigoletto*, 156
visitor, 121
visual aids, 65

"Watch your Route, Drivers" (game), 130
What Is...? (song), 193
What is Your Name? (song), 189
Where are Horse and Dog? (play), 198–209
Where do you live? (song), 245

E. GATEVA

L' ITALIANO

BELLA ED ANTICA

Manuale di lingua italiana
per gli artisti

a cura di Gheorghi Kirilov Losanov
Dottore in scienze mediche
Direttore dell'Istituto
di suggestologia

Sofia 1978

ISTITUTO SCIENTIFICO DI SUGGESTOLOGIA

© E. Gateva
   G. Lozanov
© N. Tiurkegiev
c/o Jusautor, Sofia, 1978

Fotografie
SCALA/Firenze
Copertina e pag. 36, 42, 47, 51, 63, 65, 93
Musées Nationeaux – Paris
pag. 15

Stiftelsen Pedagogisk Utveckling
(The Foundation for Educational Development)
Box 18
S-815 00 TIERP
Sverige (Sweden)

Löjdquist Tryckeri AB, Tierp 1984

In copertina:
Melozzo da Forlì (1438-1494), Angelo Musicante
Roma, Pinacoteca Vaticana   ISBN 91-970527-I-X

PREFAZIONE

Il presente manuale di lingua italiana è stato elaborato secondo le ultime esigenze del sistema didattico suggestopedico. Tutta la materia d'apprendimento è strettamente collegata alla comunicazione viva della vita quotidiana. Seguendo la favola lieta della storia che è raccontata e nello stesso tempo comprendendo i diversi aspetti della psicologia dei personaggi e le varie particolarità dell'Italia, con la sua cultura antica e contemporanea, lo studente penetra a poco a poco la bellezza della lingua straniera.

Il manuale è conforme alle basi suggestologiche, ai principii ed ai mezzi della suggestopedia. Applicandolo correttamente, l'insegnante potrà aiutare lo studente a canalizzare il complesso di tutte le sue risorse, cioè l'insegnante aiuterà lo studente ad assimilare la materia didattica nella maniera più piacevole e al livello più creativo, senza fatica, senza influire negativamente sul sistema nervoso; anzi si procura di far assimilare la materia esercitando un influsso positivo ed educativo, sempre più fortemente motivato.

A parte l'integrità della favola, della commedia didattica, il manuale si prefigge altre priorità, basate sul punto di vista suggestopedico.

1. Il massimo cumulo didattico, 850 parole nuove e la parte più importante della grammatica, viene proposto già nella prima lezione. Così sono mobilitate tutte le peculiarità suggestive del "primo incontro", quello in cui la persona che studia assimila con la massima facilità. Nello stesso tempo lo studente ha una vasta possibilità di scegliere parole, locuzioni, frasi, forme grammaticali e modelli nelle ore di elaborazione della materia.

Gli studenti non si sentono mai "condizionati" o limitati da modelli e da parole prefissati nell'esprimere i loro pensieri nella lingua straniera.

Nelle lezioni successive le nuove acquisizioni lessicali e grammaticali vanno via via diminuendo, così rendendo più facile l'apprendimento.

2. Ad alcune parti delle proposizioni ed a certe locuzioni, altre si sono collocate su una riga diversa, in modo da renderle sostituibili. Così, in pratica, è possibile imparare centinaia di modelli di lingua parlata. Pur evitando di cadere nello strutturalismo fine a se stesso, esso viene utilizzato in modo inavvertito, naturale e di grande profitto.

3. Tutte le illustrazioni del manuale sono legate al soggetto con una visualizzazione globale senza illustrare i singoli elementi della lingua, sicché l'audiovisualizzazione si svolge razionalmente e su due piani, aprendo ai discenti possibilità creative nel corso del processo didattico e nello stesso tempo evitando che essi rimangano condizionati nei limiti di una piccola quantità di elementi visualizzati tutti provenienti dal mondo degli oggetti.

4. La musica e il testo delle canzoni rispondono alle esigenze di "un'introduzione" emotiva alle più importanti unità semantiche, fonetiche e grammaticali.

5. La traduzione di ogni lezione è sempre a disposizione dello studente affinché egli possa definire con esattezza il suo primo lessico, e anche ai fini del processo conoscitivo stesso come si configura nell'adulto. Questo vale per le prime due fasi del processo didattico suggestopedico, le cosidette "decifrazione" e "sessione attiva" musicale. Il giorno seguente la traduzione gli viene tolta, conformemente allo scopo che l'insegnamento di una lingua straniera si prefigge, arrivare il più presto possibile a pensare nella lingua straniera.

La competenza sia musicale che filologica dell'autrice ha reso possibile una fusione completa dell'influsso suggestivo dell'arte con le esigenze didattiche suggestopediche dell'insegnamento di una lingua straniera.

Il presente manuale è stato presentato e sperimentato interamente o in parte oltre che in Bulgaria e nell'Unione Sovietica, anche negli Stati Uniti, in Francia, Austria, Svizzera e Svezia.

Il manuale rappresenta un modello metodologico per la preparazione di altri manuali di lingue straniere conformi al sistema didattico suggestopedico.

Si raccomanda l'uso del manuale con un insegnante ben addestrato al sistema suggestopedico. Con la seconda metà del corso incomincia la preparazione degli studenti all'apprendimento anche individuale.

Questo manuale, destinato in primo luogo a specialisti delle varie arti, potrebbe essere utilizzato anche da altri.

Istruzioni più dettagliate per il lavoro dell'insegnante e degli studenti si possono trovare nella monografia, che concerne tutti e tre gli aspetti della suggestopedia: l'istruzione, l'educazione e la cura.

GHEORGHI LOSANOV
Dottore in scienze mediche
Direttore l'Istituto di suggestologia
Sofia

Настоящият учебник по италиански език е съобразен с последните изисквания на сугестопедичната учебна система. Учебният материал е изведен на житейско комуникативно ниво. С проследуването на фабулата в лекия дидактичен разказ и свързаното с нея опознаване на различни страни от психологията на героите и особеностите на Италия с нейната древна и съвременна култура обучаващият се навлиза в красотата на чуждия език. Така трудностите при овладяването на чуждия език се преодоляват неусетно, на втори план.

Учебникът е съобразен с основите на сугестологията и принципите и средствата на сугестопедията. При неговото правилно прилагане преподавателят може да подпомогне обучаващите се в реализирането на резервния комплекс, т.е. в значително по-лесното усвояване на материала на творческо ниво и без неприятна умора, без вредно въздействие върху нервната система, с положително възпитателно въздействие и с нарастваща мотивация.

Освен цялостта на фабулата в предлаганата дидактична пиеса, учебникът има и следните нови преимущества от гледна точка на сугестопедията:

1. Най-голямата част от учебното съдържание – 850 нови думи и значителна част от основната граматика – се дава още в първия урок. Така се оползотворяват сугестивните особености на „първата среща", когато се усвоява най-лесно. Същевременно така обучаващите се имат голяма свобода в избора на думи, изрази, модели и граматични форми в часовете за разработка на новия материал. Те не се чувстват „кондиционирани" и ограничени в рамките на няколко думи и модели за изразяване на мислите си на чуждия език. В следващите уроци новата лексика и граматика намаляват, което създава лекота в усвояването им.

2. Отделните части на изреченията, както и словосъчетанията, разположени на отделен ред, са подбрани така, че да са заменими. Така на практика се усвояват стотици заменими части на модели от естествения говорим език. Без да се изпада в самоцелен структурализъм, той се оползотворява неусетно, естествено и с голям замах.

3. Онагледяването с картини в учебника е свързано със сюжета глобаризирано, а не илюстрира отделни елементи от изучавания език. Така и аудиовизуализацията се осъществява на смислово и двупланово ниво с голяма свобода за творческа изява, като се избягва кондиционирането в тесните рамки на онагледени малък брой елементи от предметния свят.

4. Песните, музикално и текстуално, отговарят на сугестивните изисквания за емоционално „въвеждане" на важни семантични, фонетични и граматични единици.

5. Преводът към всеки урок в учебника се дава на курсистите за уточняване на първоначалната лексика и съгласно нуждите на познавателния процес на възрастния в първите две фази на сугестопедичния учебен процес – дешифровка и активен концертен сеанс. На втория ден преводът се отнема – този път съгласно нуждите на чуждоезиковото обучение за по-бързото преминаване към мислене на чуждия език.

Двойната специалност на авторката – филология и музика – позволи да се постигне по-пълно сливане на сугестивното влияние на изкуството с дидактичните сугестопедични изисквания в преподаването на чужд език.

Настоящият учебник е – изцяло или отчасти – демонстриран и експериментиран освен в България и Съветския съюз още и в: САЩ, Франция, Австрия, Швейцария и Швеция.

Учебникът представлява примерно методическо ръководство за изготвянето и на други учебници за чуждоезиковата сугестопедична учебна система.

Учебникът е предвиден за работа с преподавател, който трябва да бъде обучен по сугестопедичната учебна система. Във втората половина на обучението курсистите се подготвят и за самостоятелна работа. Този учебник е предвиден за специалисти в различни области на изкуството, но може да се ползва и от други курсисти.

Подробни указания за работата на преподавателя и на курсистите се дават в методичното ръководство за цялостното сугестопедично обучение-възпитание-лечение.

Георги ЛОЗАНОВ
доктор на медицинските науки

BELLA ED ANTICA

Personaggi:

Giovanni Civinini, cantante del Teatro dell'opera
Il dottor Walter, medico psicoterapeuta
La signora Walter, sua moglie, regista
Elsa, la loro figlia, studentessa
Francesco ed Emilio, i loro figli, studenti
La famiglia del dottor Rossi
Impiegati, operai ed altri cittadini

Ai nostri giorni

"TU SE' LO MIO MAESTRO
 E 'L MIO AUTORE;
 TU SE' SOLO COLUI
 DA CU' IO TOLSI LO BELLO STILE
 CHE M'HA FATTO ONORE"

   Dante /1265 - 1321/
   Inferno, Canto I

PARTE PRIMA

"E CANTERÒ DI QUEL SECONDO REGNO
DOVE L'UMANO SPIRITO SI PURGA
E DI SALIRE AL CIEL DIVENTA DEGNO"
/Dante, Purgatorio, Canto I/

QUADRO PRIMO

CONOSCENZA IN AEREO

L'aeroporto di Berlino.
La famiglia Walter <u>parte</u>
per Roma.
L'aèreo è <u>pieno di</u>
viaggiatori.

Giovanni Civinini: Scusi, signore.
È lìbero questo <u>posto</u>?

Il dottor Walter: Sí, prego!
Si accòmodi!
Ma che sorpresa!
Lei è il signor Civinini,
il famoso cantante
della Scala di Milano.
Lei non mi conosce.
Ma io La conosco.
Sono un amico
di Suo padre.
Suo padre è un uomo
di grande ingegno.

G. Civinini: Lieto di conòscerLa.
Con chi ho l'onore?

Il dott. Walter: Mi chiamo Richard Walter.
Sono mèdico,
psicoterapèuta di Berlino.

/sono   siamo
sei   siete
è   sono
<u>èssere</u>/

7

	Ecco il mio biglietto da vísita.	/il biglietto - i biglietti un biglietto - dei biglietti/
G. Civinini:	Grazie. Ecco il mio. Lei parla l'italiano molto bene.	/parl- o parl - iamo parl- i parl - ate parl- a pàrl - ano parl-are 1/ /il francese, l'inglese, il tedesco. lo spagnolo, il búlgaro, l'ungherese, il russo, il greco, il giapponese.../
Il dott. Walter:	Grazie. Ho studiato all'Università di Roma.	

Ho studiato insieme a Suo padre.
Signor Civinini,
Lei ha un grande successo
a Berlino.
Lo spettacolo dell'Aida
è meraviglioso.

/lo spettàcolo – gli spettàcoli
uno spettacolo – degli spettacoli/

G. Civinini: Il successo non è
soltanto mio.
Canto con i miei colleghi:
Lucia Vittorini
e suo marito Giuseppe Pellico.
Ottimi cantanti.
Ottima coppia.
Un matrimònio felice.
Hanno sei bambini.

/ho   abbiamo
hai   avete
ha   hanno
              avere/

Anche loro ritornano
Viàggiano in treno.
Ma si perde tanto tempo.

Il dott. Walter: Sì,
e noi abbiamo sempre fretta.
Perché?

G. Civinini: Lei ha ragione.
Chi sa perché?

Il dott. Walter: Mi permetta di
presentarLe la mia famiglia.
La signora Walter è regista.

G. Civinini: Tanto piacere, signora.

La signora Walter: Mio marito parla spesso
di Suo padre.
Le piace la città di Berlino?

G. Civinini: Sì, mi piace molto.
E'una bella città.

Il dott. Walter: Posso presentarLe
la signorina Elsa,
mia fìglia?
E'studentessa.
Studia canto al Conservatorio.

G. Civinini: Parla anche Lei l'italiano?

Elsa: Certamente, lo parlo.
I musicisti pàrlano l'italiano:
L'italiano non è difficile.
E'fàcile.
E'una lingua bella e sonora.
Chi vuole cantare,
l'italiano deve parlare.

9

G. Civinini: Proprio cosí!

Il dott. Walter: Alle nostre spalle
sono seduti
i nostri figli.
Sono studenti,
sono bravi ragazzi.
Il maggiore si chiama Franz-
Francesco.
Suona pianoforte.
Il minore si chiama Emil -
Emilio.
Dipinge.

G. Civinini: Io non sono sposato.
Ho trent'anni.

/l'anno -gli anni/
un anno - degli anni/

Viaggio troppo.
Da cínque anni
àbito a Milano
con mia madre, con mio padre
e con mia sorella.
Sono nato a Roma.
Roma mi manca continuamente.
E' diventata proprio un museo.
Ma io ho bisogno
della sua bellezza.
Mia madre ha cinquant' anni.
Mio padre ha cinquantatrè.
Mia sorella ha vent' anni.

/la sorella - le sorelle
una sorella - delle sorelle/

E' molto intelligente.
Assomiglia al babbo.
Studia filología romanza.
Siete già stati in Italia?

Il dott. Walter: Dopo i miei studi
ci sono stato
alcune volte
per ragioni di servízio.
Ai congressi
ci incontriamo con Suo padre.
Molti anni fa
sono venuto a casa Sua.
Lei era bambino.
Conosco tutta la Sua famiglia.
L'anno scorso
sono stato a Roma.
L'Italia è un bel paese..
E' il piú ricco museo
d'Europa.
Adesso sono invitato
al Congresso degli psicoterapeuti.
I miei vèngono
per la prima volta.
Vogliamo fare un giro.
Un giro per l'Italia.
Vogliamo visitare
i luoghi cèlebri.

10

G. Civinini:	Quanto tempo rimanete?
Il dott. Walter:	Dieci giorni.
G. Civinini:	Dunque ci rivedremo.
Il dott. Walter:	Sí. Ed i Suoi fratelli?
G. Civinini:	Gianni è ingegnere in chímica. Lavora in uno stabilimento industriale a Torino. Sua moglie è professoressa in una scuola elementare. Hanno quattro figlie. Luigi è giurista. Lavora in una ditta commerciale. La moglie è ragioniere in una ditta d'importazione e d'esportazione. Carlo è professore in una scuola mèdia. Insegna lèttere. Si è laureato recentemente. Sua moglie è molto gióvane. Hanno un bambino. Vivono a Pàdova.
La signora Walter:	Siete una sòlida famiglia.
Elsa:	Signor Civinini, quando possiamo sentirLa?
G. Civinini:	Ecco il mio programma per la pròssima settimana: lunedì canto nella Traviata. martedì nella Norma, mercoledì canto nella Sonnàmbula, giovedì non canto; è il mio giorno di riposo. Venerdì ho un concerto. Avrà luogo a Roma. Sàbato canto nel Barbiere di Siviglia. Domènica nel Rigoletto.
Elsa:	Babbo, forse il Rigoletto...
Il dott. Walter:	Forse... Ecco viene la hostess. Ci porta qualcosa da bere. Avete sete?
La hostess:	Prego, signora, che cosa desídera? Una tazza di tè, una tazza di caffé, una tazza di caffelatte, un bicchiere di birra o di vino rosso o bianco oppure succo di frutta.

| | Ci sono anche:
limonata, aranciata,
spremuta d'arancio,
spremuta di limone. |
|---|---|
| La signora Walter: | Per favore, un succo di frutta. |
| La hostess: | Prego, signora.
E Lei, signore? |
| Il dott. Walter: | Vorrei un caffè
senza zúcchero. |
| Elsa: | Un'aranciata, per favore. |
| G. Civinini: | Preferisco un tè
con limone. |
| Francesco: | Vorremmo del vino rosso. |
| La signora Walter: | Ma che vergogna!
Scusi, signorina,
i ragazzi schèrzano. |

/l'aranciata – le aranciate
un'aranciata – delle aranciate/

	Vògliono dell'acqua minerale.
Francesco:	Emilio, non siamo adulti, noi? Sono stufo! Ci tràttano sempre da bambini. Non è vero?
Emilio:	Eh, sí! Ma che cosa possiamo fare?
G. Civinini:	Sono stupefatto! Parlate benìssimo l'italiano. Con una corretta pronuncia. Dove l'avete imparato?
Elsa:	All'Istituto per la ricerca scientífica di mètodi nuovi con un sistema psicològico. In un mese.
G. Civinini:	Impossìbile!
Elsa:	Perché no? Lei sa il caso di Toscanini: in un giorno ha imparato a memoria tutt'un'òpera.
G. Civinini:	E' vero, è vero. Vorrei imparare il tedesco. Ho bisogno di questa lingua.
Il dott. Walter:	Sono amico del Direttore dell'Istituto. Quest'anno in settembre cominciamo un lavoro insieme. Viene con me?
G. Civinini:	Volentieri! Mi interessa molto! Che bell' occasione! La ringrazio.
Il dott. Walter:	Prego! Non c'è di che!
Francesco:	Sentite la música? Chi canta?
Elsa:	E' la voce del signor Civinini.

Mamma,
ti voglio tanto bene!
Mamma,
tu mi aspetti sempre.
Guardo il tuo viso
un po' invecchiato,
capisco molto bene
i tuoi sacrifici,
la gioia, il dolore,
l'amor per tutti noi,
nascosto nel tuo cuore.
E cerco, cerco sempre
la strada bella e vera,
e vengo innocente
a riposàr da te...

Terra mia cara,
bella ed antica!
Guardo le montagne,
il cielo piú sereno,
i laghi, i fiumi,
le valli,
il mare piú azzurro-
l'ànimo agitato
trema di giòia pura.
Terra mia cara,
abbraccia con amore,
con fede e speranza
un figlio che torna!

G. Civinini: Siamo arrivati.
Ecco la mia patria.
Fra poco
siamo a Roma-
la città eterna.
Ragazzi, vedete laggiú?

/vedo	vediamo
vedi	ved - ete
ved - e	vèd - ono
	ved-ere 2 /

Leonardo da Vinci /1452-1519/, La Gioconda
Parigi, Louvre

	Ecco Roma.
	Fra poco viene il púllman.
	Siamo all'aeroporto.
	Il controllo dei passaporti.
L'impiegato:	Prego, signore,
	il <u>Suo</u> passaporto.
	Grazie.
	Oh, il passaporto <u>non è válido</u>!
Il dott. Walter:	Impossíbile!
	<u>Lei sbaglia</u>.
	Il mio passaporto è <u>prorogato</u>
	per un anno.
	Ecco <u>il visto d'ingresso</u>
	e d'<u>uscita</u>.
L'impiegato:	Scusi, signore.
	<u>Tutto in règola</u>.
	<u>Riempia</u>, per favore,
	questo <u>mòdulo</u>:

Cognome
Nome

Nazionalità
Professione
Luogo di nàscita
Domicilio
Luogo di partenza
Destinazione
Frontiera
Data
Firma

Il doganiere:	<u>Di chi</u> è questa valigia?
Il dott. Walter:	<u>La valigia</u> è mia.
Il doganiere:	Per favore,
	<u>deve aprire</u> la valigia.
	<u>Che cosa è questo</u>?
Il dott. Walter:	Un film.
	<u>Partécipo a</u> un Congresso
	di medicina a Roma.
	La mia esposizione
	<u>viene accompagnata</u>
	dal film.
Il doganiere:	<u>Va bene</u>, va bene.
	Porta dei <u>regali</u>?
	Ha <u>valuta</u>?

	Ha <u>denaro</u>? Quanti soldi ha?		
Il dott. Walter:	Ho degli assegni, ho un po' di lire. Devo <u>scrivere</u> qui?	/devo devi deve	dobbiamo dovete devono <u>dovere</u>/
G. Civinini:	Mi dispiace, ma <u>dobbiamo</u> <u>lasciarci</u>. Parto <u>subito</u> per Milano.	/parto parti parte	partiamo part - ite pàrtono part-<u>ire</u> 3/
	Buon giorno. Vi <u>à uguro</u> salute, felicità e divertimenti.		
Il dott. Walter:	Grazie. <u>Altrettanto</u>.		
G. Civinini:	Qual è il vostro albergo?		

Il dott. Walter:	Hotèl L e o n e
	in via Vittorio Vèneto.
La signora Walter:	Tanti saluti alla famiglia!
Emilio:	Tante belle cose!
Francesco:	Fra una settimana
	ci rivedremo.
Elsa:	Buon viaggio!
Tutti:	ArrivederLa!
Il dott. Walter:	Ora dobbiamo cercare
	un tassi
	La città si trova
	lontano da qui.
Francesco:	Ecco un tassi.
	Scusi, è libero?
L'autista:	Sí
	Dove?
Il dott. Walter:	L'albergo L e o n e
	in via
L'autista:	Vittorio Vèneto.
	Va bene.
	Andiamo.

La famiglia Walter arriva
al centro di Roma.
La bellezza della città
impressiona.

Il dott. Walter:	Cari miei,
	respirate l'aria di Roma!
Francesco:	Con l'odore di benzina.
La signora Walter:	La civilizzazione ci porta
	di tutto
L'autista:	Questo è vero, signora.
	Guardate il tràffico!
	Senza disciplina ed órdine
	non possiamo vìvere.

/posso	possiamo
puoi	potete
può	pòssono
	potere/

	Siamo arrivati.
Il dott. Walter:	Quanto Le devo?

L'autista indica la somma,
la riceve e se ne va.
La famiglia entra nell'albergo.

Il dott. Walter:	Buona sera. Vorrei tre càmere con bagno. Due a due letti, una a un letto.
L'albergatore:	Le ha prenotate? No? Quanto tempo vuole rimanere?

/voglio   vogliamo
vuoi   volete
vuole   vògliono

volere/

Dieci giorni?
Dove desidera le camere?
Al primo, al secondo,
o al terzo piano?

Il dott. Walter:	Le preferisco al secondo piano.

prefer-isc-o   preferiamo
prefer-isc-i   preferite
prefer-isc-e   prefer-isc-ono

prefer-ire 3/

	Quanto còstano le camere?
L'albergatore:	Ogni camera costa 40,000 /quarantamila/ lire.
Il dott. Walter:	Con colazione?
L'albergatore:	Senza colazione.
Il dott. Walter:	E' troppo per me.
L'albergatore:	Ma come mai, signore, il nostro albergo è di prima classe. Vuole vedere le camere? Il facchino viene con Lei. Rocco, súbito!
Il dott. Walter:	No, grazie. Prendo le camere.
La cameriera:	Buona sera. Mi chiamo Mirandolina. Sono a vostra disposizione. Le camere sono còmode e tranquille. Danno sul giardino. Accendiamo la luce! Guardate, tutto è nuovo: il tappeto, le tende, le poltrone. Il pavimento è pulito e lúcido. Sul letto c'è un cuscino. Ma nel cassettone ci sono altri cuscini. Ci sono anche le fèdere, le lenzuola e le coperte. L'armadio per i vestiti. L'attaccapanni. Le grucce. C'è uno spècchio. Il soffitto e le pareti della camera sono alti. C'è aria. Sul tavolino ci sono i giornali. Sono di oggi. Vicino alla finestra c'è una tàvola con alcuni libri. Accanto al letto c'è un comodino. Sul comodino c'è una làmpada da notte. Il telèfono. Ci sono una radio e un televisore.
Francesco:	Funziònano?
La cameriera:	Credo di sí. Sul balcone c'è

	una sedia. Nella stanza da bagno avete tutto il necessàrio: sul lavabo ci sono i saponi. L'asciugamano. Ecco la vasca e la doccia. I rubinetti per l'àcqua calda e fredda. Posso aprire le finestre?
La signora Walter:	Grazie, grazie, signora. Lei è molto gentile.
La cameriera:	Ai Suoi órdini, signora. Buona notte!
Elsa:	Ho sonno.
Il dott. Walter:	Non avete fame?
Elsa:	Non ho fame.
Francesco:	Voglio raccontarvi una barzelletta. Sentite! Rossini era un gran buongustàio. Una dama dell'aristocrazìa lo invita a cena. Un'altra dama gli chiede:
La dama:	Maestro, non si ricorda di me?
Rossini:	Mi dispiace, ma non ricordo. Dove ci siamo visti?
La dama:	In casa della marchesa Rattazzi. Lei sedeva accanto a me. Non si ricorda?
Rossini:	L'ho dimenticato.
La dama:	Ma come è possìbile? Abbiamo mangiato un magnífico pollo alla panna. Ricorda?
Rossini:	Ah, il pollo delizioso! Ricordo benìssimo...
Elsa:	Com'è bella la mùsica di Rossini: "Una voce poco fa..."

GRAMMATICA

1. Fonetica
   L'alfabeto italiano
   Particolarità della pronuncia di alcune consonanti
   Le consonanti doppie
   L'accento
   L'apocope
   L'elisione
2. Morfoligia e sintassi
   L'articolo determinativo ed indeterminativo
   Il nome: genere e numero
   I verbi ausiliari: essere ed avere
   I pronomi personali: soggetto
   Verbi regolari della I, II e III coniugazione. Presente
   Particolarità delle coniugazioni: cercare, pregare, cominciare, mangiare, vincere, dipingere
   I verbi irregolari: potere, dovere, volere
   La forma negativa dei verbi
   La forma interrogativa dei verbi
   Le preposizioni semplici ed articolate
   L'articolo partitivo
   Il verbo impersonale: c'è, ci sono
   L'aggettivo
   Participio passato
   Passato prossimo
3. Lessicologia
   Presentazione
   Professione
   Famiglia
   Lingue straniere
   I giorni della settimana
   Bevande
   Paesaggio
   All'aeroporto: il controllo dei passaporti, la dogana
   All'albergo

PATRIZIA

Vorrei raccontarvi della mia amica Patrizia.
La conoscete? No?

Patrizia è studentessa. Abita e studia a Roma. Studia violino al Conservatorio. E'una brava violinista e una brava ragazza. Non perde il suo tempo. Studia anche alcune lingue: il tedesco e il russo. Parla benissimo il francese, l'inglese e lo spagnolo. Conosce bene il greco e il latino. E'molto intelligente.

E'nata a Como. Como è una bella città vicino al lago omonimo: l'antica colonia romana, la patria dei due Plinii, di Volta... A Como abita suo padre con un'altra figlia e con il figlio maggiore.

La sorella di Patrizia si chiama Giulia. Ha dieci anni. Bella bambina! Il fratello maggiore si chiama Benedetto. E'medico. Un bravo psicoterapeuta. L'altro fratello si chiama Cesare. E'professore di italiano. Abita a Napoli. Suona pianoforte e canta. E'un poeta e musicista. Scrive per il teatro d'opera. Spesso viaggia, ma ritorna sempre a Napoli. Gli piace il cielo sereno, il mare azzurro e tranquillo. Ama molto anche Como. Si ricorda della montagna, del lago, dei fiumi, delle valli. Prende il treno e arriva a Como.

La sorella ed i fratelli di Patrizia assomigliano al padre. Patrizia assomiglia alla madre. Sua madre era napoletana.

/segue/

Ti voglio tanto bene

Moderato
Parole e musica: E. Gateva

Mamma, ti voglio tanto bene!
Mamma, tu mi aspetti sempre...
Guardo il tuo viso un po' invecchiato, capisco molto bene i tuoi sacrifici, la
gioia, il dolor, l'amor per tutti noi, nascosto nel tuo cuor. E cerco, cerco sempre la
strada bella e vera e vengo innocente
a riposar da te.

Terra mia cara

Parole e musica: E. Gateva

Moderato

Terra mia cara, bella ed antica!
Guardo le montagne, il cielo più sereno, i laghi, i fiumi, le valli, il mare più azzurro;
l'animo agitato trema di gioia pura.
Terra mia cara, abbraccia con amore, con fede e speranza un figlio che torna!

"LIBERTÀ VA CERCANDO, CH'È SÌ CARA,
COME SA CHI PER LEI VITA RIFIUTA."
/Dante, Purgatorio, Canto I/

QUADRO SECONDO
IL RISVEGLIO

Il dott. Walter: /canta/ Saluto il giorno,
saluto il sole,
saluto la grande città
che a poco a poco
si sveglia, respira-
sorride la vita.
E vedo un uomo
andare tranquillo,
pensando al mondo
che deve costruir:
un mondo nuovo,
felice e puro,
un mondo
dove
non c'è paura.

La signora Walter: Che cosa fai?

Il dott. Walter: Fàccio un po' di ginnàstica.

/faccio   facciamo
fai   fate
fa   fanno

fare-facere/

Fa bene.
Canto.
Sono di buon umore.
Oggi fa bel tempo.
È primavera.
Il sole splende.
Non fa freddo.
Tutto fiorisce.
Vieni sul balcone!
Sbrígati!
Guarda un po'!
Laggiù
un uomo vende dei fiori.
Che bei fiori!

La signora Walter: Che ora è?

Il dott. Walter: Sono le otto e mezzo.
Vieni, vieni...

La signora Walter: Mi piace restare a letto.

Il dott. Walter: Fa male alla salute.
Vieni!
Prendi un'po d'ària fresca!

La signora Walter: Un momento!
Aspetta!
Mi alzo e vengo.

/vengo   veniamo
vieni   venite
viene   vèngono
           venire/

Il dott. Walter: Che cosa fai?

La signora Walter: Mi vesto.
Mi metto le calze.
Mi metto le scarpe.
Mi lavo.

/mi lavo   ci laviamo
ti lavi   vi lavate
si lava   si làvano

lavarsi
mettersi
vestirsi/

	Mi pèttino.
	Dobbiamo prepararci.
	Oggi abbiamo molto da fare.
	Esco súbito.
Il dott. Walter:	Esci sola?
La signora Walter:	No.
	usciamo tutti insieme.

/esco   usciamo
esci   uscite
esce   èscono   uscire/

Elsa bussa alla porta.

La signora Walter:	Avanti!
Elsa:	Buon giorno, cari genitori.
	Che bel mattino!
	Come state?
Il dott. Walter:	Benone.
	E tu, come stai?

/sto   stiamo
stai   state
sta   stanno   stare/

Elsa:	Hai potuto dormire?
	Si.
	Ma sono impaziente.
	Voglio uscire.
	Voglio visitare la città.
	Voglio vedere tutto, tutto...
Il dott. Walter:	Anche tu? Come tua madre...
	Aspettate un po'!
	Sentite?
	Per il corridoio còrrono
	Francesco ed Emilio.
Francesco:	Buon giorno.
	Tutti pronti ad uscire?
	Elsa, perché non ci hai chiamato?
Elsa:	Vi piace dormire, eh!
	Chi dorme,
	non piglia pesci!
Francesco:	Dobbiamo ancora créscere.
La signora Walter:	Ah, va bene, va bene.
	Una volta siete adulti
	e un'altra volta siete bambini.
Francesco:	No, bambini, no.
	Siamo capaci di atti eròici!
	Non è vero, Emilio?
Emilio:	Non lo so, non lo so.

Elsa: Bravi,
ma avete molta fame.
Ho indovinato?

Francesco: Sí.
Non ti inganni.
Siamo tremendamente affamati.

Elsa: Sentite:
" Un fabbro ha un cane.
Quando il fabbro lavora,
il cane dorme.
Ma appena
il fabbro comincia a mangiare,
il cane si sveglia
e si avvicina al fabbro.
Che strana bèstia! -
pensa il fabbro,
e che strano udito!
Quando batto l'incúdine, dormi,
e appena muovo i denti,
ti svegli! "

Francesco: Elsa,
che cosa vuoi dire?

Il dott. Walter: Io vado in banca.

/vado   andiamo
vai   andate
va   vanno
                 andare/

Devo cambiare dei soldi.
Poi devo telefonare ai colleghi,
devo prepararmi per il Congresso.
Intanto,
voi potete visitare la città.
Eccovi una guida di Roma.
Dentro c'è una pianta.
Prima però
facciamo colazione!
Dove volete farla?
Nel ristorante dell'albergo
oppure fuori.
Possiamo andare in quel caffé,
lí di fronte all'albergo.

Elsa: Andiamo al ristorante.

Il ristorante dell'albergo
è quasi vuoto.
Súbito viene il cameriere
ed offre alla famiglia Walter
molte cose:
formaggio, burro, marmellata,
panini imbottiti, brioche,
caffelatte, succo di frutta.
Dopo la colazione il dottor Walter
domanda al cameriere quando
deve pagare.
Il cameriere risponde che
si paga dopo, tutto insieme
con il conto delle càmere.
Il dottor Walter ed Emilio
vanno alla Banca.

Il dott. Walter: Ecco qui c'è il cambio
della valuta <u>èstera</u>.
Per favore,
può cambiarmi <u>gli assegni</u>?
<u>Qual è il corso ufficiale?</u>

L'impiegato: Riempia, per favore,
questo mòdulo.
Qual è il Suo <u>indirizzo</u>?
Firmi qui!
<u>Favorisca</u> alla cassa!
Ecco le lire.

/uno, due, tre, quattro	1.2.3.4
cinque, sei, sette	5.6.7
otto, nove, dieci	8.9.10
ùndici, dòdici	11.12
trèdici, quattordici	13. 14
quìndici, sèdici	15.16
diciassètte, diciotto	17.18.
diciannove, venti	19.20
ventuno, ventidue...	21.22
trenta, quaranta,	30.40
cinquanta, sessanta	50.60
settanta, ottanta,	70.80
novanta, cento	90. 100
centoventicinque	125
duecento, trecento.	200.300
quattrocento	**400**
cinquecento, seicento	500.600
settecento, ottocento	700.800
novecento, <u>mille</u>	900.1000
<u>duemila</u>, diecimila	2000.10.000
centomila	100.000
un milione	1000.000

29

Il dott. Walter:	Grazie.
	Emilio, <u>andiàmocene</u>!
Emilio:	<u>Babbo</u>,
	c'è vicino
	un'edícola di giornali?
	Eccola.
	Per favore,
	<u>mi dia</u> un giornale d'oggi.
	Quanto costa <u>la rivista</u>?

Padre e figlio ritornano all'albergo.

Il dott. Walter:	<u>Pronto</u>!
	Una línea in città?
	<u>Non si può</u>?
	<u>Allora</u>
	<u>mi metta in comunicazione</u>
	col número 22 38 45.
	Grazie.
	<u>E'occupato</u>?
	Devo <u>attèndere</u>?
	Pronto!
	Chi è?
	Chi parla?
	Vorrei parlare con il dottor Rossi.
	<u>E'in casa</u>?
	<u>Non ho capito,</u> non ho capito.
	Scusi.
	Aspetto.
	Grazie.
	Giulio, buon giorno.
	Sono io, Richard Walter.
	Sono a Roma.
	Come stai?
	Come sta la famiglia?
La voce del dottor Rossi:	Riccardo,
	quando posso vederti?
	<u>Dove hai preso alloggio</u>?
Il dottor Walter:	<u>Al sòlito posto</u>.
	Sono venuto con la mia famiglia.
	<u>Dopodomani ci vedremo</u>
	al Congresso.
Il dottor Rossi:	No, no.
	Aspetta,
	<u>quanti ne abbiamo, oggi</u>?
	Sì, sì, oggi è <u>il tre</u> maggio.

/<u>il primo</u> maggio
mille novecento settantatrè/

	<u>Che giorno è oggi</u>?
	Ma <u>certo</u>, oggi è martedì.
	<u>Il pomeríggio</u> e <u>la sera</u>
	sono molto occupato.
	Ma <u>domani</u>,sí.
	Siete líberi
	domani sera?
	Vi invito a cena.
	<u>D'accordo</u>?
	<u>Verrò a prèndervi</u>.

Il dottor Walter:	Accetto con piacere.
	Tanti saluti alla famiglia! Emilio, dammi gli occhiali e il taccuino!
Emilio:	Ti do anche la biro.

/do   diamo
dai   date
dà   danno
            dare/

Il dott. Walter:	Emilio, abbi coraggio! Parla con piú sicurezza! Non pensare tanto! Crédimi, sarà meglio.
Emilio:	Io sono piú tímido di mio fratello. Sai, sono l'allievo piú tímido della classe.
Il dott. Walter:	Non importa. Non è un difetto. Anzi è una qualità. Devi però amministrarla bene. Tu sei modesto e buono. Mentre telèfono, prendi questo libro! Leggi! Sono racconti italiani. Pàgine bellìssime!

Emilio: /legge/ Michelángelo Buonarroti /Secondo E. Damiani/
E' nato il sei marzo 1474
a Caprese.
La famiglia deve <u>cambiar casa</u>.
Il padre dà <u>il píccolo</u>
a una bàlia,
moglie di un o scalpellino.
Essi vìvono a Firenze.
Michelangelo <u>non ha inclinazione</u>
<u>per</u> gli studi.
Preferisce fantasticare
con <u>le matite</u>,
con <u>i colori</u>
e con gli scalpelli.
Il padre <u>non è contento</u>.
Suo figlio non stùdia.
<u>Si òccupa di</u> scultura,
<u>cioè</u> di mestieri
poco <u>ùtili</u>.
<u>Ma come si può andare</u>
contro la natura?
Michelangelo ha un amico,
un certo Francesco Grannacci.
Francesco studia
da maestro Ghirlandaio.
Michelangelo <u>va</u> spesso <u>a trovare</u>
il suo amico
nella <u>bottega del bravo pittore</u>.
<u>Qui prova</u> a maneggiare
<u>gli arnesi</u> del mestiere
e <u>dà</u> forma alla sua arte.
Finalmente <u>convince</u> suo padre.
Diventa allievo del Ghirlandaio.
<u>Nello stesso tempo</u>
a Firenze vive
Lorenzo dei Mèdici.
Egli ha una scuola
di scultura,
<u>diretta</u> dal maestro Bertoldo.
Un giorno Bertoldo va dal Ghirlandaio.
Vuole dei gióvani
<u>inclini</u> alla scultura.
Il Ghirlandaio gli <u>propone</u>
Granacci e anche <u>Michelangelo</u>.
Nella scuola
Michelangelo lavora
<u>senza sosta</u>:
disegna,
studia i modelli antichi,
abbozza, <u>corregge</u>.
Un giorno <u>addocchia</u>
un <u>pezzo di marmo</u>.
Sul pezzo vede
un fàuno abbozzato.
- Questo fauno lo voglio fare io, -
<u>dice</u> Michelangelo.

/dico   diciamo
dici   dite
dice   dícono
                   <u>dire</u>-dicere/

<u>Passa</u> Lorenzo.
Vede la scultura.
Ne resta sorpreso.
- Bravo, ragazzo! -
dice a Michelangelo.
Fai di questi lavori
e Bertoldo non mi dice nulla.
- Eccellenza, il maestro non lo <u>sa</u>.

/so	sappiamo
sai	sapete
sa	sanno

<u>sapere</u>/

Non lo dico mai a <u>nessuno</u>.
- Però vedi, -
gli dice il Magnífico,
<u>hai fatto</u> un fauno vecchio,
ma con tutti <u>i denti</u>.
Lorenzo se ne va.
<u>In un bàtter d'òcchio</u>
Michelangelo <u>leva</u> un dente
al fáuno.
Il fauno diventa <u>vécchio</u>.
Ripassa Lorenzo.
Ne resta stupefatto!
Da quel giorno lo prende
a casa sua.

GRAMMATICA

1. Verbi irregolari: andare, dare, fare, stare, sapere, venire, uscire, dire, proporre
2. I verbi riflessivi
3. Gerundio presente dei verbi
4. L'imperativo
5. Gradi di comparazione
6. La comparazione irregolare
7. L'aggettivo bello
8. I numerali cardinali e ordinali
9. Aggettivi dimostrativi

Lessicologia

1. Il risveglio
2. Colazione
3. L'ora, il giorno, l'anno, il secolo
4. Invito a cena
5. Telefonate
6. L'arte della scultura

PATRIZIA

Mi sveglio. Il sole splende. L'aria pura e fresca entra dalla finestra. E'primavera. Mi piace restare a letto. Non penso a nulla. Fa male alla salute. Lo so. Tutti lo sanno. Tutti lo dicono. Quanti ne abbiamo, oggi? Ah, ecco, comincio a pensare! Quanti ne abbiamo, oggi? Vediamo. Guardo nel taccuino. Oggi è il primo aprile. Primo aprile! Che giorno sarà? Martedì. Sentite? Oggi è il primo aprile mille novecento settantatre! Vado al balcone. A poco a poco la grande città si risveglia.

Laggiù al secondo piano vive Patrizia. Entro in camera. Voglio parlare con Patrizia. Vado al telefono. "Pronto? Chi è? E'Lei, signor Falchi? Vorrei parlare con Patrizia. Dorme ancora? E sono le sei? Impossibile! Lei s'inganna. Oh, scusi, signore, scusi..." E' vero. Sono le sei del mattino. Ma io non posso più dormire. Che strana ragazza è Patrizia! Dorme ancora. Che bel tempo! Oggi ho molto da fare. Devo uscire. Vado a lavorare. Mi faccio un caffé. Esco. Fuori un uomo porta dei fiori. Che bei fiori! "Quanto costano tutti i fiori?"-gli domando. "Non so."-mi risponde l'uomo. "Ma come non lo sa? Non li vende i fiori?" " No" -dice lui e se ne va.

Ecco Patrizia. Apre la finestra. Poi apre la porta del balcone. Esce. Non mi vede. Respira. Entra di nuovo. Si prepara per uscire: si veste, si lava, si mette le calze, le scarpe, si pettina. Fa colazione: caffelatte con panino imbottito.

Patrizia ha un cane. Quando suona il violino, il cane dorme. Ma appena Patrizia comincia a mangiare, il cane si sveglia. La guarda. Aspetta. Fanno sempre colazione insieme. Poi Patrizia prende il violino e va al Conservatorio. Patrizia non mi invita mai. Assomiglio al suo cane. Il suo cane però è più felice di me. Che vita! Ma che cosa posso fare? Le persone timide sono buone, ma chi se ne interessa. Mio padre non è contento di me. Non ho inclinazione per gli studi. Mi occupo di scultura. E'un mestiere poco utile. Si può fare qualcosa dopo Michelangelo? Però io faccio belle cose. Lo dice il mio professore. E'molto contento di me. "Aspetta, aspetta, convinciamo tuo padre" mi dice spesso.

Aspetto.

/segue/

Saluto il giorno

Parole e musica: E. Gateva

Allegro

Saluto il giorno, saluto il sole, saluto la grande città che a poco a poco si sveglia, respira; sorride la vita. E

Andante

vedo un uomo andare tranquillo, pensando al mondo che deve costruir; un

Allegro

mondo nuovo, felice e puro, un mondo dove non c'è paura!

Michelangelo Buonarroti /1475-1564/. La Pietà
Vaticano, Basilica S. Pietro

"MA DIMMI: VOI CHE SIETE QUI FELICI,
DESIDERATE VOI PIÚ ALTO LOCO
PER PIÚ VEDERE E PER PIÚ FARVI AMICI?"
/Dante, Paradiso, Canto III/

QUADRO TERZO
LA CITTÀ ETERNA

Il dottor Walter:	Siete già tornati? È tardi. Dove siete andati?
Elsa:	Siamo stanchi morti. Siamo andati fino al Vaticano. Abbiamo visitato i musei vaticani. Abbiamo visto la Basílica di San Pietro con la famosa cúpola di Michelangelo e all'interno della Basílica abbiamo visto La Pietà. L'artista ha scolpito questo capolavoro quando aveva solo venticinque anni. Il gruppo è creato con una dolcezza e compostezza di linea che conquista. Sopratutto colpisce la sofferenza calma e rassegnata della Vérgine giovinetta e l'abbandono del corpo del bellíssimo Cristo, che non ha la rigidezza della morte ma pare àssopito in un sonno che prelude alla sua resurrezione." /E. Pucci/
Il dott. Walter:	E la Cappella Sistina?
Elsa:	Indimenticàbile! Soprattutto gli affreschi della volta, l'òpera di Michelangelo: 1. La creazione dell'uomo. 2. Il peccato originale e la cacciata dal Paradiso. 3. La creazione della donna. 4. Dio separa la luce dalle tenebre. 5. Le sibille ed i profeti. 6. Il giudízio universale. Quando visiteremo Fírenze?
La signora Walter:	Chi va piano, va sano e va lontano.

Francesco:	Chissà! Non mi pare!
Elsa:	Tu sei un filòsofo... Rifletti sempre.
Francesco:	Non lo sono, ma lo sarò.
La signora Walter:	Che avventure abbiamo avuto! Sapete, prima abbiamo preso l'àutobus. Abbiamo sbagliato fermata. Siamo saliti su un altro àutobus.
Emilio:	Succede.
La signora Walter:	Siamo arrivati stanchi in Vaticano.
Emilio:	Io andrò col babbo. Sarà molto piú interessante.
Il dott. Walter:	Domani andremo, figlio mio.
Elsa:	Non vi abbiamo raccontato tutto. Siamo tornati al centro di Roma.
Emilio:	Che cosa è accaduto?
Elsa:	Per strada abbiamo chiesto ad un uomo: - Scusi, dove si tròvano il Foro Romano, il Colosseo, le Catacombe... L'uomo ci ha risposto: - Prendete la prima via a destra, poi a sinistra, andate sempre diritto, attraversate la piazza, poi andate verso il ponte, lí domandate di nuovo!
Emilio:	Era un pazzo?
Francesco:	Niente affatto! Abbiamo incontrato Figaro.
Emilio:	E come lo avete riconosciuto?
Figaro:	"La ran la lera, la ran la ra, Largo al factotum della città! Largo! La ran la la ran la la ran la la! Presto a bottega, ché l'alba è già, presto! La ran la la ran la la ran la la! Ah che bel vívere, che bel piacere, /2/ per un barbiere di qualità,

di qualità!
Ah bravo Figaro, bravo,
bravìssimo, bravo!
La ran la la ran la la ran la la!
Fortunatissimo per verità,
bravo!
La ran la la ran la la ran la la!
Fortunatìssimo per verità, /2/
La la ran la la la ran la la ran! /2/
Presto a far tutto,
la notte, il giorno
sempre d'intorno in giro sta.
Miglior cuccagna
per un barbiere,
vita piú nòbile
no non si dà,
la le ran /6/
Rasori e pèttini,
lancette e fòrbici /2/
al mio comando
tutto qui sta.
V'è la risorsa
poi del mestiere,
colla donnetta,
col cavaliere,
colla donnetta,
la le ran le ra,
col cavaliere,
la la ran la la la!
Ah che bel vívere,
che bel piacere, /2/
per un barbiere
di qualità /2/
Tutti mi chièdono,
tutti mi vògliono,
donne, ragazzi,
vecchi, fanciulle,
qua la parrucca,
presto la barba,
qua la sanguigna,
presto il biglietto,
tutti mi chièdono,
tutti mi vògliono /3/
qua la parrucca,
presto la barba,
presto il biglietto,
Figaro! /9/
Oimè, oimè, che fúria,
oimè che folla,
uno alla volta
per carità /3/
uno alla volta /3/
per carità.
Figaro!
Son qua.
Ehi! Figaro!
Son qua.
Figaro qua, Figaro là, /2/,
Figaro sù, Figaro giù /2/,
pronto, prontissimo
son come un fúlmine,
sono il factotum
della città /5/.
Ah bravo, Figaro, /2/
bravo, bravissimo
a te fortuna /3/
non mancherà,
la la ran /8/,
a te fortuna /3/
non mancherà
sono il factotum della città. /2/
della città /3/"

Francesco: Ed io gli ho chiesto:
"Dimmi un po'

	la tua bottega per trovarti dove sta?
Figaro:	La bottega non si sbaglia, guardi bene, èccola quà! Número quíndici, a mano manca, quattro gradini, facciata bianca, cinque parruche nella vetrina, sopra un cartello: pomata fina, mostra in azzurro alla moderna, v'è per insegna una lanterna, là senza fallo mi troverà!" /Atto I da Barbiere di Siviglia di G. Rossini/
Francesco:	Ho detto: "Ho ben capito". Tutti siamo scoppiati a rídere.
La signora Walter:	Poi l'uomo ci ha spiegato: – Non sono barbiere, nè sono il factotum della città. Sono proprietario di una trattoría. Guadagno poco, spendo molto. Ho una grande famiglia. Otto figli. Immaginàtevi! Schiavo sono io, schiavo e niente piú! Tutti i miei figli sono suonatori ambulanti. Il mio locale è semplice e silenzioso. Non c'è molta gente. C'è sempre però qualche cosa da mangiare. Venite con me! Noi ci guardiamo. Siamo d'accordo. Seguiamo l'uomo. Ben presto giungiamo davanti al piccolo ristorante. Il nostro condottiero índica un cartello che sta affisso sulla porta. Leggiamo: "E' vietato l'ingresso ai fumatori." L'uomo dice: "Odio il tabacco. Non posso soffrire i fumatori. Sono impertinenti." Sotto quel cartello c'è un finestrino. Egli bussa. Ci àprono.

	Entriamo.
	Tutto è pulito.
	Tutto è ben disposto.
	Le tavole sono coperte
	di tovaglie càndide.
	Ci sediamo.
	Immediatamente viene
	l'único cameriere.
	E'molto cortese.
	Ci saluta e ci domanda
	che cosa vogliamo.
	Ci porta le posate:
	i cucchiai, le forchette,
	i coltelli, i cucchiaini.
	Abbiamo mangiato bene.
	Tutto era molto gustoso.
	Abbiamo pagato
	e siamo usciti contenti.
	Fuori,
	davanti alla trattoria,
	c'è una piazza
	piena di carrozze.
	Non rídere!
	Davvero!
	I vetturini ci vèngono incontro
	e ci invìtano a portarci
	in carrozza.
	Dapprima rifiutiamo.
	Poi decidiamo di salire.
	Le risate e le grida
	sono state infinite.
	Abbiamo fatto una corsa tremenda.
	Una ruota si è staccata.
	Il vetturino si è arrabbiato.
	Elsa stupita ha protestato.
	Finalmente èccoci qui.
Emilio:	Non vi credo.
Il dott. Walter:	Ma perché non avete preso
	un tassì?
La signora Walter:	I tuoi figli non hanno voluto.
	Sai,
	nei mezzi di trasporto
	chièdono:
	- Scusi, scende?
	- Scusi, sale?
	- Permesso, permesso!
	E rídono come bambini
	maleducati.
	Che ne dici?
Il dott. Walter:	Siete rimasti contenti?
	E'la cosa piú importante.
Elsa:	Siamo felici e contenti.
	Il pomeriggio
	abbiamo visitato Roma antica:
	il Foro romano,
	ricco di tèmpli, di basìliche,
	di costruzioni monumentali,
	di bellìssime statue.

41

Michelangelo Buonarroti, Il Mosè
Roma, S. Pietro in Vincoli

" Si capisce l'orgoglio
dei romani
dell'età repubblicana
e di quella imperiale.
Infatti qui si è svolta
intensamente
la vita política, civile
e religiosa del pòpolo.
Impressionanti sono:
l'Arco trionfale di Tito,
l'arco di Settímio Severo,
i Fori imperiali di Traiano
e di Augusto,
il Colosseo –
quel grandioso Anfiteatro Flavio
per 50 000 spettatori.
Ha la forma ellíttica,
si svolge su quattro piani.
L'asse maggiore misura 188 metri,
quello minore 156,
la sua circonferenza 527,
mentre la màssima altezza
misura 57 metri. " /E.P./

Emilio: Domani visiteremo anche
le Catacombe.

Elsa: Siamo andati anche
alla Chiesa di San Pietro
in Víncoli
ad ammirare il Mosè
di Michelangelo.
" Il grande legislatore
del pòpolo ebràico,
dallo sguardo sdegnòso
e irritato
contro gli ebrèi idolatri,
è qui la síntesi
di una somma di sentimenti
umani e divini.
Il capolavoro è anche
un riflesso dello stato d'ànimo,
del caràttere e dei sentimenti
piú profondi
dell'artista stesso. " /E.P./

Emilio: Andiamo a pranzare!

Elsa: Ma guarda un po'!
Che ora è?
Sono le sette.
Fa buio.
Andiamo a cenare.

Emilio: Facciamo una passeggiata?

Il dott. Walter: Dopo la cena.

La famiglia Walter va a cenare.

Il dott. Walter: Cameriere,
è líbera questa tavola?

43

Il cameriere: Sì, signore, prego.
Accomodàtevi.
Ecco la lista.

La signora Walter legge la lista.

Antipasto
Prosciutto
Salame
Sardine
Olive
Gàmberi
Aragosta
Acciughe
Burro
Funghi
Antipasto misto

Primo piatto
Minestre
Brodo
Zuppa di pesce
Zuppa di verdura
Pizza
Ravioli
Risotto
Spaghetti

Secondo piatto
Carne
Arrosto
Bistecca
Lesso
Braciola di maiale
Costoletta /alla milanese,
alla bolognese/
Rognoni
Fègato
Manzo
Agnello
Vitello
Pollo /arrosto, bollito/
Lombo
Maiale

Pesce
Pesce fritto
Merluzzo
Rombo
Tonno
Trota
Contorno /verdura/
Patate fritte /lesse/
Purè di patate
Spinàci
Piselli
Fagiolini
Cavolfiore
Asparagi

Insalata
Insalata di cetrioli
Insalata di patate
Insalata di pomodori
Insalata verde

Uova
Uova alla coque
Uova sode
Uova al tegame
Uova all'occhio di bue
Frittata. Omelette.

Frutta, formaggio, dolci

Mele
Pere
Pesche
Uva
Banane
Prugne
Albicocche
Ciliege
Melone
Arance
Fràgole
Dàtteri
Mandorle
Budino
Pasta
Biscotti
Gelato
Torta

Formaggio
Cacio
Mozzarella

Vino, Birra

Vino bianco, rosso,
    dolce, secco,
      da pasto
Barbèra, Chianti, Frascati, Orvieto
Birra chiara, scura

Il dott. Walter:	<u>Avete scelto</u>?
Francesco:	Ci vuole tempo per <u>scégliere</u>.
Elsa:	Mio fratello sempre...
Il dott. Walter:	Elsa, <u>lascia stare</u>! Tuo fratello è un filòsofo. Ha sempre dei <u>desideri</u> speciali.
Elsa:	Mia madre e mio padre lo <u>difèndono</u> sempre. Noi abbiamo dei desideri sémplici. Non è vero, Emilio?
Emilio:	Io mangio di tutto. Che buon odore sento!
Il dott. Walter:	Per favore, signore, ci porti le migliori <u>pietanze</u>! E che cosa bevete?
La signora Walter:	Vorrei <u>bere</u> un succo di frutta.
Elsa:	Un'aranciata.
Francesco:	Sempre con quest'aranciata!
Il dott. Walter:	Basta, ragazzi! <u>Bevo</u> alla vostra salute, miei cari! <u>Siete content</u>i?

Michelangelo Buonarroti
Sibilla Eritrea
Vaticano, Cappella Sistina

GRAMMATICA

1. Aggettivo e pronome possessivo
2. Forme irregolari del participio passato
3. Passato prossimo: verbi transitivi e intransitivi
4. I verbi: sedersi, scegliere, bere
5. Verbi impersonali
6. Il modo infinito

Lessicologia

1. Per la città
2. Pranzo e cena
3. L'aria di Figaro

PATRIZIA

Oggi è domenica. Bel mattino. Sono le otto. Mi alzo. Esco subito. Dove? Non me lo chiedete, per favore! Lo sapete benissimo. Vado sotto il balcone di Patrizia. Non sento il suo violino da tre giorni. E' partita? Ah, eccola! Oggi non ho paura. "Buon giorno, Patrizia. Come stai?" Patrizia appena mi guarda. "Come mai cosí presto! Dove vai?" Parla tranquilla. Prende qualche cosa dal balcone e vuole rientrare. Ma io dico subito: "Patrizia, vuoi fare una passeggiata? Oggi fa bel tempo....." Perdo il coraggio. Patrizia non dice nulla. Guarda il cielo, il sole. Poi entra nella stanza. Non mi muovo... Il tempo passa. E' passata un'ora. Non mi muovo. Si avvicina un amico. Mi dice qualche cosa. Io non lo sento. Mi prende la mano. Dice: "Sei un pazzo. Capisci? Sei un pazzo ed io non ti conosco piú. Senti?" Non sento niente. L'amico se ne va. Non mi muovo.

Patrizia apre la porta. Si avvicina. "Andiamo! Dove?", dice tranquilla. Dove? Non lo so. Sono sbalordito. Sono il piú timido ragazzo del mondo. Penso: Ho pochi denari. Dove possiamo andare? Dico: "Patrizia, non possiamo prendere l'auto. Non ho denaro per l'auto. Sai, la settimana che viene..."Patrizia ride: "Anche io non ho denaro. Andiamo alle Catacombe!" Dico: "Possiamo però pranzare in un ristorante. Posso pagare il pranzo." Patrizia ride di nuovo: "Anche io posso pagare un pranzo. E cosí possiamo anche cenare. Bella vita! Eh?" Tutti e due scoppiamo in una risata.

Patrizia è una ragazza meravigliosa. Mi ha raccontato molte cose meravigliose. E' venuta da un altro mondo. Perciò suona il violino cosí... Vorrei andare anch'io in quel mondo. Forse lí c'è una scuola diretta dal grande maestro Michelangelo. Forse... Ho chiesto a Patrizia. Ella ride: "Sei un pazzo!"

"CHIARE, FRESCHE E DOLCI ACQUE,
OVE LE BELLE MEMBRA
POSE COLEI CHE SOLA A ME PAR DONNA"

Francesco Petrarca /1304-1374/

QUADRO QUARTO
LE STAGIONI

La signora Walter /canta/:
    Nella primavera
    tutto fiorisce:
    àlberi e prati
    pieni di fiori,
    spàrgono profumo,
    spargono bellezza,
    nel cuore stretto
    nasce la speranza.
    Ricca, trionfante,
    calda, abbondante
    ségue l'estate.
    Tutto ciò che ama
    non vuol'bruciarlo;
    sa che giorni d'oro,
    giorni d'autunno
    tra poco verranno,
    portando freschezza,
    portando salvezza,
    pioggia,
    poi neve,
    il sole invernale,
    il primo bucaneve.
    Sempre primavera!

Il dott. Walter: Ti sei già alzata?

La signora Walter: Sí.
    Ho riposato bene.
    Non sono piú stanca.
    Sono disposta ad uscire.
    Quale àutobus,
    fílobus o tram
    dobbiamo prèndere
    per andare a Villa Borghese?

Il dott. Walter: No, cosí non si può.
    Prenderemo un tassi.

La signora Walter: Anche a me piace
    il trasporto urbano.

Il dott. Walter: Ma come mai?
    Roma è una capitale grande.

La signora Walter: Ti sono gratìssima
    di tutto...

Il dott. Walter:	Quest' è bella!
	Mi fa piacere, lo sai.
Elsa:	Buon giorno.
	Siamo pronti.
	Fuori tira vento.
	Il cielo è coperto
	di núvole.
	Il pomeriggio
	non farà bel tempo.
	Pioverà.
Francesco:	In primavera è cosí.
	Grandi cambiamenti
	della natura e della vita.
Elsa:	Comincia a filosofare.
Francesco:	Per favore,
	silenzio,
	date retta a un giovinetto
	del nuovo sècolo!
	Vorrei recitare un'òpera mia
	dedicata all'anno 2000.
Elsa:	Be', sentiàmola!
Francesco:	Benvenuto, due mila!
	"Per noi
	ogni nuovo anno è un amico,
	che ci porta una bracciata
	di doni
	e di speranze d'oro.
	Tu m'allungherai i baffi,
	m'aggiungerai due dita
	di statura
	e mi libererai dal greco
	e dal latino.
	E tu aprirai le porte
	del nuovo sècolo,
	del sècolo nostro,
	del mio;
	poiché quello,
	che muore con te,
	è il sècolo della generazione
	vecchia
	che ci tiene alla cavezza.
	Sarà nostro il venturo
	che ci si apre davanti,
	come un continente misterioso...
	Sino a mezzo /alla metà/
	del venturo io vivrò, spero,
	e regnerò, forse.
	O pòveri vecchi
	che non vedrete!
	Noi rinnoveremo le lettere
	e trasformeremo le arti,
	daremo a ogni scienza
	uno spintone...
	e troveremo sieri infallíbili
	per tutte le infermità,
	e viaggeremo sopra le núvole
	e in fondo all'ocèano,

Michelangelo Buonarroti, La creazione dell'...
Vaticano, Cappella Sistina

| | e <u>udremo</u> la música nuova,
| | e <u>converseremo</u> con gli amici
| | da un capo all'altro d'Europa,"
| | da <u>Est</u> a <u>Ovest</u>,
| | da Nord a Sud,
| | in tutto il mondo.

| Emilio: | Bravíssimo!
| | L'<u>hai scritto</u> tu?

| Francesco: | Sí, ti piace?

| Emilio: | Molto.

| Elsa: | Dio mio,
| | che impertinenza!
| | Che <u>bugiardo sei</u> tu!
| | Questo è un <u>brano</u>
| | di Edmondo <u>De Amícis</u>
| | dal suo <u>Capo d'anno</u>.

| Francesco: | Elsa!
| Il dott. Walter: | Domani sera
| | <u>andremo</u> dal dottor Rossi
| | <u>di cui</u> vi ho parlato.
| | Ci ha invitato a cena.
| | Abbiamo un <u>appuntamento</u> qui
| | all'albergo.
| | Verrà lui a prènderci.
| | E'molto simpàtico.
| | <u>Trascorreremo</u> una bella serata.
| | <u>Vedrete</u>.
| | Anche lui <u>prende parte</u> al Congresso
| | <u>per cui</u> sono venuto.
| | E'un bravo medico.
| | Il suo nome è noto.
| | Pronto, per favore,
| | può chiamarmi un tassì?
| | Me lo <u>màndano</u> sùbito?
| | Grazie.
| | Andiamo.

La famiglia Walter scende. Davanti all'albergo
li aspetta un tassì.

| Il dott. Walter: | Signore, per favore,
| | facciamo un giro:
| | Piazza Navona,
| | Piazza Venezia,
| | Il Campidoglio,
| | Il Palazzo del Quirinale,
| | La Fontana di Trevi,
| | La piazza di Spagna,
| | Villa Borghese.

| Elsa: | Babbo,
| | scendo al primo ufficio postale
| | che vediamo.
| | Voglio <u>imbucare</u> /<u>impostare</u>/ le lèttere
| | che ho scritto.

| Emilio: | Anche io.
| | Ho scritto a un <u>malato</u>

	con cui /il quale/ siamo amici. L'Italia lo interessa molto. Gli spedisco delle cartoline. Gliele spedirò raccomandate.
Alla posta Elsa:	Quanto costa un francobollo per l'èstero? Per una lèttera raccomandata? /semplice, via aèrea/ Mi faccia pesare le lèttere! Sono un po' pesanti. Fino a che ora è aperta la posta? Mi dia, per favore, dieci buste! Grazie.
Corre Francesco. Francesco:	Vengo per spedire un telegramma alla nonna. L'abbiamo dimenticata. Per favore, quanto costa a parola?
Emilio:	Aspetta, aspetta! Il babbo le ha telefonato. Non l'ha dimenticata.

Francesco:	Perbacco! Il bene lo faccio sempre in ritardo! Eppure glielo spedirò! Emilio, préstami 2000 lire!
Emilio:	Eccotele!
Francesco:	Mille grazie, fratello!

I Walter prosèguono il loro itinerario.

Elsa:	Papà, che edificio è questo? E' un Duomo?
Il dott. Walter:	Questo è il Pàntheon. Dopo il Colosseo questo è il monumento piú interessante e meglio conservato della Roma augustea. Nel suo interno custodisce le tombe dei reali d'Italia e quella del grande Raffaello.
Elsa:	Vorrei visitarlo. E' chiuso. Quando è aperto?
L'autista:	Da alcuni mesi il Pàntheon è in ricostruzione. Non si può entrare.
Elsa:	Peccato! E quella statua? Di che època è?
Il dott. Walter:	La bellìssima statua equestre in bronzo è d'età imperiale /originariamente dorata/. E' dell'Imperatore Marco Aurelio. Ecco la Villa Borghese. E' un parco che si estende per 6 chilòmetri. Il cardinale Borghese vi ha raccolto oggetti artistici. La Villa è costruita ai primi del XVII sècolo. Ci sono pitture preziose, sculture dello stile Barocco, eccètera.
La signora Walter:	Che bel parco! Una vera armonìa tra arte e natura. Come si chiàmano questi fiori di tutti i colori: giallo, rosa, viola, celeste, turchino, e quegli screziati?

Dopo la visita alla Villa.

Emilio: Babbo,
voglio visitare
una biblioteca centrale.
Cerco un libro di storia
composto di molti volumi.
Voglio saperne di piú
su Mazzini e su Garibaldi.
Mi interessa molto
il Risorgimento italiano
come movimento nazionale
e anche il Romanticismo
italiano
come corrente letteraria.
Vedremo il monumento di Garibaldi?
Conoscete questo fatto
della vita di Garibaldi?
E'avvenuto durante
la guerra di liberazione
italiana del 1859-1860,
condotta alla vittoria
dall'eroe del pòpolo italiano
Giuseppe Garibaldi.
Un gruppo di soldati,
comandati da un sergente
taglia legna in un bosco.
I soldati lavòrano con zelo
e il sergente senza fare nulla
solo comanda, grida e rimprèvera
i soldati.
Passa in quel momento un uomo
a cavallo
che si ferma a guardare
e chiede al sergente:
- Perché gridi tanto?
- Perché abbiamo fretta
e devo fare lavorare
i miei soldati.
- E se avete fretta,
perché non aiuti anche tu?
- Ma io sono il sergente
e devo solo comandare.
- Ho capito,
ora vengo ad aiutare
un poco anch'io.
Il cavaliere scende
da cavallo
e si mette a tagliare legna.
Quando ha fatto un bel fascio
lo porge al sergente,
che nel frattempo
contínua a dare òrdini
e a gridare qua e là.
- Grazie - dice il sergente.
- Non c'è bisogno di ringraziare,
dice il cavaliere,
ognuno ha il dovere
di aiutare in un caso símile.
Se un'altra volta
hai bisogno di me,
puoi chiamarmi.
- Con piacere...ma chi è Lei?
- Io sono il generale Garibaldi.

Elsa:	Grandi uòmini ci sono nella storia del mondo.

La sera. La famiglia Walter riposa davanti al televisore.

La signora Walter:	Che cosa c'è stasera alla televisione?
Francesco:	Stasera sarà rappresentata e sarà anche trasmessa per radio l'opera B o h è m e di Giácomo Puccini.
Elsa:	Accendiamo il televisore! Spegniamo la luce! Silenzio! Non fate chiasso! Comincia lo spettacolo. Nella parte di Mimi c'è la signora Vittorini. Tutto il complesso è òttimo. Vale la pena di sentirlo. Che voci mòrbide, commoventi!

GRAMMATICA

1. I pronomi personali: soggetto, complemento diretto, complemento indiretto, raggruppamenti di pronomi personali
2. I pronomi relativi
3. Aggettivi e pronomi indefiniti
4. Gli avverbi
5.' Le particelle avverbiali e pronominali: ci-vi-ne
6. Il verbo <u>andarsene</u>
7. I verbi: tenere, morire, apparire, udire
8. Futuro semplice
9. Particolarità del futuro semplice

    Lessicologia
1. Le stagioni
2. Roma monumentale
3. Alla posta
4. I colori
5. Giuseppe Garibaldi
6. La televisione e la radio
7. Paganini al ristorante. Paganini e il vetturino. Scipione ed Ennio

PAGANINI AL RISTORANTE

Paganini è a Milano. Mentre passeggia per le vie con il suo meraviglioso violino sotto il braccio, sente odore di pesce fritto che a lui piace molto. Segue l'odore e giunge davanti a una trattoria. Entra, ma, immediatamente il proprietario gli va incontro e lo prega di uscire dal locale. Paganini stupito e arrabbiato vuole protestare, ma il proprietario gli indica un cartello che sta affisso sulla porta e sul quale è scritto: E'vietato l'ingresso ai suonatori ambulanti.

PAGANINI E IL VETTURINO

Paganini dà concerti a Parigi. Una sera si avvicina a una carrozza e domanda al vetturino quanto costa una corsa fino alla sala del concerto.
- Venti franchi - risponde il vetturino.
- Sono cosí care le carrozze a Parigi? - domanda il maestro.
- Caro signore, - dice il vetturino, che ha riconosciuto il maestro - quando si guadagnano 4 mila franchi per suonare su una corda sola si possono dare anche venti franchi per una corsa in carrozza.

Paganini non risponde nulla e sale in carrozza. Quando giungono davanti alla sala scende e paga al vetturino solo due franchi dicendo:
-Gli altri diciotto franchi te li darò quando potrai portarmi su una ruota sola.

braccio, m
passeggiare
corda, f

SCIPIONE ED ENNIO

Scipione, famoso condottiero romano, ha bisogno di parlare al poeta Ennio. Va a casa sua e lo chiama dalla strada. Una schiava risponde che Ennio non è in casa, ma Scipione sente che proprio Ennio le dice di rispondere cosí. E se ne va.
Dopo qualche giorno Ennio bussa alla porta di Scipione.
- Non sono in casa - dice Scipione.
- Ma come, dice Ennio, io sento la tua voce.
- Tu sei poco cortese, risponde Scipione. L'altro giorno io ho creduto alla tua schiava, quando mi diceva che non eri a casa e ora tu non vuoi credere a me stesso?

diceva /dire/
eri /essere/

Sempre primavera

Andante
Parole e musica: E. Gateva

Nella primavera tutto fiorisce!

Alberi e prati, pieni di fiori,

spargono profumo, spargono bellezza;

nel cuore stretto nasce la speranza.

Ricca, trionfante, calda, abbondante

rit.
segue l'estate.

a tempo
Tutto ciò che ama non vuol bruciarlo;

sa che giorni d'oro, giorni d'autunno

tra poco verranno, portando salvezza, portando freschezza, pioggia, poi neve, il

sole invernale, il primo bucaneve. Sempre primavera!

"CHE FAI TU, LUNA, IN CIEL? DIMMI, CHE FAI,
SILENZIOSA LUNA?
SORGI LA SERA, E VAI
CONTEMPLANDO I DESERTI."
/Giacomo Leopardi 1798-1837/

QUADRO QUINTO

I MESI

Francesco /canta/: Che gèlida manina,
se la lasci riscaldar...
Cercar che giova?
Al buio non si trova.
Ma per fortuna
è una notte di luna
e qui la luna
l'abbiamo vicina.
Aspetti signorina!
Le dirò con due parole:
chi son, chi son,
e che faccio,
come vivo?
Vuole?
Chi son? Chi son?
Sono un poeta.
Che cosa faccio?
Scrivo.
E come vivo?
Vivo...

Elsa /canta/: Sí,
mi chiamano Mimì,
ma il mio nome è Lucía.
La storia mia è breve;
a tela o a seta
ricamo a casa e fuori.
Son tranquilla e lieta
ed è mio svago
far gigli e rose.
Mi piàccion quelle cose
che han sì dolce malìa,
che pàrlano d'amore,
di primavere...
che pàrlano di sogni
e di chimere,
quelle cose
che han nome poesía.

/G. Puccini – Boheme/

Elsa: Lei m'intende?

Francesco: Sí.
Noi ci intendiamo
senza parlare.

Emilio: Che cosa volete dire?

Francesco: Te lo traduco sùbito.
Un filòsofo e una cantante
si intèndono facilmente.
Capisci?

Emilio:	Capisco.
Francesco:	Finalmente! Lo dico sempre che il pittore pensa piú del filòsofo.
Emilio:	Mi fai dei rimpròveri?
Francesco:	Per carità! Non ti faccio niente.
Elsa:	Basta, ragazzi! E'tardi. Vado con la mamma dal parrucchiere. Stasera andiamo a trovare il dottor Rossi. Dobbiamo prepararci.
Francesco:	Veniamo anche noi.

Vicino all'albergo c'è un salone.

La parrucchiera:	Che cosa desidera, signora?
La signora Walter:	Tutte e due vorremmo fare la messa in piega.
Elsa:	Vorrei farmi tagliare un po' i capelli.
Il parrucchiere:	Signore, devo accorciarLe un po' i capelli. Sono troppo lunghi.
Francesco:	Mi faccia la barba, per favore!
Il parrucchiere:	Le piàcciono i baffi e le basette?
Francesco:	Sí, signore. Mi piàcciono, ma...
Il parrucchiere:	Vorrebbe l'acqua di Cologna, brillantina, crema?
Francesco:	No, no, grazie. Quanto Le devo?
Il parrucchiere:	Alla cassa, per favore.
Francesco:	Scusi, non ho spíccioli.
Il cassiere:	Non si preòccupi! Ecco il resto.
Elsa:	Scusi, signore, sà dirmi dove c'è una lavandería a secco?
Il cassiere:	Dietro il nostro salone, signorina.

Elsa:	Grazie. Buon giorno.
	Tutti e quattro cércano e tròvano súbito la lavandería a secco. Entrano. In fondo alla sala vèdono una ragazzina. Elsa si rivolge a lei
Elsa:	Per favore, signorina, mi faccia pulire questa gonna. Vi ho fatto una macchia.
Emilio:	Anche la mia giacca.
Elsa:	Saranno pronte stasera?
La ragazza:	No, per domani alle cinque.
Elsa:	Scusi, signorina, ma non posso lasciarle. Ho bisogno di...
La ragazza:	Mi dispiace, ma non posso fare nient'altro. Buon giorno.

La signora Walter:	Sapete? Ho bisogno di un calzolaio.
	Mi faccio riparare il tacco.
Elsa:	Che cosa faremo?
Emilio:	Aspetteremo il babbo.
	Egli tornerà dal Congresso.
	Allora decideremo.
	Mentre lo aspettiamo
	vi racconterò del mio sogno.
Francesco:	Il sogno di un...
La signora Walter:	Tu devi sempre canzonare.
	Emilio, ti ascolto.
Emilio:	Stanotte ho visto in sogno
	tutti i dodici mesi
	come persone vive.
	Erano figli dell'Anno
	e della Terra.
	GENNAIO sembrava un gigante.
	Aveva occhi azzurri,
	fronte alta.
	La barba, le sopracciglia
	ed i capelli
	èrano bianchi.
	Il volto ed il corpo gióvani.
	Era un saggio.
	Assomigliava a Leonardo da Vinci.
	Intorno a lui c'era freddo,
	ma anche - tranquillità.
	Teneva per mano suo figlio
	il Capodanno.
	Al contrario del padre
	il figlio era allegro.
	Veniva da una stella
	e portava ai nonni
	e al padre la Risurrezione.
	Tutti gli volèvano molto bene.
	Vedevo i quadri di Raffaello,
	sentivo la música di Mozart.
	FEBBRAIO era il figlio minore.
	Era di bassa statura.
	La testa di un romano nòbile.
	I lineamenti molto fini.
	I capelli brizzolati.
	Era magro, pàllido,
	era di cattivo umore.
	A volte gli mancava
	qualcosa
	e fuggiva a cercarla.
	Era piccolo,
	ma spaventava tutti.
	Diceva:
	"E'bene farsi amare,
	ma è meglio farsi temére.
	Farsi odiare, no.
	Giova quindi il timore
	che non ha affinità con l'òdio."
	/Il Principe - N. Machiavelli,
	1469-1527/
	Era Machiavelli? No, no...

Raffaello Sanzio, /1483-1520/, Madonna della Seggiola
Firenze, Palazzo Pitti

MARZO aveva le spalle larghe,
il collo lungo,
il naso di un greco.
Orecchi piccoli.
Petto forte.
Svelto!
Ora sorrideva come un Dio,
ora gettava uno sguardo
da bestia feroce.
Allora le mani
gli si stringèvano in pugni.
Io avevo davvero paura.
Si arrabbiava,
poi sorrideva,
portàndoci un bucaneve.
Tutti i figli vivèvano
all'estremo Oriente
su una montagna altìssima.
  APRILE era un entusiasta.
Giudicava con giustizia.
Metteva tutto in órdine:
gli èsseri e la natura "morta".
Aspettava il maggio
e cantava allegro:
"Maggio risveglia i nidi,
maggio risveglia i cuori,
....
le donne han nei capelli
rose, negli occhi il sol."
/Giosué Carducci 1835-1907/
  MAGGIO era bello,
dai capelli ricciuti,
dalle guance paffute
e le labbra piene.
Respirava a pieni polmoni.
Un vero Apollo.
Giocava con la gente,
con gli uccelli,
con gli animali.
Si nascondeva in un cespuglio,
o in un boschetto,
o in un bosco fitto,
poi entrava nella gola
dell'usignuolo.
La dolce melodía
si udiva dappertutto.
Altri uccelli ed insetti
lo aiutàvano.
Tuonava,
si avvicinava GIUGNO.
  Maggio,lo accoglieva
come sé lo meritava:
cadèvano i fúlmini,
gran chiarore, poi silenzio.
Il profumo delle rose
veniva da ogni parte.
Le rose erano coperte di
gocce di pioggia.
Le beveva LUGLIO,
uomo dal corpo ardente,
dagli occhi scuri, penetranti.
Accendeva un fuoco,
il segnale d'inízio
della mietitura.

Michelangelo Buonarroti. David
Firenze, Galleria dell'Accademia

Veniva AGOSTO.
Il frumento, il granoturco,
tutti i cereali
èrano maturi.
I raggi del sole
riscaldàvano la schiena
del contadino.
Le gambe,i piedi, il dorso
gli dolèvano.
I ginocchi si piegàvano.
Tutto il corpo si sforzava.
Ma egli era contento.
Il granaio scricchiolava
dal peso.
Le cantine si riempìvano di
vìveri.
    SETTEMBRE veniva dal mare.
Con passo leggero.
Con l'aria distratta.
Càrico di frutta.
Biondo, bruciato.
I fratelli andàvano a trovare
i loro genitori,
portando sempre ricchi regali:
la neve sòffice, il sole,
la pioggia, la frutta.
    OTTOBRE era tièpido,
serio,
dai capelli castani, lisci.
Era snello e orgoglioso.
I suoi fratelli erano venuti
prima di lui.
Avevano lavorato bene.
Avèvano adornato le foglie
e l'erba.
Avèvano appeso delle nùvole
variopinte.
Avèvano mandato alcuni uccelli
per il mondo.
E gli uccelli vòlano,
annunciando un nuovo Rinascimento.
    NOVEMBRE E DICEMBRE
mi sussuràvano all'orecchio:
"Lenta la neve fiocca, fiocca, fiocca.
Senti: una zana dòndola pian piàno.
Un bimbo piange, il pìccol dito in bocca,
canta una vecchia, il mento sulla mano.
La vecchia canta: Intorno al tùo lettino
C'è rose e gigli, tutto un bel giardino.
Nel bel giardino il bimbo s'addormenta.
La neve fiocca lenta, lenta, lenta."
/Giovanni Páscoli 1855-1912/

La signora Walter:	Che strano sogno! Ne farò una messa in scena. Tuo fratello e tua sorella penseranno alla mùsica. Tu dipingerai le decorazioni. Tuo padre sarà il giùdice.
Francesco:	Finché c'è vita, c'è speranza!
La signora Walter:	Smetti di ridere! Lo dico sul sèrio.

GRAMMATICA

1. Aggettivi e pronomi interrogativi
2. I verbi: tradurre, condurre, produrre
3. Il verbo causativo: fare
4. L'imperfetto
5. Il trapassato prossimo

Lessicologia

1. Vari servizi: dal parrucchiere, dal calzolaio, alla lavanderia a secco
2. I mesi
3. Il corpo ed il carattere umano
4. Le barzellette: I due piaceri, La fine del mondo

I DUE PIACERI

- Ascoltami! Devo parlarti di una cosa che mi riguarda.
- Parlamene pure!
- Devi farmi due grandi piaceri. Te ne sarò gratissimo.
- Dimmi ciò che desideri: sono dispostissimo a fare tutto ciò che mi sarà possibile.
- Il primo piacere che ti chiedo è di prestarmi subito mille lire: anzi, se puoi, prestamene due mila. Il secondo piacere è di non dirlo a nessuno.
- Ecco, il secondo piacere te lo posso fare volentieri, da vero amico. Il primo, mi dispiace, ma proprio non posso.

LA FINE DEL MONDO

Un conferenziere spiega al pubblico che, secondo alcuni astronomi la fine del mondo accadrà fra trenta milioni di anni.
- Come? Come ha detto? - grida spaventato un uomo, alzandosi. - Quando sarà la fine del mondo?
- Fra trenta milioni di anni.
- Ah! esclama l'uomo - rimettendosi a sedere, con un sospiro di sollievo. - Avevo capito fra tre milioni!

esclamare
sospirare, sospiro, m.
sollievo, m.

"NELLE OPERE TEATRALI IL PUBBLICO
È IL SUPREMO GIUDICE!"
　　　Vincenzo Bellini 1801-1835

QUADRO SESTO
AL CONCERTO

La signora Walter: Vi racconterò di quando
sono andata a Teatro
per la prima volta.
"-Abbiamo fatto tardi -
dice mia nonna.
Infatti,
quando entriamo nel palchetto,
il primo atto è già finito.
Cala il sipario.
Nel teatro si riaccèndono
le luci.
Io, dapprima,
non vedo l'impressionante folla.
Poi vedo le file dei palchetti,
poi la platèa,
tutta nera di teste,
il sipario, la ribalta.
Poi alzo la testa
e ammiro il lampadàrio.
- Ti piace? - mi chiede la nonna.
- Sí, è tanto bello.
- Vedi,
questi sono i palchi
in prima fila,
quello è il loggione,
dove i prezzi sono bassi
e dove puoi rimanere schiacciata.
Ti piacerebbe èssere lassú ?
- Oh!
- Quelle sono le poltrone,
quelli - i posti distinti,
i posti in piedi...
- E quello, nonna?
Indico la cuffia del suggeritore.
- Oh, - dice la nonna,
è un po'diffícile spiegarti.
Quando a scuola
una tua compagna
non sa la lezione,
un'altra le suggerisce
piano, piano...
in modo che la maestra
non senta.
- La maestra se ne accorge
sempre.
- Anche il pùbblico se ne accorge
quando gli attori non sanno
la parte.

"Oh, Dio, adesso tu non sai
che cosa è la parte.
Abbi pazienza, bambina!
Ma bisogna
che tu stia attenta.
La nonna mi dice
che dietro il sipario
c'è il palcoscènico
e che lo spettácolo è là,
sul palcoscènico.
Si alza il sipario
e appare l'interno
d'un convento
e due mònache...
La nonna mi fa cenno
di ascoltare e di stare zitta...
Io non comprendo: sto buona,
sto zitta, ma non capisco.
La mamma è là: perché è là?
E'in convento?
Si è fatta suora?
Perché?
Perché non mi hanno detto
nulla?
E'la mamma,
non c'è piú nessun dubbio...
Tendo le braccia a mia madre,
ma il sipario cade
in quel momento
e copre tutto.
Il convento è sparito." /Secondo M. Moretti/

Emilio: Non ho mai sentito
di questa storia.
Perciò ti sei fatta regista.

La signora Walter: Non sono sicura
se proprio questo fosse
il motivo e la causa, ma...

Francesco: Poco prima ho letto
un fatto della vita di Puccini.
"Si rappresentava a Vienna
la Butterflay.
Puccini aveva preso alloggio
in un albergo.
Portàrono un mucchio di posta
per lui.
Il maestro la sfogliava
distrattamente:
inviti a feste,
a ricevimenti, a pranzi,
complimenti di gente illustre.
Tutta roba
che non lo interessava.
Ma ad un tratto
gli capitò fra le mani
ia lèttera di un giovanotto
che si qualificava studente
e innamorato...
innamorato di una bionda ragazza
viennese;
e siccome era pòvero

>
> chiedeva due poltrone
> per ascoltare la musica
> del maestro
> insieme alla sua ragazza.
> Puccini ne fu tanto commosso
> che andò lui stesso
> a comprare i due biglietti
> e poi li spedì al giovanotto."

Emilio: Credi
che oggi possa accadere
una cosa símile?

Elsa: Di una cosa símile
oggi si dice:
"Vedi tempi antichi"!

Èmilio: Ma perché, perché?

Elsa: Perché siamo troppo intelligenti.

Francesco: Elsa, che cosa dici?
L'umanésimo esiste!

In quel momento ritorna il dottor Walter dal Congresso. Suona il telèfono.

Il dott. Walter:	Pronto!
	Chi parla?
La voce del dott. Rossi:	Riccardo, buona sera.
	Vi aspetto nel ridotto
	con una pìccola sorpresa.
Il dott. Walter:	Scendiamo sùbito.
	Ma chi si vede?
	Signor Civinini!
	Lo sapevo io!
	Lei conosce il dottor Rossi!
	Inghe, ti presento il dottor Rossi.

I Walter e il dottor Rossi
fanno conoscenza fra di loro.

Il dott. Rossi:	Il signor Civinini
	ci ha telefonato.
	Ci ha invitato al suo concerto.
	Io gli ho detto
	che non possiamo andare
	perché stasera aspettiamo
	alcuni òspiti di Berlino.
	Egli mi ha detto il tuo nome.
	Poi...èccoci qui.
	Prima andiamo al concerto,
	poi a casa mia.
	D'accordo?
Il dott. Walter:	Pensavo di proporvi lo stesso.
Il dott. Rossi:	E'chiaro.
	C'è la telepatìa!
	Andiamo!
	La mia famiglia ci aspetta.
	Laura, ti presento la famiglia
	Walter.
	La signora Laura Rossi,
	mia moglie, la mia
	collaboratrice, segretaria,
	e compagna.
	Ella è responsàbile
	di tutto il buono o il cattivo
	che mi può accadere.
	Lolita, nostra figlia,
	attrice famosa
	ma senza denaro.
	L'altra figlia Giovanna
	frequenta il collegio.
	Il suo sogno è quello
	di finire il piú presto possìbile
	gli studi a scuola.
	Nostro figlio Antonio,
	scrittore, redattore,
	giornalista e operaio.
	Infatti è un ingegnere
	ricercatore.
Antonio:	Oh, papà!

Il dott. Rossi: Ed io,
mèdico sémplice
e capo della prodigiosa famiglia.
Curo dei disturbi,
gravi o leggere malattíe.
Mi viene un paziente
e dice:
– Dottore, mi sento molto male.
Ed io:
– Che cosa Le fa male?
Egli:
– Mi fa male la testa.
Può darsi che il cervello...
Io:
– Può darsi...
Ma egli mi interrompe
con un gesto nervoso:
– Mi duole la gola,
la lingua è bianca.
Ho mal di stòmaco,
gli intestini...
Ho la tosse.
Credo di avere la febbre alta.
Ho comprato dalla farmacía
questa medicina.
Me la consiglia?
Io:

	– Vediàmola!
	Credo
	che fosse meglio
	buttarla via.
	Ha la pressione alta?
	....
	No, non l'ha.
	Ecco, Lei non ha niente.
	Ha preso un raffreddore.
	Ha dei disturbi intestinali.
	Deve stare a dieta.
	Guarito, vada súbito
	in campagna!
	L'aria fresca Le farà bene.
	Addío!
Antonio:	Papà,
	smetti con queste bugíe!
Il dott. Walter:	Ah, tu sei sempre lo stesso!
Il dott. Rossi:	Andiamo!
	Il concerto comincia.
Emilio:	Signor Civinini,
	che cosa ascolteremo?
G. Civinini:	Nella prima parte
	l'Orchestra da càmera eseguirà
	I Concerti grossi di A. Corelli
	e Le quattro stagioni di A. Vivaldi.
	Io canterò nella seconda parte
	due canzoni: L'Ideale di Tosti
	e la Mattinata di R. Leoncavallo
	e l'aria di Calaf.
	Il soprano Bianca Merelli eseguirà
	l'aria di Rosina.
	Ascolterete il basso Giuliano Brunetti
	che canterà l'aria della Calunnia.
	Tutti e due sono dall'Accademia
	Santa Cecilia di Roma.
Il dott. Rossi:	Dopo il concerto
	ci riuniamo presso le àuto.
Tutti:	In bocca al lupo, signor Civinini!

GRAMMATICA

1. Il passato remoto
2. I piu importanti verbi irregolari al passato remoto
3. Il modo congiuntivo
4. Il congiuntivo presente
5. Il congiuntivo passato

Lessicologia

1. Al teatro, al concerto
2. Presentazioni
3. Dal medico
4. Le barzellette: Il dottore ed il sarto, Ciascuno ama i suoi simili

IL DOTTORE E IL SARTO

Il dottore di campagna va dal sarto del paese dove lavora.
- Buon giorno, desidero un vestito.
- Si accomodi, signore ! Le prendo subito le misure !
- Il vestito deve essere per tutti i giorni, perché per i vestiti belli vado dal sarto di città.
- Lei allora fa proprio come me. Quando ho solo un piccolo disturbo, vengo da Lei. Quando la malattia è seria, vado dal dottore di città.

CIASCUNO AMA I SUOI SIMILI

Dante, perseguitato nella sua patria, fu costretto a fuggire a Verona, dove il principe Albonio della Scala mostrava a quest'uomo di genio meno stima che al buffone che teneva alla sua corte. Ad un tale, che gli mostrava la sua sorpresa per una tale preferenza, Dante rispose:
- Ciascuno ama i suoi simili!

costringere
mostrare
stima, f.
corte, f
simile, agg.

"CIASCUNO AMA I SUOI SIMILI."

QUADRO SETTIMO
L'AMICIZIA

Tutti:	Bravo, signor Civinini, bravo!
Il dott. Walter:	Mi pare di aver sentito Gigli in persona!
G. Civinini:	Oh, Lei sta esagerando!
Emilio:	Proprio cosí!
Francesco:	Ottima interpretazione! I suoi colleghi sono perfetti. L'Orchestra è di alto livello. Gli archi, il gruppo degli strumenti a fiato, gli ottoni, gli strumenti a percussione hanno suonato con impegno. Il Direttore d'orchestra ha fatto una bella figura. Non impone a forza la sua interpretazione, ma ti lascia líbero. Così si può concepire meglio la filosofía del compositore.
Il dott. Rossi:	L'osservazione del gióvane è vera. Insomma questa è una verità generale. Andiamo a casa!
Elsa:	Dove sono parcheggiate le macchine?
Francesco:	Non te ne sei accorta? Io invece ho visto le scritte: "Senso único", "E'vietato il parcheggio." "E'riservato alle màcchine autorizzate".
Elsa:	Non ti è sfuggito niente.
Francesco:	Dottor Rossi, è lontano la Sua casa?
Il dott. Rossi:	Sí, è un po'lontano. Non possiamo andare a piedi. Si trova in periferia, in un bel quartiere.

	Non ci sono centri residenziali nè condòmini. Vicino alla casa si trova l'ospedale ed il policlínico dove lavoro io.
	....
La signora Rossi:	Eccoli. Antonio, è chiuso a chiave. Apri il cancello! Entrate pure! Sentítevi come se foste a casa vostra.
La signora Walter:	Non credevo che aveste una casa cosí bella!
La signora Rossi:	Sí, è còmoda. Non è grande, è vecchia, ma ci siamo abituati. Non mi piace l'appartamento, benché sia piú fàcile da mantenerlo. Anche Rossi è della stessa opinione. Finita la guerra,

	siamo venuti in questa casa.
	Non c'è rumore.
	La casa e un'eredità.
	E'stata costruita dai genitori
	di Rossi.
	Un giorno, però, la perderemo.
	Lo Stato ha cominciato a
	costruire anche qui.
	Rossi non è contento
	perché con l'età
	i nostri costumi, le nostre pretese...
Il dott. Rossi:	Non voglio sentire
	che tu mi parli dell'età.
	Nessuno può arrestare
	lo sviluppo della tècnica.
	Io non credo
	che la nostra vita àbbia límite.
	Il tempo, lo spazio e cosi via
	sono nozioni filosòfiche...
	Che cosa ce ne dìcono i gióvani?
	Di che cosa state conversando?
Antonio:	Sto raccontando di
	"Una grande pàgina della mia vita.
	Fra le mie piú memoràbili glorie
	giovanili,
	figura anche la modificazione
	di un'importante legge
	delle scienze físiche.
	Questa legge pretende
	che un animale, o un fiore,
	al quale venga tolta l'aria
	mediante la "campana pneumàtica"
	muoia per mancanza di ossígeno.
	- Domani - aveva annunziato
	con la sua flèbile voce il professore
	di físiça alla scolaresca della Terza
	Liceo B-
	eseguiremo l'esperimento
	della campana pneumàtica.
	Rinunceremo a sacrificare
	una bestiola e ci serviremo
	di un fiore.
	Anzi: qualcuno di voi porti
	senz'altro questo fiore.
	- Io! - scattai primo
	fra trentadue compagni,
	con quello zelo
	che tanto mi distingueva
	quando mi trovavo in classe,
	e non esiliato nel corridoio
	per ingiusta punizione.
	L'indomani, dunque, mi recai
	al Liceo,
	alle due meno un quarto,
	tenendo fra le dita
	un bellìssimo garòfano screziato.
	L'assistente sta appunto preparando
	la campana pneumàtica per l'esperimento:
	gli dico che per órdine superiore
	ho portato il garofano
	e che m'incombe anche l'obbligo

77

di collocarlo sotto la campana.
Il mìope vecchietto mi risponde
con un gesto rassegnato,
ed eseguo in pochi àttimi
l'importante operazione.
Il professore guarda la campana
e il fiore,
mi ringrazia con un sorriso
búrbero-paterno ed esordisce.
- Oggi, dunque, eseguiremo l'esperimento
di cui parlammo ieri.
Toglieremo gradualmente l'aria
dalla campana di vetro,
e vedremo, via, via,
il garòfano sullo stelo reclinare
e avvizzire.
Prego di far attenzione.
Molinelli, incominci!
Molinelli è il vecchietto assistente:
costui, a un cenno del professore,
incomincia a far girare l'ampia ruota
il cui movimento deve togliere
l'aria dalla campana:
e dopo un paio di minuti
di sforzi, si riposa.
- L'aria - disse il professore -

è ora tolta in piccola quantità;
il fiore non ne risente ancora:
fra breve, gli efetti della mancanza
d'aria saranno evidenti.
Molinelli, avanti!
Con un'espressione di martire
cristiano,
Molinelli riprende a far girare
la ruota.
Sessantaquattro pupille sono
fissamente spalancate sul garòfano,
che mantiene con fierezza
la propria posizione
ad onta del tentativo di asfissiarlo.
- Bisogna perseverare:
si faccia silenzio!
Molinelli, continui a togliere
l'aria senza interruzione.
Il pòvero assistente,
già soverchiato dalla fatica,
ricomincia la sua pena
fino a congestionarsi.
Ormai le posizioni sono chiare,
e la lotta è aperta
fra il professore,
sicuro del fatto suo,
e il fiore ben deciso
a non lasciarsi sopraffare.
Il mormorío riprende
in tono maggiore.
- Avanti! - órdina il professore
al disgraziato Molinelli,
oramai all'estremo.
Ma il formidabile garòfano
non piega, non si flette,
non oscilla, non cede.
L'altro da capo ad affannarsi
sulla ruota:
ciascuno da noi capisce
che ormai i minuti sono contati:
non per la vita del fiore,
ma per quella dell'assistente.
- C'è ancora dell'aria?
si esacerba il professore.
Risate, urla; colpo di scena inatteso:
Molinelli ha cessato di girare
la ruota e si è abbattuto su una sedia;
il professore si avvicina alla campana,
vi immette nuovamente l'aria,
si impadronisce del fiore,
lo esàmina. Un àttimo.
Poi mi fissa con uno sguardo
che intimorirebbe un'àquila;
uno sguardo terríbile,
da giustiziere.
- Si alzi e si giustífichi!
Mi alzo, sentendomi intorno
il pàlpito dell'affettuosa solidarietà
dei compagni, e mi giustífico:
- Avrei voluto
che si facesse una breve aggiunta,
forse non inútile,
alla legge física

	da Lei enunciata ieri: i fiori ai quali viene tolta l'aria per mezzo della campana pneumatica reclìnano sullo stelo e avvizzìscono; si sottràggono però a questo fenòmeno i fiori di cellulòide." /A. Frattini/
Il dott. Rossi:	Che cosa vi ho detto io?
Antonio:	Che Antonio è un furbo e mascalzone fin da bambino! Papà, la televisione trasmette vìdeo registrazioni di sport: partite di calcio, di pallacanestro, di pallavolo, di nuoto, sci e pattini, pugilato e scherma, sollevamento pesi. Vuoi gettare un'occhiata?
Il dott. Rossi:	No! Andiamo al campo di battaglia! Alle armi! Alla tàvola, amici!

GRAMMATICA

1. Voce passiva
2. Azione finita
3. Modo congiuntivo: imperfetto e trapassato
4. Il modo congiuntivo in proposizione principale
5. La coniugazione perifrastica

Lessicologia:
1. La casa
2. Una grande pagina della mia vita
3. Lo sport

LA PROVA

Un contadino accusa un suo compaesano davanti al magistrato di aver rubato un animale. Il giudice domanda all'accusatore:
- Sei sicuro che egli l'abbia rubato?
- Sicurissimo!
- Ne hai delle prove?
- Posso presentare uno che l'ha veduto.
- Ed io, dice l'accusato, posso presentarle venti che non m'hanno veduto.
- Se è cosi, risponde il giudice, venti valgono più di uno.
E lo manda assolto.

IL PEZZO DIFFICILE

Un signore durante un concerto ascolta impaziente un violinista che gratta furiosamente e rapidamente il suo violino e desidera solo che finisca al più presto possibile.
- Ti avverto, gli dice un amico, che è un pezzo molto difficile.
- Ahimè! Vorrei che fosse addirittura impossibile!
- Ma sai, non può piacere molto, perché la sala è sorda.
- Quanto la invidio in questo momento!

accusare
rubare
prova, f
assolto, agg.

grattare
avvertire
sordo, agg
invidiare

"...CHI HA GLI OCCHI
NELLA FRONTE E NELLA MENTE,
DI QUELLI SI HA DA SERVIRE
PER ISCORTA."
Galileo Galilei 1564 - 1642.
Dialogo dei massimi sistemi/

QUADRO OTTAVO
ARRIVEDERCI ROMA

Il dottor Walter:	A mezzogiorno partiremo per Firenze. Poi ci aspetta Milano con gli spettácoli nella Scala. Vostra madre ed Elsa se ne interèssano tanto! Voglio farvi vedere Venezia che è única per la sua bellezza. Ma prima vado all'Ufficio informazioni. Devo prenotare i biglietti per il nostro ritorno. E voi?
La signora Walter:	Vorremmo andare ai negozi.
Elsa:	Vorremmo fare delle spese.
Il dottor Walter:	Va bene, va bene. Fàtele, perché presto diremo addio, Italia!

In Ufficio informazioni

Il dottor Walter:	Scusi, signorina, vorrei cinque posti sull'aèreo per Berlino. Per il 14 maggio. Ce ne sono? A che ora parte l'aereo?
L'impiegata:	Alle otto e mezzo. Ma alle sette e mezzo, al piú tardi, dovete èssere all'aeroporto.
Il dottor Walter:	Senz'altro. Grazie.
	Mentre il dottor Walter si òccupa dei biglietti, fa le último telefonate ai colleghi,

la signora Walter e i figli
entrano nei negozi.
Nelle vetrine è riflessa l'immàgine
della città moderna: industriale
e stravagante.
Ecco i Walter in via del Tritone,
in via Barberini, in via del Babbuino,
in Corso...

Elsa: In questa vetrina sono esposti
molti tessuti di lana,
di seta e di cotone
per àbiti, vestiti, camicie,
camicette.
Entriamo!
Per favore,
mi faccia vedere questa stoffa!
Quanto costa al metro?
Me ne dia tre metri!

La commessa: Le faccio sùbito
lo scontrino e il pacco,
signorina.

Elsa: Qui c'è la biancherìa fine.
Qui ci sono camicie, maglie,
cravatte.
Francesco, Emilio,

                        vi piàcciono quelle
                        camicie e maglie?
                        Ne compriamo tre paia!
                        Che begli scarpe e stivali!
                        Sono a buon mercato.
                        Vorrei provare quegli stivaletti marroni.
                        Anche un paio per te, mamma.

Francesco /brontolando/:
                        Non slanciarti per afferrare
                        tutto!
                        Sai, il proverbio dice:
                        "Chi troppo vuole,
                        nulla stringe."

Elsa: Oh, tu sei insopportàbile!
                        Mamma,
                        qui ci sono guanti,
                        valige e borse di pelle.
                        Gioiellería e orologi.
                        Profumería.
                        Giocàttoli: che belle bàmbole!

Emilio: Qui sono esposti
                        materiali elèttrici:
                        stufe e cucine,
                        lavatrici e frigoríferi,
                        ferri da stiro,

magnetòfoni, radioline e pile.
Dolciumi:
scàtole di cioccolatini,
cioccolate. Pasticceria.
Panetteria.
Ortaggi e frutta.
E' mezzogiorno.
Dobbiamo tornare.

La signora Walter: Andiamo!

La famiglia Walter va alla stazione centrale
in un tassì, ma...

L'autista: Ho un guasto alla màcchina!
Devo fermare all'autorimessa.
E' per un àttimo solo.
Devo verificare tutto:
le ruote, i copertoni,
i freni, il cambio,
le candele e il volante.
Forse il lubrificante...
Oh, un fanale e un parafango
sono quasi caduti!
Il pedale dell'acceleratore
è rotto.

Elsa:	Ve l'ho detto io!
Francesco:	Forse le manca la benzina. Oppure c'è sciòpero?
L'autista:	Non c'era niente. Píccola cosa. Tutto in órdine. Andiamo!
Elsa:	Arriveremo mai?
L'autista:	Ma certo. Io sono in gamba! Guido a grande velocità.
La signora Walter:	Piano, per favore.
L'autista:	Eccoci alla stazione. Buon giorno e buon viaggio!
Il dottor Walter:	Dove è l'orario ferroviario? No, è meglio chièdere allo sportello. Per favore, a che ora c'è un treno per Firenze?
L'impiegato:	Alle due.

Il dottor Walter:	Prego, cinque biglietti prima classe con posti riservati.
L'altoparlante:	Attenzione! Il treno per Firenze delle ore due parte dal terzo binario. Si prègano tutti i viaggiatori di salire.
Francesco:	Ecco la nostra vettura e il nostro scompartimento.
La signora Walter:	Spero che non sia per fumatori. Posso chiúdere il finestrino?
Emilio:	Il paesaggio che si vede dal treno è molto pittoresco. Si vèdono le città, i villaggi, i campi, pochi contadini che lavòrano la terra, giardini e bei cipressi e le loro ombre, le stalle, le màcchine agrícole, mercati e molta gente. L'autostrada è molto moderna.
Francesco:	Vi leggerò una novella dal Decameron di Giovanni Boccaccio. Il cuoco Chichibio /Secondo Boccaccio/ Currado Gianfigliazzi della città di Firenze è un nòbile cittadino e gran buongustaio di selvaggina. Un giorno uccide una gru grassa e giòvane e la manda al suo cuoco di nome Chichibio. Gli órdina di arrostirla bene per cena, perché avrà degli òspiti. Chichibio prepara la gru e la mette al fuoco ad arrostirla. Dopo poco un odore appetitoso si sparge nella strada. Lí passa una giòvane donna alla quale Chichibio da gran tempo fa la corte. Il profumo delizioso della gru arrostita dà alla donna una gran voglia di assaggiarla. Ed ella chiede al cuoco una coscia. Risponde lui: – Non posso dàrtela, ragazza, non posso. La gru è del mio padrone il quale stasera avrà degli ospiti. Ma la donna insiste tanto che finalmente Chichibio cede. Stacca una delle cosce e la dà alla ragazza. A cena il padrone si accorge che alla gru manca una coscia e fa chiamare il cuoco.

- Dove è andata l'altra zampa? -
gli chiede severamente.
Il furbo Chichibio risponde:
- Signore, le gru hanno una sola zampa!
Allora il padrone arrabbiato dice:
- Domattina voglio vedere
quello che tu hai detto.
Ti giuro, però,
se sarà altrimenti
ti acconcio bene io.
Bada!
La mattina seguente
il padrone e i suoi òspiti
mòntano i cavalli
per andare alla caccia.
Il padrone órdina a Chichibio
di montare anche lui il ronzino
e di accompagnarli.
Ed ecco sopra la riva di un fiume
dódici gru che dòrmono,
come di sòlito,
appoggiate a una zampa sola.
Chichibio se ne avvede
e dice súbito:
- Signore, ben può vedere
quelle gru che hanno una zampa sola.
Io non ho mentito.
Il signore ferma il cavallo,
batte con le mani, gridando: ho, ho...

Le gru, svegliàndosi,
màndano giú l'altro piè.
- Che te ne pare, ghiottone? -
grida il padrone.
Risponde súbito Chichibio:
- Messer, ieri sera,
quando ho portato la gru arrostita,
Lei non ha battuto le mani
e non ha gridato: ho, ho...
Se l'avesse fatto
anche quella avrebbe stesa
l'altra gamba.
Piace al padrone la pronta
e spirituosa risposta del cuoco
e Chichibio èvita la mala ventura.

Elsa: E'vero.
Gli italiani hanno una mente dúttile.
Fanno delle scoperte interessantìssime.
Pochi però rièscono a trarre vantaggi
materiali dalle loro trovate.

Il dott. Walter: Firenze!
Siamo arrivati alla città
dei piú grandi e illustri italiani:
Giotto, Dante, Michelangelo,
Machiavelli, Cellini, Donatello
e tanti altri!

Il vero Rinascimento del mondo
è cominciato da qui.
Ci sono tanti luoghi cèlebri
da vedere!
Il tempo però è cosí insufficiente.
Domani dobbiamo alzarci presto.
Adesso prendiamo alloggio
alla pensione S I L L A
lungo l'Arno!

Ormai è calata la sera.

Elsa /canta pianíssimo/:
Scende la notte incoronata di stelle,
luce di luna abbraccia il mondo.
Tutti abbiamo trovato la calma.
Silenzio!
Dopo un giorno pieno di moto
l'alma agitata vuole riposo...

Silenzio

Parole e musica: E. Gateva

Andante

Scende la notte incoronata di stelle.

Luce di luna abbraccia il mondo.

Tutti abbiamo trovato la calma. Silenzio...

Dopo un giorno pieno di moto,

rit...

l'alma agitata vuole riposo...

GRAMMATICA

1. Modo condizionale: presente e passato
2. Periodo ipotetico

Lessicologia:
1. In Ufficio informazioni
2. Alla stazione. Viaggio in treno
3. Negozi
4. In auto
5. Il cuoco Chichibio

IL CANE E LA CARNE

Un cane passa su un ponte che attraversa un fiume. Tiene in bocca un pezzo di carne. Mentre passa, guarda nell'acqua e vede riflessa la sua immagine.
Oh, guarda, -dice-un altro cane con un altro pezzo di carne. Ora lo prendo e cosí avrò due pezzi di carne.
Mentre cosí dice, apre la bocca, si slancia per afferrare l'altro pezzo, ma... resta senza l'uno e senza l'altro.
Famoso è il proverbio: "Chi troppo vuole, nulla stringe."

I TRE BICCHIERI

Un contadino lavora in un campo di grano. Ad un certo momento si sente molto stanco e dice:
- Sono stanco, devo riposare un poco e bere un bicchiere di vino, poi riprenderò il lavoro.
Si siede sotto un albero, all'ombra, prende la bottiglia e si versa un bicchiere di vino. Si sente riposato, e ricomincia il lavoro. Dopo poco, però, si sente nuovamente stanco.
- Devo bere ancora un bicchiere-dice, smette il lavoro e 'va a bere ancora un bicchiere.
Riprende il lavoro, ma poco dopo si sente piú stanco di prima e decide di bere un terzo bicchiere. Alla fine si addormenta vicino alla bottiglia e si sveglia quando è già buio. Allora il contadino si arrabbia e ritorna a casa brontolando, perché ha perduto una giornata di lavoro.

UN FANCIULLO ED UN PANETTIERE

Un fanciullo entra in una panetteria per comprare un pezzo di pane da 50 lire. Gli sembra che il pane sia troppo piccolo, e dice al panettiere che è certo che il pane non abbia il peso voluto.
- Che importa! - risponde il panettiere, - avrai meno da portare.
- E'giusto, interrompe il fanciullo, e getta sul banco quaranta lire.
- Fermati! - dice il panettiere, - tu non mi hai pagato quanto mi spetta.
- Che importa! - risponde il fanciullo, -avrà meno da contare.

bottiglia, f   spettare
versare   contare

Firenze
Il Duomo e il Campanile di Giotto

Bologna, 15 Maggio 1973

LORENZ EFFENBERGER
Sigfridstraße 26
BERLIN

Caro amico,

Sono molto contento del nostro viaggio in Italia. Avevi ragione! Conoscendo la storia e la cultura di un paese e di un popolo, si può capire meglio la vita attuale, la natura ed il carattere stesso di ogni singola persona. Io ormai ho deciso: studierò filologia italiana. Ai nostri giorni è difficile studiare le lingue classiche: il greco ed il latino. Quasi tutti dicono che sono lingue morte. Macché, altro che morte! E l'italiano non è un latino volgare? Vorrei conoscere più profondamente la storia umana. Certo, gli avvenimenti non si ripetono mai, ma si assomigliano assai.

L'anno prossimo visiteremo insieme, tu ed io, la Grecia, l'Egitto e l'Italia. Che ne dici? Sei d'accordo? Ho raccontato il mio piano al babbo. Ci darà il denaro.

Tanti affettuosi saluti
Emilio

Bologna, 12 Maggio 1973

Spett.Ditta Cesare
Via Rubicone 37
TORINO
Italia

Egregi Signori,

Ho letto il V/pregiato nome in una guida commerciale. Da un collega mio e V/cliente, il Dott. Rossi, sono venuto a sapere che nella V/città dirigete una grande ditta di apparecchi ed impianti di medicina. Perciò mi permetto di rivolgermi a Voi con la seguente domanda:

Io sono psicoterapeuta e scienziato. Ho un laboratorio vecchio. Ho bisogno di rinnovarlo di vari apparecchi moderni. Cerco di comprare alcuni apparecchi molto sensibili che possano registrare ogni minimo mutamento nella psiche umana. Mutamenti che si compiono sotto l'influsso di vari agenti esterni ed interni. Per esempio: vari cambiamenti del polso, della circolazione del sangue, della corrente biologica, ecc. o sotto l'influsso di un discorso o di una parola sola, o della musica o di certi accordi, oppure sotto l'influenza di un'autorità o della pura logica individuale, ecc.

Perché possiate avere un'idea completa della mia commissione, Vi rimetto numerosi disegni e fotografie di tutto ciò che mi interessa e mi occorre.

So che possedete una fabbrica che è una delle più grandi per questi prodotti e li esporta in tutti i paesi del mondo. So anche che i V/prodotti trovano facile e corrente mercato, perché sono in grado di soddisfare ogni cliente.

Ho raccomandato la V/ditta a un'altra ditta del mio paese che è molto interessata di aver più diretto contatto con Voi ed aumentare così il volume dei propri affari. Farà di tutto per aiutarVi con prezzi atti a battere ogni concorrenza e con condizioni speciali di pagamento. Un rappresentante della menzionata ditta verrà da Voi con l'offerta della mia commissione.

In attesa della V/risposta distintamente Vi saluto

Dott. Richard Walter

ELSA E GIOVANNI CIVININI A VIENNA

Ma chi si vede? La signorina Elsa e il signor Civinini! Eccoli uscire dal Teatro dell'opera di Vienna. Che gioia rivederli! Un breve incontro e veniamo a sapere molto. Si sono recentemente sposati. "Tanti auguri di felicità! Tanti auguri di ogni bene!"

E'vero, c'è una cosa spiacevole che disturba la vita dei due giovani. Ve ne accorgete?

Il signor Civinini non voleva che sua moglie si dedicasse al teatro. Il signor Civinini è un vero italiano: geloso, pieno di scrupoli. E la signora Elsa, invece, difende la sua propria dignità e i suoi diritti di una donna moderna. Su questo argomento discutono disperatamente...

G.Civinini: Elsa, tu potresti lavorare dovunque ti piacesse. Ho tanti amici che lavorano presso vari ministeri. Per esempio...

Elsa: Sí, sí. Li conosco abbastanza bene: quelli del Ministero dell'Istruzione. No, non mi piace essere una stupida professoressa di canto. E'ripugnante. Oppure mi dirai che per me sarebbe molto più conveniente prendere un posto nel Ministero dell'Edilizia, del Commercio estero o interno, degli Affari esteri, della Sanità, dell'Assistenza sociale, dei Trasporti. Che onore essere una segretaria del Ministro delle Finanze! Ma tu, cosa credi? Io preferisco fare la semplice operaia nell'Industria tessile, alimentare, meccanica, energetica o mineraria. Mi sentirò independente e forte.

G.Civinini: Elsa, finíscila! Tu non capisci niente. Povera ragazza! Quante volte te l'ho detto e quante volte dovrei ripetertelo! Basta uno che sia vittima di questa miserabile vita d'artista. Tutte queste liti mi danno già noia.

Elsa: Ma certo. Ci credo. Cosí la finiremo al Palazzo di Giustizia.

G. Civinini: Senti, abbiamo un programma abbastanza denso. Gettiamo un'occhiata al nostro calendario; dopo la Pasqua ho degli spettacoli negli Stati Uniti, in Belgio, Danimarca, Francia, Gran Bretagna, Grecia, Svizzera, Giappone, Cina, Algeria, nell'Unione Sovietica, Canadà. Dobbiamo prendere parte a quel grande concerto organizzato dall'ONU. Per le ferie andremo in Italia. Poi festeggeremo il Natale in Germania con i tuoi e la Pasqua dove vuoi, come lo dice il proverbio.

Elsa: Hai vinto come sempre! Andiamo!

GRAMMATICA

Quadro primo

FONETICA

L'alfabeto italiano

A a	a		M m		emme
B b	bi		N n		enne
C c	ci		O o		o
D d	di		P p		pi
E e	e		Q q		qu
F f	effe		R r		erre
G g	gi		S s		esse
H h	acca		T t		ti
I i	i		U u		u
L l	elle		V v		vi /vu/
			Z z		zeta

K, k /cappa/, X, x /ics/, Y, y /i greco/, W, w /doppia vi/ – Queste lettere si incontrano in voci non italiane.

IN ITALIANO NON SOLO LE VOCALI TONICHE, MA ANCHE QUELLE ATONE VANNO PRONUNCIATE CON NITIDEZZA E PRECISIONE.

Le vocali atone non si dileguano mai, nè si degradano, nè sfumano. La melodia propria della lingua italiana, il fascino musicale dell'italiano è insito in quel principio di chiarezza, nettezza, purezza: stabilità di timbro di ogni vocale. /I. Petkanov, La grammatica italiana, Sofia – 1956/

PARTICOLARITÀ DELLA PRONUNCIA DI ALCUNE CONSONANTI

c	ce	certamente, felice, successo
	ci	Civinini, Lucia
	ca	cantante, Scala, domenica
	co	Conservatorio, ecco, Pellico
	cu	cuore, scuola
	cia, cio	cominciamo, sacrificio /i atona-cia, cio non viene pronunciata/
	chi, che	chiedere, marchesa
g	ge	dipinge, intelligente
	gi	giro, regista
	ga, go, gu	ragazzo, Rigoletto, guardo
	gia, gio	viaggiano, Giovànni /i atona non viene pronunciata/
	ghe, ghi	colleghe, colleghi
	gli	figlio, biglietto
	gn	signore, ingegno, montagna
h		ho, hai, ha, hanno, hostess /h non viene pronunciata mai/
q	qu	quando, acqua, tranquillo
s		a/ sempre, studentessa, posto, respirare
		b/ francese, casa slavo, sbagliare
	sce	conoscenza
	sci	cuscino, scientifico
	sca, sco, scu	Scala, preferisco, scusi
z		a/ zucchero, zero
		b/ servizio, ragazzo, scherzano

96

LE CONSONANTI DOPPIE
ba<u>bb</u>o, raga<u>zz</u>o, a<u>bbr</u>acciare, repu<u>bbl</u>ica

L'ACCENTO

1. Parole piane:
    2 1   2 1   2 1   2 1
sign<u>o</u>re, cant<u>a</u>nte, m<u>a</u>re, r<u>o</u>sso
2. Parole tronche:
citt<u>à</u>, universit<u>à</u>
3. Parole sdrucciole:
    3 2 1   3 2 1   3 , 2 1   3 2 1
tel<u>e</u>fono, l<u>i</u>bero, z<u>u</u>cchero, p<u>a</u>rlano

L'APOCOPE /Troncamento/
buo<u>n</u> giorno /buon<u>o</u> giorno/
gra<u>n</u> buongustaio /grand<u>e</u> <u>b</u>uongustaio/

L'ELISIONE
trent' <u>a</u>nni /trent<u>a</u> <u>a</u>nni/
<u>l</u>'amico

MORFOLOGIA E SINTASSI
L'articolo determinativo e indeterminativo
Il nome: genere e numero

Maschile

Singolare   Plurale

1. Nomi che terminano in -o
a/ nomi che cominciano con una consonante tranne la z, s impura, ps:
<u>il</u> /<u>un</u>/ bigliett<u>o</u>   <u>i</u> /<u>dei</u>/ bigliett<u>i</u>
il quadro, il successo, il marito, il matrimonio, il figlio, il ragazzo, il museo, il congresso, il giro, il luogo /i luoghi/, il giorno, il bambino.

b/ nomi che cominciano con <u>s</u> impura /<u>s+consonante</u>/, z, pn, ps, j:
<u>lo</u> /<u>uno</u>/ <u>s</u>pettacolo   <u>gli</u> /<u>degli</u>/ <u>s</u>pettacoli
lo stabilimento, lo specchio, lo psicologo, lo zucchero
c/ nomi che cominciano con vocale:
<u>l'</u> /<u>un</u>/ anno   <u>gli</u> /<u>degli</u>/ <u>a</u>nni
l'italiano, l'aeroporto, l'istituto, l'albergo /gli alberghi/ l'amico, /gli amici/
2. Nomi che terminano in -<u>e</u>
il /un/ padr<u>e</u>   i /dei/ padr<u>i</u>
il cantante, il viaggiatore, il direttore, il professore, lo studente, gli studenti, lo scrittore, l'autore /gli autori/

3. Nomi che terminano in -<u>a</u>
il /un/ musicist<u>a</u>
il collega, il pianista, il poeta, il sistema, lo psicoterapeuta   i /dei/ musicist<u>i</u>
4. Nomi che terminano in consonante:
il /un/ fil<u>m</u>, ba<u>r</u>   i /dei/ fil<u>m</u>, ba<u>r</u>
5. Particolarità del plurale
il lenzuol<u>o</u>
                                                                             <u>le</u> lenzuol<u>a</u>

Femminile

Singolare   Plurale
1. Nomi che terminano in -<u>a</u>
a/ nomi che cominciano con consonante:
<u>la</u> /<u>una</u>/ <u>s</u>orell<u>a</u>   <u>le</u> /<u>delle</u>/ <u>s</u>orell<u>e</u>
la strada, la famiglia, la signora, la lingua, la ragazza, la tazza, la sorpresa, la bellezza, la gioia, la valigia

b/ nomi che cominciano con vocale:
l' /un'/ aranciata   le /delle/ aranciate
l'italiana, l'opera, l'amica /le amiche/, l'uscita, l'acqua
2. Nomi che terminano in -e
la /una/ madre   le /delle/ madri
la moglie, la cantante, l'importazione, l'occasione, la canzone, la voce, l'ungherese,
la francese
la scrittrice /lo scrittore/   le /delle/ scrittrici
3. Nomi che terminano in -o
la /una/ mano   le mani
la radio, l'auto   le radio, le auto
4. Plurale dei nomi tronchi:
la /una/ città   le /delle/ città

I VERBI AUSILIARI: ESSERE ED AVERE
I pronomi personali - soggetto

                          Essere

1. /Io/   sono   italiano.
2. /Tu/   sei   un bambino!
3. /Egli/ /Lui/   è   inglese.
   /Ella/ /Lei/   è   italiana.
   /Lei/   è   molto gentile.

1. /Noi/   siamo   a Roma.
2. /Voi/   siete   studenti.
3. /Essi/ /Loro/   sono   ragazzi.
   /Esse/ Loro   sono   ragazze.
   /Loro/   sono   molto gentili.

                                  Lei e Loro - forme di cortesia

                         Avere

1.   Ho   un figlio.
2.   Hai   un fratello?
3.   Ha   due fratelli.

1.   Abbiamo   molti amici.
2.   Avete   tanti libri!
3.   Hanno   grandi successi.

                  VERBI DELLA I, II e III. CONIUGAZIONE, PRESENTE

I coniugazione   II coniugazione
cant - are   cred - ere
1. cant- o   cant- iamo   credo   crediamo
2. cant- i   cant- ate   credi   cred- ete
3. cant- a   cant- ano   cred- e   cred- ono

studiare   abbracciare   perdere   permettere
presentare   pregare   scrivere   piacere
suonare   viaggiare   prendere   sedere
lavorare   ritornare   potere   dipingere
abitare   parlare   dovere   rivedere
mancare   entrare   volere   vivere
assomigliare   chiamarsi   chiedere   ricevere
invitare   interessarsi   vedere   accendere
visitare   cominciare   rimanere   conoscere

portare	laurearsi		III coniugazione
scherzare	diventare		
scusare	insegnare		
trattare	indicare		
imparare	respirare	part- ire	
ringraziare	prorogare		
aspettare	partecipare	parto	partiamo
guardare	accompagnare	parti	part- ite
riposare	lasciare	parte	partono
tremare	augurare		
tornare	trovare		
arrivare	impressionare	preferire	aprire
sbagliare	mangiare	capire	salire
firmare	prenotare		venire
desiderare	costare		sentire
raccontare	ricordare		riempire
dimenticare	funzionare		
cercare			

PARTICOLARITÀ DELLE CONIUGAZIONI

I coniugazione

cercare		cominciare	
cerco	cerchiamo	comincio	cominciamo
cerchi	cercate	cominci	cominciate
cerca	cercano	comincia	cominciano
pregare		mangiare	
prego	preghiamo	mangio	mangiamo
preghi	pregate	mangi	mangiate
prega	pregano	mangia	mangiano

II coniugazione

vincere		conoscere	
vinco	vinciamo	conosco	conosciamo
vinci	vincete	conosci	conoscete
vince	vincono	conosce	conoscono
dipingere		rimanere	
dipingo	dipingiamo	rimango	rimaniamo
dipingi	dipingete	rimani	rimanete
dipinge	dipingono	rimane	rimangono

Verbi irregolari

potere	
posso	possiamo
puoi	potete
può	possono
volere	
voglio	vogliamo
vuoi	volete
vuole	vogliono
dovere	
devo	dobbiamo
devi	dovete
deve	devono

III coniugazione'

capire		salire	
capisco	capiamo	salgo	saliamo
capisci	capite	sali	salite
capisce	capiscono	sale	salgono

LA FORMA NEGATIVA DEI VERBI
Giovedí non canto; è il mio giorno di riposo.

LA FORMA INTERROGATIVA DEI VERBI
Sentite la musica?

LE PREPOSIZIONI SEMPLICI ED ARTICOLATE

a
Abito a Milano.

a+ il= al	a+ i = ai	a+ la= alla	a+ le = alle
a+ lo= allo	a+ gli= agli	a+ l'= all'	
a+ l'= all'			

Studia al Conservatorio.

da
Da cinque anni abito a Milano.

da+ il= dal	da+ i= dai	da+ la= dalla	da+ le= dalle
da+ lo= dallo	da+ gli= dagli	da+ l'= dall'	
da+ l'= dall'			

Vengo dall'aeroporto.

di
Sono amico di Suo padre.

di+ il= del	di+ i= dei	di+ la= della	di+ le= delle
di+ lo= dello	di+ gli= degli	di+ l'= dell'	
di+ l'= dell'			

Le pareti della camera sono alte.

in
Viaggiano in treno.

in + il= nel	in + i = nei	in + la = nella	in + le = nelle
in + lo = nello	in + gli = negli	in + l' = nell'	
in + l' = nell'			

Nell'armadio per i vestiti ci sono molte grucce.

su
Sulla tavola ci sono i giornali /su + la = sulla/

per
Vengono per la prima volta.

L'ARTICOLO PARTITIVO
Vogliono dell'acqua minerale.
Non vogliono acqua minerale.

IL VERBO IMPERSONALE   c'è, ci sono

Sul letto c'è un cuscino.
Sul letto ci sono due cuscini.

L'AGGETTIVO
1. Lo spettacolo è meraviglioso.
   Gli spettacoli sono meravigliosi.

   La camera è comoda e tranquilla.
   Le camere sono comode e tranquille.

2. Francesco è un ragazzo intelligente.
   Francesco ed Emilio sono due ragazzi intelligenti.
   Elsa è una ragazza intelligente.
   Elsa e la sua amica sono ragazze intelligenti.

PARTICIPIO PASSATO

I coniugazione   II coniugazione   III coniugazione

cant - are   cred - ere   part - ire
cant - ato   cred - uto   part - ito

PASSATO PROSSÌMO

Ho cantato   Abbiamo cantato
Hai cantato   Avete cantato
Ha cantato   Hanno cantato

Abbiamo mangiato un magnifico pollo alla panna.

Sono partito /maschile/, partita /femminile/   Siamo partiti, -e
Sei partito, -a   Siete partiti, -e
E' partito, -a   Sono partiti, -e

Siamo arrivati.

Avere   ### Essere

ho avuto   abbiamo avuto   sono stato, -a   siamo stati, -e
hai avuto   avete avuto   sei stato, -a   siete stati, -e
ha avuto   hanno avuto   è stato, -a   sono stati, -e

Hanno avuto grande successo.   Siete stati in Italia?

GRAMMATICA
Quadro secondo

I VERBI IRREGOLARI: fare, dare, stare, andare
                    sapere, venire, uscire

I VERBI RIFLESSIVI: lavarsi /I/, mettersi /II/, vestirsi /III/

io mi lavo   io mi metto /le scarpe/   io mi vesto
tu ti lavi   tu ti metti   tu ti vesti
egli si lava   egli si mette   egli si veste
noi ci laviamo   noi ci mettiamo   noi ci vestiamo
voi vi lavate   voi vi mettete   voi vi vestite
essi si lavano   essi si mettono   essi si vestono

Devo prepararmi
Devi prepararti
Deve prepararsi
Dobbiamo prepararci
Dovete prepararvi
Devono prepararsi

GERUNDIO PRESENTE DEI VERBI: cantare - cantando
                             credere - credendo
                             partire - partendo

lavàndo<u>mi</u>, lavando<u>ti</u>, lavando<u>si</u>, lavando<u>ci</u>, lavando<u>vi</u>, lavando<u>si</u>
mettèndo<u>mi</u>
vestèndo<u>mi</u>

L'IMPERATIVO

Emilio, <u>parla</u> con piú sicurezza!
<u>Non pensare</u> tanto!
Leggi!

	parl<u>are</u>		
1. -	parliamo!		<u>non</u> parliamo!
2. parl<u>a</u>!	parl<u>a</u>te!	<u>non parlare</u>!	non parlate!

	cred<u>ere</u>		
1.	crediamo!	-	non crediamo!
2. credi!	credete!	non credere!	non credete!

	part<u>ire</u>		
1. -	partiamo!	-	non partiamo!
2. parti!	partite!	non partire!	non partite!

	lav<u>arsi</u>		
1. -	laviàmo<u>ci</u>!	-	non laviàmoci!
2. làva<u>ti</u>!	lavàte<u>vi</u>!	non lavar<u>ti</u> =	non lavàtevi =
		non <u>ti</u> lavare!	non vi lavate!

GRADI DI COMPARAZIONE

grado positivo: il ragazzo modesto - i ragazzi modesti
                   la ragazza modesta - le ragazze modeste
grado comparativo: La ragazza è <u>piú modesta del</u> ragazzo.
                   Il ragazzo è <u>meno modesto</u> della ragazza.
                   Il ragazzo è /<u>cosí, tanto</u>/ modesto <u>come</u> /<u>quanto</u>/ la ragazza.
grado superlativo: Emilio è <u>il piú timido</u> /modesto/ allievo della classe.
                     / i piú timidi
                     la piú timida
                     le piú timide /
grado superlativo assoluto: modest<u>issimo</u> = molto modesto
                           bellissimo = molto bello

LA COMPARAZIONE IRREGOLARE

pos.	comp.	superl.
buono	migliore	ottimo
cattivo	peggiore	pessimo
grande	maggiore	massimo
piccolo	minore	minimo

gli avverbi:

bene	meglio	benissimo
male	peggio	malissimo

L'AGGETTIVO BELLO

fiore bello - fiori belli
<u>bel</u> fiore - <u>bei</u> fiori   bella ragazza - belle ragazze
<u>bello</u> spettacolo - begli spettacoli
<u>bell'</u>amico - begli amici   bell' amica - belle amiche

I NUMERALI

a/ cardinali:
    un libro, uno studente, una ragazza
    due libri, due ragazze

Che ora è?
Che ore sono?
Sono le undici.
Sono le undici e mezzo
Sono le dieci e un quarto.
Sono le dodici e venticinque.
Sono le dodici meno un quarto.
Sono le dodici meno dieci.
E l'una.

3 + 4 = 7 /3 più 4 fa 7 /
8 - 2 = 6 /8 meno 2 fa 6/
2 x 5 = 10/2 volte 5 fa 10/
6 : 3 = 2 /6 diviso 3 fa 2/

il Duecento = il secolo XIII
il Trecento = XIV
il Quattrocento = XV
il Cinquecento = XVI
il Seicento = XVII
il Settecento - XVIII
l'Ottocento = XIX
il Novecento = XX

b/ ordinali:

primo
secondo
terzo
quarto   -a, -i, -e
quinto
sesto
settimo
ottavo
nono
decimo

undicesimo/decimoprimo/
dodicèsimo /decimosecondo/
tredicesimo /decimoterzo/
quattordicesimo /decimoquarto/
. . . .

ventesimo

AGGETTIVI DIMOSTRATIVI

Questo fauno lo voglio fare io.
Possiamo andare in quel caffé...

questo libro - questi libri
quest' amico - questi amici

questa ragazza - queste ragazze
quest' amica - queste amiche

quel libro - quei libri
quello studente - quegli studenti
quell'amico - quegli amici

quella ragazza - quelle ragazze
quell'amica - quelle amiche

codesto - codesti
codesta - codeste

IL VERBO IRREGOLARE: PROPORRE

propongo   proponiamo
proponi   proponete
propone   propongono

GRAMMATICA
Quadro terzo

1. Aggettivo e pronome possessivo

I tuoi figli non hanno voluto.
Sono amico di Suo padre.
Tuo fratello è un filosofo.
Mia madre è mio padre, lo difendono sempre.
Sòno venuto con la mia famiglia.
Michelangelo va spesso a trovare il suo amico.
I miei vengono per la prima volta.

mio padre, mio marito, suo figlio, vostro fratello, il loro figlio, tua madre, nostra figlia, la loro sorella, tua moglie

singolare		plurale	
mio	fratello	i miei	fratelli
tuo	fratello	i tuoi	fratelli
suo	fratello	i suoi	fratelli
nostro	fratello	i nostri	fratelli
vostro	fratello	i vostri	fratelli
il loro	fratello	i loro	fratelli
mia	sorella	le mie	sorelle
tua	sorella	le tue	sorelle
sua	sorella	le sue	sorelle
nostra	sorella	le nostre	sorelle
vostra	sorella	le vostre	sorelle
la loro	sorella	le loro	sorelle

però: la mia cara madre, la mia mamma, la mia sorellina, il mio caro padre, il mio babbo, il mio fratellino

2. Forme del participio passato.

accendere - acceso
prendere - preso
difendere - difeso
scendere - sceso

chiudere - chiuso
ridere - riso
decidere - deciso

spargere - sparso
correre - corso
perdere - perso, perduto

vincere - vinto
dipingere - dipinto
spingere - spinto

scegliere - scelto
togliere - tolto

trarre - tratto
dire - detto
leggere - letto
scrivere - scritto
correggere - corretto
dirigere - diretto
condurre - condotto
produrre - prodotto
esprimere - espresso
concedere - concesso
succedere - successo
muovere - mosso

cadere - caduto
volere - voluto
bere - bevuto
sapere - saputo
piovere - piovuto
crescere - cresciuto

cogliere - colto
risolvere - risolto
chiedere - chiesto
rimanere - rimasto
nascondere - nascosto
rispondere - risposto
porre - posto

essere - stato, -i, -a, -e
avere - avuto

conoscere - conosciuto
nascere - nato
piacere - piaciuto
vedere - visto, veduto
fare - fatto
mettere - messo
vivere - vissuto
costringere - costretto
venire - venuto
apparire - apparso
coprire - coperto
morire - morto
soffrire - sofferto

3. Passato prossimo indica un'azione passata che ha qualche contatto con il presente.

a/ verbi transitivi /la cui azione passa su un complemento diretto/ al passato prossimo si coniugano con il verbo avere
Abbiamo visto la Basilica.
Abbiamo preso l'autobus.
Non vi abbiamo raccontato tutto.
b/ verbi intransitivi /la cui azione non passa su un complemento diretto/, i verbi riflessivi, la voce passiva si coniugano con essere.

Siamo tornati al centro di Roma.
Sono arrivato. Sono arrivata.
La casa e costruita dai genitori.
Mi sono preparata subito.
Dove ci siamo visti?
andare, arrivare, cadere, diventare, giungere, morire, nascere, rimanere, restare, tornare, uscire, venire, crescere, invecchiare, entrare - si coniugano con essere

4. I verbi:

sedersi	scegliere	bere /bevere/
mi siedo	scelgo	bevo
ti siedi	scegli	bevi
si siede	sceglie	beve
ci sediamo	scegliamo	beviamo
vi sedete	scegliete	bevete
si siedono	scelgono	bevono

5. Verbi impersonali:
a/ piove, tuona, lampeggia
succede, accade, basta, ci vuole, bisogna
b/ fa caldo, fa freddo, fa buio
è possibile, non è possibile, è facile, è vero.
c/ va bene, non importa, mi pare, mi piace /mi piacciono/
d/ si paga dopo

6. Il modo infinito: cantare, credere, partire
a/ i verbi modali /senza preposizione/ + infinito:
Non posso sopportare i fumatori.
Voglio visitare i musei.
Devo partire subito per Milano.
Lascia stare[1]
b/ altri verbi con preposizione + infinito
Prego di pagare
Decidiamo di salire.
Ci invitano a portarci in carrozza.
Andiamo a pranzare.
Cominciamo a lavorare.

Sono pronto ad uscire.

Abbiamo molto da fare.

c/ l'infinito = sostantivo
   Ah che bel vivere, /il vivere/
   che bel piacere! /il piacere/

GRAMMATICA
Quadro quarto

1. I pronomi personali
a/ soggetto

<u>Egli</u> /Lorenzo dei Medici/ ha una scuola di scultura.

<u>singolare</u>

1 persona
io
2 persona
tu
3. persona
egli - per persona   ella - per persona
lui - per persona   lei - per persona
esso - per oggetto   essa - per oggetto e persona

<u>plurale</u>

1 persona
noi
2 persona
voi
3 persona
essi - per persone e oggetti   esse - per persone e oggetti
                                   loro - per persone

b/ complemento diretto

<u>forma tonica</u>   <u>forma atona</u>

Francesco guarda <u>me</u>   Francesco   <u>mi</u> guarda.
                 te   ti
                 lui, lei, se   lo, la, si
                 noi   ci
                 voi   vi
                 loro   li, le

Voglio veder<u>ti</u>. /-lo, -la, -vi, -li, -le/
Vuoi veder<u>mi</u>? /-lo, -la, -ci, -li, -le/
Francesco vuole veder<u>mi</u>. /-ti, -lo, -la, -ci, -vi, -li, -le/
Vogliamo veder<u>ti</u>. /-lo, -la, -vi, -li, -le/
Francesco ed Elsa vogliono veder<u>mi</u>. /-ti, -lo, -la, -ci, -vi, -li, -le/
Vogliono vedere loro.

Guàrda<u>mi</u>! /-lo, -la, -ci, -li, -le/ Guardàte<u>mi</u>! /-lo, -la, ci, -li, -le/
Vedèndo<u>mi</u>... /-ti, -lo, -la, -ci, -vi, -li, -le/
Ècco<u>mi</u>! /-ti, -lo, -la, -ci, -vi, -li, -le/

c/ complemento indiretto
<u>forma tonica</u>
Francesco dice   a me   un aneddoto.
                    a te
                    a sè, a lui, a lei
                    a noi
                    a voi
                    a   loro

Francesco parla di lui. /di me, di te, di lei, di noi, di voi, di loro/
Francesco esce con loro. /con me, con te, con lui, con lei, con noi, con voi/

forma atona

Francesco   mi   dice un aneddoto.
                 ti
                 gli, le
                 ci
                 vi
Francesco dice   loro   un aneddoto.

Voglio dirti un aneddoto.
Vuoi dirgli un aneddóto?
Francesco vuole dirmi un aneddoto.
Francesco vuole dire loro un aneddoto
Dimmi la verità! /gli, - le, - ci/
Dìtemi la verità!
Dammi il giornale!
Fammi un favore!
Dicèndomi la verita, esce. /-ti, -gli, -le, -ci, -vi/

d/ Raggruppamenti di pronomi personali:
complemento indiretto /forma atona/ + complemento diretto /f. atona/

Francesco mi dice l'aneddoto.

Francesco   me lo   dice.
                 te lo
                 se lo, glielo, glielo
                 ce lo
                 ve lo
Francesco lo dice loro.

Francesco mi dice la verità.

Francesco   me la   dice.
                 te la
                 se la, gliela, gliela
                 ce la
                 ve la
Francesco la dice loro.

Francesco mi porta i libri.

Francesco   me li   porta.
                 te li
                 se li, glieli, glieli
                 ce li
                 ve li
Francesco li porta loro.

Francesco mi porta le lettere.

Francesco   me le   porta.
                 te le
                 se le, gliele, gliele
                 ce le
                 ve le
Francesco le porta loro.
Voglio dìrtelo. /-glielo, -velo/
Vuoi dìrmelo?
Dàmmelo! Dàtemelo! /-glielo, -celo/
Dìmmelo! Dìtemelo!
Fàmmelo! Fàtemelo!
Dàmmela! Dàtemela! Dàmmeli! Dàtemeli! Dàmmele! Dàtemele

2. Pronomi relativi

    che - soggetto
        Passa un uomo che si ferma a guardare.
        Passano degli uomini che si fermano.
        Passa la donna che si ferma.
        Passano le donne che si fermano.

    cui - complemento indiretto
        Andremo dal dottor Rossi di cui vi ho parlato.

    il cui, la cui, i cui, le cui
        Ecco lo scrittore il cui libro tu leggi. /i cui libri/
        Ecco lo scultore la cui scultura tu vedi. /le cui sculture/

    il quale, i quali, la quale, le quali
        Passa un uomo il quale si ferma. /= che/
        Ho scritto a un malato con il quale siamo amici./= con cui/

    chi - per persona
        Chi dorme non piglia pesci.

3. Aggettivi e pronomi indefiniti:

    a/ aggettivi
    ogni   Ogni camera costa 40000 lire.
    qualche   Qualche giorno ci vedremo.
    qualùnque
    qualsiasi   Prendo una camera qualsiasi
    b/ aggettivi e pronomi
    ciascuno, -a ; alcuni
    nessuno, -a   Nessuno lo sa. Non lo sa nessuno.
    molto, -a, -i, -e Non c'è molta gente.
    poco, -a, -i, -e
    tanto, -a, -i, -e
    c/ pronomi
    ognuno   Ognuno ha il dovere di aiutare...
    qualcuno
    chiunque
    nulla
    niente

4. Gli avverbi

    a/ di maniera:
        / solo   sola   solamente
        piano   piano
        buono   bene
        cattivo /   male
    b/ di luogo: qui, qua, lì, là, sotto, sopra, su, giù, fuori, dentro, vicino, lontano
    c/ di tempo: adesso, ora, oggi, ieri, domani, allora, subito, dopo, poi, già, mai, sempre.
    d/ di misura: poco, molto, abbastanza, affatto
    e/ di affermazione e di negazione:
        sì, davvero, certo   no, non, neanche
    f/ di dubbio: forse, quasi, eventualmente

5/ Le particelle avverbiali e pronominali: ci-vi-ne

    a/ avverbio di luogo: Siete già stati in Italia? Ci sono stato. /= lì, qui/ Andiàmocene. Me ne vado. /= di qui, di lì/
    b/ Pronome: Che ne dici? /= di questo, di quello/

6. Il verbo andarsene

me ne vado	ce ne andiamo
te ne vai	ve ne andate
se ne va	se ne vanno

7. I verbi:

tenere		morire	
tengo	teniamo	muoio	moriamo
tieni	tenete	muori	morite
tiene	tengono	muore	muoiono

apparire		udire	
appaio	appariamo	odo	udiamo
appari	apparite	odi	udite
appare	appaiono	ode	odono

8. Futuro semplice

Il pomeriggio non farà bel tempo. Pioverà.
Tu m'allungherai i baffi, m'aggiungerai due dita di statura e mi libererai /liberare/ dal latino e greco. E tu aprirai /aprire/ le porte del nuovo secolo ..... sarà nostro il venturo.
Il concerto avrà luogo a Roma.
Io andrò col babbo.

II coniugazione	III coniugazione	I coniugazione
credere - creder-ò	aprire - aprir-ò	parlare - parler-ò
creder-ai	aprir - ai	parler-ai
creder-à	aprir-à	parler-à
creder-emo	aprir-emo	parler-emo
creder-ete	aprir--ete	parler-ete
creder-anno	aprir-anno	parler-anno

9. Particolarità del futuro semplice

avere		essere	
avrò	avremo	sarò	saremo
avrai	avrete	sarai	sarete
avrà	avranno	sarà	saranno

andare-andrò	farè - farò	bere - berrò
potere - potrò	stare - starò	volere - vorrò
dovere - dovrò	dare - darò	tenere - terrò
vivere - vivrò	tradurre - tradurrò	venire - verrò
vedere - vedrò	porre - porrò	
	trarre - trarrò	
	dire - dirò	

GRAMMATICA
Quadro quinto

1. Aggettivi e pronomi interrogativi:
   a/ pronomi:
      chi?
      che cosa?

      Chi son/o/? Sono un poeta.
      Che cosa è questo?
      Che cosa faccio? Scrivo.

   b/ pronomi e aggettivi
      che?

      Che fai tu, luna?
      Che giorno e oggi?
      quale, quali?
      Qual è il Suo indirizzo?
      Quali lingue parla?

2. Verbi   tradurre, condurre, produrre

               tradurre /traducere/

      traduco   traduciamo
      traduci   traducete
      traduce   traducono

3. Il verbo causativo: fare
                        fare + l'infinito
      Mi faccio riparare il tacco.
      Mi faccia pulire la gonna!
      Ti fai costruire una casa?
      Lo fa chiamare.
      Mi faccio fare un vestito.

4. L'imperfetto: indica un'azione passata che avviene in modo continuato ed indeterminato.
      Assomigliava a Leonardo da Vinci.
      Aveva occhi azzurri.
      Era un saggio.
      Vedevo i quadri di Raffaello.
      Sentivo la musica di Vivaldi.

   1 coniugazione   2 coniugazione   3 coniugazione

      cantare - canta-vo
             canta-vi   vedere - vede-vo   sentire - senti-vo
             canta-va
             canta-vamo
             canta-vate
             cantà-vano
      avere - ave-vo
      essere - ero   eravamo
             eri   eravate
             era   èrano

5. Trapassato prossimo: indica un'azione passata che ha avuto luogo quando un'altra azione era stata già compiuta.
      I suoi fratelli erano venuti prima di lui.
      Avevano lavorato bene.

lavorare, vedere, sentire

    avevo lavorato /visto, sentito/
    avevi lavorato
    aveva lavorato

    avevamo lavorato /visto, sentito/
    avevate lavorato
    avevano lavorato

venire

    ero venuto,-a
    eri venuto,-a
    era venuto,-a

    eravamo venuti, - e
    eravate venuti, - e
    èrano venuti, - e

GRAMMATICA

Quadro sesto

1. Il passato remoto: indica un'azione passata che ha perduto ogni contatto con il presente.
   Portarono un mucchio di posta per lui.
   Puccini ne fu tanto commosso che andò lui stesso a comprare i due biglietti e poi li spedì al giovanotto.

1. coniugazione   2 coniugazione   3 coniugazione

portare - port-ai   credere - cred-ei /cred-etti/   spedire - sped-ii
    port-asti   cred-esti   sped-isti
    port-ò   cred-é /cred-ette/   sped-ì

    port-ammo   cred-emmo   sped-immo
    port-aste   cred-este   sped-iste
    port-àrono   cred-èrono /cred-èttero/   sped-irono

essere   avere

fui   fummo   ebbi   avemmo
fosti   foste   avesti   aveste
fu   fùrono   ebbe   èbbero

2. I più importanti verbi irregolari al passato remoto:
   1 coniugazione: dare: diedi, desti, diede, demmo, deste, dièdero
       stare: stetti, stesti, stette, stemmo, steste, stèttero
       fare: feci, facesti, fece, facemmo, faceste, fécero

2 coniugazione: volere: volli, volesti, volle, volemmo, voleste, vòllero
    sapere: seppi, sapesti, seppe, sapemmo, sapeste, sèppero
    a/ scendere: scesi, scendesti, scese, scendemmo, scendeste, scésero

    accendere: accesi
    chiudere: chiusi
    correre: corsi
    decidere: decisi
    difendere: difesi
    mettere: misi, mettesti, mise, mettemmo, meteste, mìsero
    leggere: lessi
    chiedere: chiesi
    muovere: mossi
    perdere: persi
    prendere: presi
    scegliere: scelsi
    spendere: spesi
    spargere: sparsi
    porre: posi
    rimanere: rimasi

rispondere: risposi
scrivere: scrissi
vincere: vinsi
vivere: vissi
b/ bere: bevvi, bevesti, bevve, bevemmo, beveste, bévvero
cadere: caddi
conoscere: conobbi
crescere: crebbi
nascere: nacqui
piacere: piacqui
piovere: piovve /3 p.sg./
rompere: ruppi
tenere: tenni

3 coniugazione: venire: venni, venisti, venne   venimmo, veniste, vènnero
3. Il modo congiuntivo:
In italiano il verbo in una proposizione subordinata si mette all'indicativo quando il verbo della proposizione principale indica certezza.
Se l'azione nella proposizione principale non è sicura, ma è incerta, probabile, augurabile, possibile, il verbo nella proposizione subordinata è al congiuntivo.
Le proposizioni con il verbo al congiuntivo sono introdotte dalle congiunzioni che /o composti/ o se.
  1. Sono sicura che oggi può accadere una cosa simile.
  2. Credi che oggi possa accadere una cosa simile?
  3. Non credo che oggi possa accadere una cosa simile.
  4. Spero che oggi possa accadere una cosa simile.
  5. Voglio che oggi ella venga.
  6. E' possibile /probabile, può darsi, bisogna /che oggi venga.
  7. Benchè /sebbene, in caso che/ sia tardi, aspettiamo.
4. Il congiuntivo presente:
Voglio /spero, dubito, non voglio, non sono sicura, non credo/ che ella canti

Non sono sicura che /ella, egli, tu/ senta tutto.

cantare   vedere, sentire
che io canti   veda   senta
che tu canti   veda
che egli canti   veda
che noi cantiamo   vediamo
che voi cantiate   vediate
che essi càntino   vèdano

Spero che ella sia una brava studentessa e che abbia molti successi.

essere: che io/ tu, egli/ sia, che noi siamo, che voi siate, che essi siano

avere: che io/ tu, egli/abbia, che noi abbiamo, che voi abbiate, che essi àbbiano.

Spero che andiate a trovare l'amico.
Non crede che vengano domani.
Non sappiamo se possano telefonarci.
Spero che vogliano venire.
Dubito che mi diano il libro.
Spero che stia bene.

andare: dare: stare:
che io/tu, egli/   vada   dia   stia
che noi   andiamo   diamo   stiamo
che voi   andiate   diate   stiate
che essi   vàdano   dìano   stìano

fare:
faccia
facciamo
facciate
fàcciano

volere:
voglia
vogliamo
vogliate
vògliano

potere:
possa
possiamo
possiate
pòssano

dovere:
debba
dobbiamo
dobbiate
dèbbano

sapere:
sappia
sappiamo
sappiate
sàppiano

conoscere:
conosca
conosciamo
conosciate
conòscano

venire:
venga
veniamo
veniate
vèngano

finire:
finisca
finiamo
finiate
finìscano

5. Il congiuntivo passato:

Spero che ella abbia sentito e visto lo spettacolo.
Non credo che egli sia partito.

sentire
che io abbia sentito
che noi abbiamo sentito
che voi abbiate sentito
che essi abbiano sentito

partire
sia partito, - a
siamo partiti, - e
siate partiti, - e
siano partiti, - e

GRAMMATICA

Quadro settimo

1. Modo congiuntivo - imperfetto e trapassato

Non credevo che aveste una casa così bella.
Non credeva che portasse /vedessero, sentissero/ tutto.
Speravo che tu fossi una brava studentessa e che avessi molti successi.
Dubitavano che ella desse loro il libro.
Speravo che tu stessi bene.

a/ l'imperfetto

portare
che io portassi
che tu portassi
che egli portasse

che noi portassimo
che voi portaste
che essi portàssero

vedere
vedessi
vedessi
vedesse

vedessimo
vedeste
vedéssero

sentire
sentissi
sentissi
sentisse

sentissimo
sentiste
sentìssero

essere
che io fossi
che tu fossi
che egli fosse

che noi fossimo
che voi foste
che essi fòssero

avere
avessi
avessi
avesse

avessimo
aveste
avessero

dare
che io dessi
che tu dessi
che egli desse
che noi dessimo
che voi deste
che essi dèssero

stare
stessi
stessi
stesse
stessimo
steste
stèssero

andare: andassi
fare: facessi
volere: volessi
potere: potessi
dovere: dovessi

venire: venissi
finire: finissi

b/ il trapassato

Non credeva che avessero portato /visto, sentito/ tutto.
Speravo che tu fossi stata una brava studentessa.
Non credevate che io fossi arrivata.

portare /vedere, sentire/

che io avessi portato /visto, sentito/
che tu avessi portato
che egli avesse portato
che noi avessimo portato
che voi aveste portato
che essi avèssero portato

venire

che io fossi venuto, -a
che tu fossi venuto, -a
che egli /ella/ fosse venuto, - a
che noi fossimo venuti, -e
che voi foste venuti, -e
che essi /esse/ fòssero venuti, - e

2. Il modo congiuntivo in proposizione principale
a/ imperativo:
Si alzi e si giustifichi!
Mi dia, per favore...
Mi dica, per favore...
Mi faccia...
b/ desiderio:
Almeno mi avesse detto tutto.
Almeno fossero venuti.
Venga pure!
c/ dubbio:
Che fosse partito?

3. Voce passiva: essere /venire/ + participio passato del verbo coniugato
La casa è stata costruita dai genitori.
La mia esposizione viene accompagnata dal film.

Presente

io sono accompagnato, -a

Passato prossimo

io sono stato, -a accompagnato, -a

Futuro semplice

io sarò accompagnato, -a

Trapassato prossimo

io ero stato, -a accompagnato, -a

Imperfetto

io ero accompagnato, -a

Modo congiuntivo: presente: che io sia accompagnato, -a
                  passato: che io sia stato, -a accompagnato, -a
                  imperfetto: che io fossi accompagnato, -a
                  trapassato: che io fossi stato, -a accompagnato, -a

4. Azione finita: <u>Finita</u> la guerra, siamo venuti in questa casa.
a/ con participio passato:
<u>Ricevuto</u> la lettera, egli ha capito tutto.
b/ con gerundio passato:
<u>Avendo ricevuto</u> la lettera, egli ha capito tutto.
c/ con infinito passato:
Dopo <u>aver ricevuto</u> la lettera, egli ha capito tutto.

5. La coniugazione perifrastica:
a/ azione continuata: stare /andare, venire/ + il gerundio presente
Oh, Lei <u>sta esagerando</u>!
Di che cosa <u>state conversando</u>?

b/ futuro immediato: stare per +' l'infinito di un verbo
<u>Sto per uscire</u>.

GRAMMATICA

Quadro ottavo

1. Modo condizionale: serve ad indicare un'azione che dipende da una condizione.
   Si adopera quando si rivolge una domanda, preghiera, invito, desiderio
<u>Vorremmo</u> andare ai negozi.
Messer...Lei non ha gridato: ho,'ho...Se l'avesse fatto, anche quella /gru/ <u>avrebbe stesa</u> l'altra gamba.

a/ <u>Presente</u>
I   II   III
parl-are, scriv-ere   parl-, <u>scriv</u>- erei   sent-ire <u>sent</u>-irei
                                    - eresti   -iresti
                                    - erebbe   -irebbe
                                    - eremmo   -iremmo
                                    - ereste   -ireste
                                    - erèbbero   -irèbbero

essere: sarei, saresti, sarebbe, saremmo, sareste, sarèbbero
<u>avere</u>: avrei, avresti, avrebbe, avremmo, avreste, avrèbbero

dare: darei
fare: farei
andare: andrei   dire: direi
stare: starei
dovere: dovrei   porre: porrei
sapere: saprei   tradurre: tradurrei
potere: potrei
volere: vorrei, vorresti, vorrebbe, vorremmo, vorreste, vorrèbbero
venire: verrei
bere: berrei

b/ <u>Passato</u>
   avrei parlato   sarei partito,-a

c/ Voce passiva:
Presente: io sarei accompagnato, -a
Passato: io sarei stato, -a accompagnato, -a

2. Periodo ipotetico:
a/ certezza: Se mi aspetti /aspetterai/, vengo /verrò/.
b/ possibilità: Se mi aspettassi, <u>verrei</u>.
c/ impossibilità: Se mi avessi aspettato, <u>sarei venuto</u>.
         Se mi avessi aspettato, venivo.
         Se mi aspettavi, sarei venuta.
         Se mi aspettavi, venivo.

Настоящий учебник итальянского языка составлен с учетом последних требований суггестопедической учебной системы. Учебный материал подается на житейском коммуникативном уровне. Следя за фабулой легкого дидактического рассказа и одновременно знакомясь с разными сторонами психологии героев и особенностями Италии, ее древней и современной культурой, учащийся овладевает красотой иностранного языка. При этом трудности овладения преодолеваются незаметно, на втором плане.

Учебник построен на основах суггестологии и принципах и средствах суггестопеди Правильно его применяя, преподаватель может помочь обучающимся в реализации резервного комплекса, т.е. значительно легче усваивать материал на творческом уровне и без неприятной усталости, без вредного воздействия на нервную систему: при этом налицо положительное воспитательное воздействие и нарастающая мотивация.

Помимо цельности фабулы в предлагаемой дидактической пьесе, учебник обладает следующими новыми преимуществами с точки зрения суггестопедии:

1. Основная часть учебного содержания - 850 новых слов, равно как и значительная часть основной грамматики — поданы уже в первом уроке. Тем самым использованы суггестивные особенности „первой встречи", когда процесс усвоения является наиболее легким. В то же время обучающиеся имеют большую свободу в выборе слов, выражений, моделей и грамматических форм в часы разработки нового материала. Они не испытывают обстановки „кондиционирования" и ограничения в рамках нескольких слов и моделей для выражения своих мыслей на иностранном языке. При следующих уроках объем новой лексики и грамматики сокращается и это обеспечивает легкость в их усвоении.

2. Отдельные части фраз, а также словосочетания, расположенные на отдельной строке, подобраны таким образом, что их можно менять. Так, на практике усваиваются сотни заменимых частей моделей естественного разговорного языка. Не впадая в самоцельный структурализм язык воспринимается незаметно, естественно и с большим замахом.

3. Наглядность картинок в учебнике связана с сюжетом, причем это делается глобализированно, а не иллюстрируя лишь отдельные элементы изучаемого языка. Точно так же и аудиовизуализация осуществляется на смысловом и двуплановом уровне при большой свободе для творческого выявления, что устраняет кондиционирование в узких рамках представленного небольшого числа элементов предметного мира.

4. Песни в музыкальном и текстовом отношении соответствуют суггестивным требованиям эмоционального „введения" важных семантических, фонетических и грамматических единиц.

5. Перевод при каждом уроке учебника подается курсистам /для уточнения первоначальной лексики, а также в зависимости от нужд познавательного процесса взрослого/ в первых двух фазах суггестопедического учебного процесса - дешифровки и активного концертного сеанса. На второй день перевод убирается - на этот раз в соответствии с условиями обучения иностранным языкам для скорейшего перехода к мышлению на незнакомом языке.

Автор, будучи специалистом как в области филологии, так и в сфере музыки, сумел добиться более полного слияния суггестивного влияния искусства с дидактическими суггестопедическими требованиями преподавания иностранного языка.

Настоящий учебник - целиком или частично - демонстрировался и экспериментировался и экспериментировался не только в Болгарии и в Советском Союзе, но еще и в США, Франции, Австрии, Швейцарии и Швеции.

Учебник является примерным методическим руководством для выработки других учебников на базе суггестопедической системы обучения иностранным языкам.

Учебник рассчитан на работу с преподавателем, специально обученным по суггестопедической учебной системе. Во второй половине обучения курсисты готовятся и к самостоятельной работе. Этот учебник предназначен для специалистов в разных сферах искусства, но приложим и для других курсистов.

Подробные указания о работе преподавателя и курсистов содержатся в методическом руководстве по общему суггестопедическому обучению-воспитанию-лечению.

Георгий ЛОЗАНОВ
Доктор медицинских наук

The present text-book of the Italian language is consistent with the latest requirements of the suggestopedic system. The material is drawn from life on a communicative level. Following the plot of the light didactic story, the students become familiar with various aspects of the characters' psychology, with the characteristic features of Italy and its ancient and modern culture; they penetrate into the beauty of the foreign language. In this way the difficulties of mastering the language recede into the background and are overcome imperceptibly

The text-book is consistent with the basis of suggestology, as well as with the principles and techniques of suggestopedia. Its correct use makes it possible for the teacher to help students to realize the reserve complex, i.e. to learn the material with considerable ease at a creative level and without unpleasant fatigue, with no harmful effects on the nervous- systemß with favourable educational effects and with ever-growing motivation.

Besides giving the whole plot of the didactic play, this text-book has the following new points, advantages from the standpoint of suggestopedia:

1/ Most of the subject—matter /850 new words and a considerable part of the essential grammar/ is given already in the first lesson. So use is made of the particular suggestive features at the "first meeting", when learning is the easiest. At the same time, the students have a wide choice of words, phrases, models and grammatical forms in all the classes for the elaboration of the new material. They do not feel "conditioned" and restricted within the framework of a few words and models when expressing their thoughts in the foreign language. In the following lessons, the number of new words and grammar units decreases, so that learning them is easier.

2/ The different parts of the sentences, as well as the word groups, have been put in separate lines so that they can be changed. In this way, hundreds of parts of models of the spoken language that can be changed are learnt more easily. Without falling into structuralism per se, it is used imperceptibly, naturally and usefully.

3/ The visual aids in the text-book are connected with the subject-matter and globalized, and do not illustrate only single elements. In this way, audio visualization is carried out at a semantic and double-plane level, with great liberty for creative initiative, avoiding conditioning within the narrow framework of a small number of visualized elements.

4/ The music and the words of the songs are consistent with suggestive requirements for the emotional "introduction" of important semantic, phonetic and grammatical units.

5/ Students are given translations of every lesson in the text-book in order to grasp the starting vocabulary better and in order to satisfy the needs of the adults' cognitive process in the initial two phases of the suggestopedic process of learning: deciphering and active concert session. On the second day, the translations are taken away from the students. This is in line with the requirements for learning the foreign language and for rapid transition to thinking in the foreign language.

The author's dual specialty: philology and music, has made it possible for her to achieve a better fusion of the suggestive influence of art and the suggestopedic requirements of teaching the foreign language.

The present text-book has been demonstrated and experimented with, partly or wholly, in Bulgaria and the Soviet Union, as well as in the United States, France, Austria, Switzerland and Sweden.

The text-book can serve as a model methodical handbook for compiling other similar ones for the suggestopedic system of teaching and learning foreign languages.

The text-book is for working with a teacher, who has been trained in the suggestopedic system. During the second half of the course, students are already trained to study independently as well. The text-book is intended for specialists in different fields of art, but it could also be used for other students.

Detailed instructions for the way teachers and students should work with the text-book are to be found in the methodical handbook for the whole suggestopedic teaching-education-remedial system

Georgi Lozanov, M.D., M.Sci.D.

Denna italienska lärobok har utarbetats enligt det suggestopediska systemets senaste krav. Hela materialet är nära knutet till det dagliga livets kommunikation. Genom att följa den lätt didaktiska historiens handling lär eleverna samtidigt känna olika sidor av personernas psykologi och Italiens särdrag med sin antika och samtida kultur; de tränger så småningom in i det främmande språkets skönhet.

Läroboken överensstämmer med suggestologins grunder och suggestopedins principer och teknik. Genom att använda den korrekt kommer läraren att kunna hjälpa eleverna att utnyttja sina reserver. Läraren kommer alltså att hjälpa eleven att assimilera materialet på ett mycket behagligt sätt och på en mycket kreativ nivå utan ansträngning, utan negativ inverkan på nervsystemet; man låter istället materialet assimileras med gynnsam inlärningseffekt, under allt starkare motivation.

Förutom det didaktiska skådespelets hela handling har läroboken följande drag, fördelar ur suggestopedins synpunkt.

1. Den största delen av materialet, 850 nya ord och den viktigaste delen av grammatiken presenteras redan under första dagens lektioner. På så sätt drar man nytta av alla suggestiva inslag vid första mötet då inlärningen är lättast. På samma gång har den studerande en omfattande möjlighet att välja ord, uttryck, fraser, grammatiska former och modeller vid bearbetningen av materialet under lektionerna.

Eleverna känner sig aldrig beroende eller begränsade av modeller och på förhand givna ord då de uttrycker sina tankar på det främmande språket.

Under de följande lektionerna minskar så småningom antalet nya ord och grammatiska moment så att inlärningen av dessa blir lättare.

2. De olika delarna av fraserna så väl som ordgrupperna, har placerats på olika rader, så att de kan bytas ut. På detta sätt lär man sig lättare hundratals delar av modeller för det talade språket. Utan att låta strukturalismen bli ett mål i sig, används den omärkligt, naturligt och till stor nytta.

3. Alla illustrationer i läroboken är knutna till ämnet som helheter och illustrerar därför inte enstaka element i språket. På så sätt genomförs audiovisualiseringen rationellt och på två plan, med stor frihet för kreativa initiativ samtidigt som man undviker att eleverna blir begränsade inom ramen för ett litet antal visualiserade element.

4. Musiken och sångtexterna motsvarar kraven för en känslomässig introduktion till de viktigaste semantiska, fonetiska och grammatiska enheterna.

5. Översättningen till varje lektion finns alltid till elevens förfogande för att denne exakt ska kunna definiera sitt första ordförråd och tillfredställa behoven i de vuxnas kognitiva process under de två första faserna i den suggestopediska inlärningsprocessen, textintroduktion och aktiv konsertsession. På den andra dagen tas översättningarna bort från eleverna. Detta överensstämmer med kraven på inlärningen av det främmande språket och snabb övergång till tänkande på det främmande språket.

Författarens filologiska och musikaliska kompetens har gjort det möjligt för henne att uppnå en bättre sammansmältning av det suggestiva inflytandet av konst och de suggestopediska kraven på undervisning av främmande språk.

Denna lärobok har demonstrerats och utexperimenterats helt eller delvis, förutom i Bulgarien och Sovjetunionen, även i USA, Frankrike, Österrike, Schweiz och Sverige.

Läroboken representerar en metodisk modell för utformande av andra läroböcker i främmande språk enligt det suggestopediska systemets undervisningsmetodik.

Läroboken är avsedd för arbete med lärare som har tränats i den suggestopediska metodiken. Under den andra halvan av kursen är eleverna redan tränade att även studera självständigt. Läroboken är avsedd för specialister på olika områden inom konst, men den kan också användas för andra elever.

Detaljerade instruktioner för hur lärare och elever ska arbeta med läroboken finns i den metodiska lärarhandledningen för hela det suggestopediska systemet, med dess kurativa och undervisande aspekter.

GEORGI LOZANOV, M.D.

INDICE

1. CONOSCENZA IN AEREO — 7
   PATRIZIA /I/ — 22
2. IL RISVEGLIO — 25
   PATRIZIA /II/ — 34
3. LA CITTÀ ETERNA — 37
   PATRIZIA /III/ — 48
4. LE STAGIONI — 49
5. I MESI — 59
6. AL CONCERTO — 68
7. L'AMICIZIA — 75
8. ARRIVEDERCI ROMA — 82
9. GRAMMATICA — 96